Community over Chaos

STUDIES IN RHETORIC AND COMMUNICATION
General Editors:
E. Culpepper Clark
Raymie E. McKerrow
David Zarefsky

James A. Mackin, Jr.

Community over Chaos
An Ecological Perspective on Communication Ethics

The University of Alabama Press   Tuscaloosa and London

∞

The paper on which this book is printed meets the minimum requirements of American National Standard for Information Science–Permanence of Paper for Printed Library Materials, ANSI Z39.48–1984.

Library of Congress Cataloging-in-Publication Data

Mackin, James A.
   Community over chaos : an ecological perspective on communication
ethics / James A. Mackin, Jr.
      p. cm. — (Studies in rhetoric and communication)
   Includes bibliographical references and index.
   ISBN 0-8173-0860-1 (alk. paper)
      1. Communication—Moral and ethical aspects. I. Title.
   II. Series.
   P94.M23 1997
   174—dc20   96-34776

British Library Cataloguing-in-Publication Data available

To all of us who struggle to live ethical lives

Contents

Acknowledgments

I have not written this book with any sense of moral superiority; I am all too aware of the difficulty of leading an ethical life. I wrote this book because I feel a moral obligation to contribute what I can to the scholarly community that has supported me. If this book succeeds at all, then this scholarly community—by arguing with, correcting, and developing the ideas presented here—will eventually strengthen the larger communicative ecosystem that supports it. If the book fails, the failure is mine, because I have not lacked nurturing support from the community.

The first level of community to which I am indebted is my immediate family—Jo Anne, Erin, and Catherine Mackin—and my mother, Marion Mackin. The ethical theory here was not developed in an ivory tower. In part because of my own ethical inadequacy, my marriage dissolved as I was writing this book. Nevertheless, because of the courage and loyalty of my family, our family bonds have held together. I am living through a narrow triumph of community over chaos.

The second level of community to which I am indebted comprises my colleagues and former colleagues at Tulane University's Department of Communication—Connie Balides, Van Cagle, Kelly Coyle, Marsha Houston, Gaye LeMon, Ana Lopez, John Patton, Ed Rogge, Carole Spitzack, Kathie Turner, and Kittie Watson. Despite the extraordinary pressure of being understaffed for their academic mission and yet productive of scholarly research, my colleagues always found time to help me through both my personal and professional struggles. This project would never have been completed without their support.

The third level of community that has nurtured me is the larger community of scholars in the field of communication and in related fields. My inquiry into communicative ethics began as a dissertation under the direction of Rick Cherwitz at the University of Texas. James Kinneavy was especially helpful by pointing out the inadequacy of that initial approach to the problem because of its failure to confront the issues raised by postmodernism. This book rose out of the ashes of my somewhat naive dissertation. I am especially indebted to Ray McKerrow for his moral support and prodding criticism of my manuscript. Ray has also served me as a model of the ethical scholar, supporting my project even as we disagreed on fundamental questions. In addition to scholarly advice, Rod Hart and Beth Macom helped sustain me through my personal struggles. I also benefited greatly from advice and encouragement given by Tom Frentz, Jan Rushing, Carol Jablonski, John Lucaites, Don Ochs, and others too numerous to name. Furthermore, I gathered many insights from the discussions of the Peirce List on the Internet, led by Joe Ransdell of Texas Tech. The Peirce List illustrates the potential of the Internet when the participants are aware of their ethical obligations.

The fourth level of community that has supported me includes my friends and neighbors here in the New Orleans area. Living in New Orleans provides a constant reminder of the need to respect both diversity and community. As the favorite local metaphor has it, New Orleans is a gumbo. I am indebted to my neighbors, most of whom are black blue-collar workers who have experienced the consequences of excessive divisiveness firsthand, and to my friends around the horseshoe at Fat Harry's for reminding me that common sense deserves our critical respect. I am also thankful that I live in a national community that, despite its defects, allows criticism and dissent, enabling us to pursue our ethical obligation to make our communicative ecosystem more nurturing of all its members.

Finally, I thank the University of Alabama Press, especially Nicole Mitchell, for patient support of this project. Nicole's forbearance in encouraging me through my many problems despite the damage to her production schedule accounts for the fact that you now hold a book in your hands. I am especially grateful to the press's readers, who scrutinized my original manuscript and offered thorough and useful criticism. I am also indebted to the members of the press who have shepherded this project through production. I am sorry that limitations of space and time preclude my recognition of everyone who has helped me. Writing these insufficient acknowledgments has reminded me once again how much I depend upon the communicative ecosystem that supports me.

Community over Chaos

1

Our Postmodern Ethical Quandary

Are we in an era of ethical decline? In recent years we have seen high-ranking officials in the executive branch of government admit without remorse that they lied to Congress. A major network's news department confessed under pressure that it had rigged a demonstration of an automotive fuel tank explosion for dramatic effect. The story was supposed to be a fair investigation of the likelihood of such an explosion in an accident. We also are caught up in a national debate about "political correctness" in our communication. Is politically correct discourse *ethically* correct? Does ethical correctness mean anything anymore? Does anyone care?

I think ethical correctness does mean something, and I think most people still care about being ethical in their communication. We are, however, caught up in a period of ethical questioning. Such questioning is, at bottom, theoretical; and it indicates the importance of theory in our practical life. Theory tells us why and how things happen or should happen. Most of us still believe it is wrong to lie, but we are no longer certain why it is wrong or how exceptions might occur. Are our ethical judgments merely a result of our feelings—our sentiments, as Hume put it? Or are they based in something beyond the normal appearances of nature, in a transcendent human nature that leads us to follow general laws out of duty, as Kant would have it? Could our ethical judgments even be reasonable assessments of situations and outcomes, and if so, what principle distinguishes a *good* outcome from a *bad* one? The principle I recommend in this book is the principle of ecological reciprocity, our obligation to support the ecosystem that supports us. Most of us recognize that pollution of our physical ecosystem is wrong. We should also recognize that our social systems are communicative ecosystems, which are also vulnerable to pollution. An ecological perspective on ethical theory can restore confidence in the possibility of ethical behavior in practice.

Our current theoretical quandaries reflect our lack of ethical roots. Back in the age of modernism, we cut our links to the past in order to see what they were made of. Those links did not survive such destructive testing. In the 1930s, Kenneth Burke observed that modernism had set society adrift by its critique of the past:

In contrast with modern enlightenment, all previous schemes of adjustment looked like mere superstition. Modern mankind was detached: as regards its relationship with the continent of previous thought, it was insular. . . . The race distrusted its parentage, and children distrusted their parents. In this respect the era was one long record of symbolic parricide: no wonder many came to consider the "Oedipus complex" as the basis of human motivation.[1]

Since Burke first wrote these words, we have turned our parricidal tendencies loose upon modernism itself in what we call the *postmodern* age. Having undermined the traditions of the past, modernism constructed new foundations. Those foundations are today under deconstruction.

Modernism and postmodernism may seem to be arcane academic topics. The consequences of our inability to justify communicative ethics, however, reach far beyond the ivory tower. The quality of our communication affects the quality of our communities. We cannot act together with common purpose unless we can communicate with each other. The much maligned term *rhetoric* referred in ancient times to an art of community leadership—an art that through the years has been abused by unethical practitioners. Our failure to recover or reinvent a concept of rhetoric as the process of communal deliberation allows unethical rhetors to continue to pollute what Farrell calls our "rhetorical culture."[2] The fact that unethical rhetors abound does not mean that an ethical rhetoric is impossible. What stance should we take toward the claim "everyone is doing it"? This book takes the position that the community must protect its communicative ecosystem in order to continue to support all of its members. What everybody is doing may be polluting that communicative system, just as what everyone does often pollutes our biological ecosystems. In both cases, such pollution is unethical. Audiences and speakers are moral agents, responsible for the results of their communicative actions on the larger ecosystem.

I intend to show that a critical use of common sense and a reconsideration of some classical concepts in light of the modern and postmodern critique will provide us with a common ground for ethical judgment. Because postmodernism raises questions about both the concept of community and the concept of sense-making that are crucial to my project, in this first chapter I will consider the arguments of several significant proponents of the postmodern perspective—Lyotard, Derrida, and Foucault. Each of them is clearly motivated by ethical concerns, but none of them is yet able to offer a way of sharing those concerns with others that doesn't draw upon the very edifice he has undermined. This inability to maintain a consistent ethical stance at the theoretical level has consequences at the practical level. Before addressing the theoretical questions, let's consider an example of these practical consequences at the mundane level of a comic book.

Ethical Aporia in *Animal Man*

Animal Man is a comic book that has taken to pamphleteering on behalf of animal rights. Discourse that attempts to influence community action is rhetoric in the classical tradition, although the style and medium would seem unusual to a classicist. Nevertheless, as rhetoric it carries with it certain ethical responsibilities derived from its nature as political discourse. Neither Aristotle nor Cicero would have much difficulty grounding the ethics of such rhetoric in the needs of the community. For Grant Morrison, the postmodern writer of *Animal Man*, however, no such grounding is available. Burned out in his attempt to create an ethical rhetoric, Morrison resigns as writer; but he does so in an unusual manner in the comic book itself, in an episode titled "Deus ex Machina."[3] In this episode, Morrison writes himself into the story and introduces himself to Animal Man, the superhero of the book. The Morrison character explains to Animal Man that he as writer is a "demiurgic power" that doesn't create anything but uses and spoils the purity of what is there. Unable to justify his power, he refuses to continue in that role.

The poststructural semiotic influence manifests itself in a confusion of levels of symbolism that allows the "real" author to enter into the symbolic creation. At the same time, the author confesses that he is not an *auctoritas*—an originating subject—but a transmitter of previously existing symbols. "You existed long before I wrote about you and, if you're lucky, you'll still be young when I'm old or dead," the Morrison character tells Animal Man. Morrison also employs Baudrillard's concept of hyperrealism by making the cartoon characters colorful while representing his own world in gray and sepia tones. Animal Man comments on the dullness: "Your world must be terrible. It seems so . . . gray and bleak." On the other hand, the hyperreal world of the superhero also has an excess of violent action. In an earlier episode, Animal Man's wife and children were murdered. "It added drama. All stories need drama and it's easy to get a cheap emotional shock by killing popular characters," Morrison explains. When Animal Man asks whether Morrison would bring his family back, Morrison responds in true Baudrillardian fashion: "Sorry, it wouldn't be realistic. Pointless violence and death is 'realistic.' Comic books are 'realistic' now."

Morrison's cynicism seems to be based in postmodern antiphilosophy and antihumanism. He denies that any metanarrative really structures life:

Animal Man: You haven't been much good at writing my life, have you? I've just wandered through a series of unconnected events, with people telling me that everything is connected.

Morrison: Yeah, well, that's the trouble with my stories— they always seem to build up to something that never actually happens. That's the trouble with my life, too.

Animal Man: My life, you mean!

If these are my stories you've been telling, if I'm the star of this "comic book," then why am I always on the sidelines? Why am I always just an observer?

Morrison: It's the same for almost everyone. We expect starring roles in our own lives but somehow we just end up with walk-on parts.

Life doesn't have plots and subplots and denouements. It's just a big collection of loose ends and dangling threads that never get explained.

Animal Man: Listen, where I come from, we expect real stories. I'm getting sick of these pseudo-existential narratives!

Morrison also denies any special rational or moral qualities to human beings:

. . . in the end it all boils down to three words. "Might makes right."
Man is able to abuse and slaughter and experiment on animals simply because he's stronger than they are. Other than that, there's no moral ground on which to justify any animal exploitation.

A child with leukemia has no more intrinsic right to life than does a white lab rat. Anyone who believes that man's "intelligence" makes him special has only to look at the way we continue to destroy our environment.

Man is not an intelligent species.

As readers, we suspect that Morrison's postmodern cynicism is born out of a disappointed idealism. The closing of the episode suggests that the problem is indeed the loss of his childhood narrative. As author, Morrison restores Animal Man to his family, which is unharmed. Morrison as character, on the other hand, returns to his childhood home in a final, futile attempt to restore his metaphysical narrative: "When I was young, I had an imaginary friend called Foxy. He lived in a vast underground kingdom. A Utopia ruled over by peaceful and intelligent foxes. I used to signal to him. My parents bought me a torch so that I could signal to him. Not a flashlight. We call them torches over here. I used to stand at the top of Angus Oval and shine my torch out towards the hills. Foxy always signalled back." The character Morrison climbs up Angus Oval and sends his signal out into the dark. "Foxy, I came back. I didn't forget. I came back. The line of the hills stays dark. There is no answering light. No light at all. Clouds pile up in the darkness, weighted with snow. Curtains are drawn. Windows blink and go dark. Wind whines in the power lines. Stars go out. Streets are empty. Goodbye." In the second bleak frame after Morrison exits from the scene, a light signal flashes from the distant hills. The metaphysical origin, as always, is deferred and unreachable.

Morrison's "Deus ex Machina" is not, of course, a good example of postmodern theorizing. It is, rather, an example of the demoralizing effects of postmodern thinking on communicative action. The reception and interpretation of postmodern thought in popular culture leads to a paralyzing cynicism about the possibility of effective and ethical rhetorical action. A young man who hoped to improve his world through communication yields to this cynicism and publicly resigns. Even as Morrison the character surrenders to his postmodern malaise, however, Morrison the author gives his readers a ray of hope in the returned signal from the hills. He will not deprive his readers of faith in some kind of Kantian thing-in-itself that is unknowable yet still grounds our morality. This remnant of optimism in Morrison the author is insufficient to motivate him to continue, but it reveals the anguish in his resignation.

The anguish of Morrison reflects the anguish of our age. We are inheritors of the initial optimism of modernism, but we cannot sustain this optimism in the shadows cast by Auschwitz, the Gulag, and, more recently, Bosnia-Herzegovina. Postmodern theorizing has, for the most part, focused on showing why our earlier optimism was unjustified. A new, corrected ground for optimism is not forthcoming, although writers like Lyotard, Derrida, and Foucault seem sincerely to wish for one. Without some cause for optimism, a workable theory of ethics is impossible. Ethics is the art of practical action, and practical action requires the motivating belief that action can improve a situation in some way, even if it be simply by improving the subject of that action. Postmodernism continues to undercut that motivating belief.

Lyotard and the Fragmentation of Community

French theorists have led the postmodern critique of modernism. Prominent among these theorists is Lyotard, who characterizes postmodernism as "the crisis of narratives." Although science criticizes narratives as fables, when it seeks to legitimize itself, it also relies on grand narratives to support its discourse of legitimation, which is philosophy. The term *modern* in Lyotard's usage designates "any science that legitimates itself with reference to a metadiscourse of this kind making an explicit appeal to some grand narrative, such as the dialectics of Spirit, the hermeneutics of meaning, the emancipation of the rational or working subject, or the creation of wealth." In contrast, the *postmodern* is simply "incredulity toward metanarratives."[4]

Lyotard describes two major versions of the modern metanarratives that were used to legitimize the claims of scientific knowledge to universality. The different versions have constructed different subjects for their stories. One version is practical and emancipatory, "humanity as the hero of liberty."[5] The other version is speculative: "The subject of knowledge is not the people, but the speculative spirit."[6] The speculative spirit is the subject of a totalizing narrative that must construct a unity to the various discourses, combining positive empirical statements with moral statements. The epitome of the speculative version is the Hegelian system based on a universal history of Spirit. "The narrator must be a metasubject in the process of formulating both the legitimacy of the discourses of the empirical sciences and that of the direct institutions of popular cultures."[7] This metasubject cannot be a historical community, not even a community of scientists, but must transcend its historical instantiations.

The practical metanarrative is supposedly more concrete. It is the story of the emancipation of the autonomous subject from external constraints. The subject rules itself with just laws because the legislators are the citizens. The autonomous subject has a right to science in order to govern itself well. In this Kantian model, moral self-governing is the end and science is the means. "Knowledge is no longer the subject, but in the service of the subject: its only legitimacy (though it is formidable) is the fact that it allows morality to become reality."[8] This Kantian model is critically dependent on Kant's essentialist humanism. Because for Kant the essence of the human being is rational, the human will can give general laws. Rational human beings are autonomous because they are subject to their own general laws. The categorical imperative and the autonomy of human beings both depend upon this essential rationalism that transcends empirical circumstances.[9]

Modernism, according to Lyotard, also developed two different models of society: "either society forms a functional whole, or it is divided in two."[10] Both models are derived from nineteenth century theories. The idea of society as a functional whole began as an organic model of society; after modification by cybernetic theory, the organic model became the self-regulating system of Talcott Parsons. Contemporary system theories of society are technocratic. "The true goal of the system, the reason it programs itself like a computer, is the optimization of the global relationship between input and output—in other words, performativity."[11] The alternative model is the Marxist model of inherent division and opposition within society, the model of class struggle. This model, according to Lyotard, barely survives in the academic traditions of critical theory.

The different models of knowledge and of society result in different concepts of communication and information in society. Various ethical principles can be derived from different combinations of these models and metanarratives. Stalinism, for example, combined the totalizing narrative of universal history with the social model of class struggle to define an ethic of conformity with the Communist party. The party leadership stood for the proletariat and its historical destiny. Propaganda that coincided with this destiny was ethical by definition. On the other hand, in capitalistic states, the news industry could portray itself as the functional representative of the people's right to know, derived from the people's autonomy as human beings. Information could then be marketed as a commodity or used to deliver an audience to an advertiser. An ethic of "objectivity" assured larger markets for the commodity and fit in with the technocratic systems model of society by portraying mass media as serving the function of "surveillance of the environment."[12]

We could imagine the comic-book writer Morrison effectively justifying his rhetoric under either of these metanarratives. He might see the animal rights movement as the inevitable next step in the history of civil rights. The few but dedicated members of the movement could be viewed as the vanguard of history. His communicative ethic would compel him to show the essential historical truth regardless of its offensiveness. Taking offense would be a sign of a kind of "bourgeois" morality. Art would be subordinated to a higher purpose. On the other hand, Morrison could have decided that his function in our society was simply to produce a commodity that people used for their own purposes as free citizens. He could then focus on "production values" to ensure that his readers received the highest-quality comic book he could produce. In the process, he could take special satisfaction if he were able to include information about how animals were treated or the state of the environment in general. His ethical problems would be limited to balancing the surveillance and entertainment functions of his work.

In either case, a supporting metanarrative could have protected Morrison from his dark night of the soul. As Lyotard points out, however, under postmodernism the "grand narrative has lost its credibility, regardless of what mode of unification it uses, regardless of whether it is a speculative narrative or a narrative of emancipation."[13] Neither narrative is able to unify the underlying disparate discourses. In postmodernism, the underlying differences are taken to be irreconcilable.

To account for what has happened, Lyotard relies on Wittgenstein's conception of language games. Different discourses operate in the same way a game of chess operates, "by a set of rules determining the properties of each of the pieces, in other words, the proper way to move them." For Lyotard's purposes, the concept of language games leads to three observations and two principles. The observations are that (1) "the players invent the rules"; (2) "if there are no rules, there is no game"; and (3) "every utterance should be thought of as a 'move' in a game." The principles that he sees as underlying his method as a whole are: (1) "to speak is to fight, in the sense of playing, and speech acts fall within the domain of a general agonistics"; and (2) "the observable social bond is composed of language 'moves.' "[14] Lyotard's approach breaks with the modern tradition's metanarratives and its alternative social models.

Under Lyotard's prodding, the speculative model falls apart into a collection of different language games. "There is erosion at work inside the speculative game, and by loosening the weave of the encyclopedic net in which each science was to find its place, it eventually sets them free. . . . The speculative hierarchy of learning gives way to an immanent and, as it were, 'flat' network of areas of inquiry, the respective frontiers of which are in constant flux."[15] The meanings within one game do not relate to other games; no secret depth, no common spirit inheres in them all. The rules are made within each game and apply only to that game. Little narratives may justify the individual games to their players, but no metanarrative can justify them all.

The deconstruction of the Kantian discourse of emancipation is more complex. Kant recognized the separate domains of speculative reason, practical reason, and judgment. Lyotard treats these as separate and incommensurable language games that should not be combined. Instead, he advocates an aesthetics of the sublime because the sublime to Kant exceeds the limits of representation. As Kant expressed it, the sublime "concerns rational ideas, which, although no adequate presentation of them is possible, may be excited and called into the mind by that very inadequacy itself which does not admit of presentation through the senses."[16] For Kant, the sublime is the experience of the imagination turning inward and finding the unpresentable idea of the supersensible. It is this indeterminate idea of the supersensible within us that provides "the point of union of all our faculties *a priori:* for we are left with no other expedient to bring reason into harmony with itself."[17]

Lyotard's translation of the faculties into language games explicitly drops out the Kantian allusion to noumenal unity of the faculties. The loss is significant because Kant also based the possibility of moral autonomy in the realm of the noumenal. Lyotard is not being quite true to the Kantian text when he uses Kant in support of his fragmented postmodern aesthetics of the sublime:

Finally, it must be clear that it is our business not to supply reality but to invent allusions to the conceivable which cannot be presented. And it is not to be expected that this task will effect the last reconciliation between language games (which, under the name of faculties, Kant knew to be separated by a chasm), and that only the transcendental illusion (that of Hegel) can hope to totalize them into a real unity. But Kant also knew that the price to pay for such an illusion is terror. The nineteenth and twentieth centuries have given us as much terror as we can take. We have paid a high enough price for the nostalgia of the whole and the one, for the reconciliation of the concept and the sensible, of the transparent and the communicable experience. Under the general demand for slackening and for appeasement, we can hear the mutterings of the desire for a return of terror, for the realization of the fantasy to seize reality. The answer is: Let us wage a war on totality; let us be witnesses to the unpresentable; let us activate the differences and save the honor of the name.[18]

Kant did, indeed, recognize a chasm between the phenomenal world that is the domain of the intellect and the noumenal world that is the domain of practical reason. For Kant, however, the faculty of judgment provided a "mediating link" between the concepts of nature (intellect) and the concepts of freedom (reason).[19] Kant further insists on a universality inherent in the judgment of taste, a validity for everyone, that is dependent upon "the supersensible substratum of humanity."[20] Kant's critique of judgment assumes a universal *sensus communis* based in the unknowable essence of humanity. This bridge between language games is missing in Lyotard's version of Kant. In fact, Lyotard argues the contrary, that such universality can be achieved only through terror.

Lyotard's misreading of Kant seems to be the result of considering Kant's emancipatory idealism from the viewpoint of postmodern pessimism. The presumed sensus communis of Kant becomes for Lyotard the promise of a community that is never realized. The mark of its failure is Auschwitz. As Pefanis summarizes Lyotard's argument, " 'Reason' in the service of the idea of humanity, in the service of its achievable end through history, stands crossed and double-crossed at the threshold of *post-history* by the signs of its historical failure."[21] Lyotard's disgust with totalizing narratives is not a result of reading Kant but a result of seeing Kant's idealism double-crossed by history. Having been double-crossed, Lyotard rejects the possibility of communality in favor of nihilistic fragmentation: "Here is a course of action: harden, worsen and accelerate decadence. Adopt the perspective of active nihilism, exceed the mere recognition—be it depressive or admiring—of the destruction of all values. Become more and more incredulous. Push decadence further still and accept, for instance, to destroy the belief in truth under all its forms."[22]

While wishing to destroy the belief in truth, Lyotard still wishes to preserve a meaning for justice. At times he expects to have his cake and deconstruct it, too. His counterpoint to Kant's suprasensible source for the autonomous will is the libido, an indeterminate source of random impulses.[23] The randomness of the libido may account for the diversity of language games, but Lyotard is unable to derive an ethical principle like justice from it. He tells us:

Consensus has become an outmoded and suspect value. But justice as a value is neither outmoded nor suspect. We must thus arrive at an idea and practice of justice that is not linked to that of consensus.

A recognition of the heteromorphous nature of language games is a first step in that direction. This obviously implies a renunciation of terror, which assumes that they are isomorphic and tries to make them so. The second step is the principle that any consensus on the rules defining a game and the "moves" playable within it *must* be local, in other words, agreed on by its present players and subject to eventual cancellation.[24]

Unfortunately, nothing in Lyotard's theory of language games makes a renunciation of terror obligatory. Language games are forms of fighting, he tells us, although the fighting is "play." Sometimes, however, the play leads to real violence. Just recently, in a Little League baseball game in California, a seventeen-year-old spectator died as the result of violence after the game. During the game, taunting and racial slurs had raised tension between the teams and between their partisan fans. After the death and another serious injury occurred, the umpire, in classic understatement, called it a breakdown in civility and attributed it to the example of professional players that the teenagers emulated.[25] The Balkans are a more terrifying example of how diverse language games may escalate from play fighting to real fighting. The various ethnic groups each have their own local rules governing how they shall operate within their own game, but no common rules govern how the different groups shall treat each other. Such common rules would require a consensus that Lyotard has eliminated as a possibility. As long as their libidos urge them on, we would expect these members of various language games to go on killing each other.

This chaos is clearly not what Lyotard has in mind in his celebration of diversity. His vision includes an opening up of information sources to the public so that groups determining their own rules would have access to information to help them in their decisions. Despite his opposition to consensus, Lyotard cannot avoid envisioning diversity against the horizon of community. He simply fails to notice that horizon, which itself makes possible his concept of justice. Lyotard's intention was to sketch "the outline of a politics that would respect both the desire for justice and the desire for the unknown." His sketch of diversity is not yet a politics, however, because politics is about community, the polis. Diversity without community can be achieved through tribal warfare. Diversity within community is, in fact, the problem of justice, as Aristotle long ago recognized.[26] Lyotard's vision requires the larger community to distribute its resources more fairly, a traditional question of distributive justice. Lyotard takes for granted a concept of justice that is rooted in a discourse tradition, or language game. Yet his own argument does not allow him to privilege any particular language game. He gives us no reason to prefer the language game of Aristotelian justice to the language game of violence, unless justice is somehow inscribed on our libidos.

In the Aristotelian tradition, justice is a basic principle of community. Communication is the condition of possibility of community.[27] So it is also in Kenneth Burke. Burke recognizes that division is a basic operating principle of rhetoric:

We need never deny the presence of strife, enmity, faction as a characteristic motive of rhetorical expression. We need not close our eyes to their almost tyrannous ubiquity in human relations; we can be on the alert always to see how such temptations to strife are implicit in the institutions that condition human relationships; yet we can at the same time always look beyond this order, to the principle of identification in general, a terministic choice justified by the fact that the identifications in the order of love are also characteristic of rhetorical expression.[28]

A principle of justice that operates between the diverse language games requires a higher order of identification that emphasizes association rather than dissociation. Some minimum consensus (sensus communis) is required for Lyotard's vision of justice to become a reality. His own theory is inadequate to his vision.

Derrida and the Deconstruction of Essence

For the last ten years or so, *deconstruction* has been a faddish term in the academic community. In part, the attention received was deserved. In the hands of a talented scholar like Derrida, deconstruction has raised serious questions about some of our metaphysical presuppositions. On the other hand, at its worst, deconstruction appears to be an evasion of serious scholarly thought and a preference for clever polemics. If not properly contextualized, deconstruction can result in a loss of faith in the ability of communication to accomplish anything worthwhile. The disheartening of the comic-book author Morrison echoes just such a simplistic acceptance of deconstruction. Morrison's futile attempt to contact the origin of his beliefs reflects the focus on origins in the Western tradition of metaphysics. Deconstruction shows that the attempt to make the origin present to one's mind is always necessarily doomed.

Deconstruction belongs to an alternative Western tradition, the tradition of skepticism. Within that tradition, some skeptics have been pragmatic, giving up certainty but seeking probable grounds for reasoned action. Others have turned cynical, allowing doubt to vitiate any attempt at constructive action. Curiously, such radical skepticism seems to require unwavering faith in the results of one's own skeptical inquiries.

Derrida's skepticism does not seem to be so very radical. He questions the possibility that essences or origins can be made present to the mind through communication. He calls the belief in the presence of such essences logocentrism. Ellis criticizes Derrida for using the term *logocentrism* because for him it obscures the connection with essentialism, which has been the object of a long history of criticism. Ellis believes that, in general, deconstruction simply uses more obscure terms to discuss problems that were already well known.[29] Ellis has a point in that Continental philosophy and Anglo-American analytic philosophy often seem unaware of their common concerns. The term *logocentrism*, however, does identify an important aspect of the metaphysical tradition derived from its early history in Greece. The knowledge of essences is connected with *logos*. Plato established dialectic (*dia*, through, by means of, thorough; *lexis*, speech) as the preferred method of metaphysics. Perception was limited to appearances; only through speaking thoroughly could knowledge of true reality be achieved. Aristotle further refined this art of thorough speaking by means of his organon of logic. The heated opposition of both Plato and Aristotle to the sophists was based in a critique of the sophistic uses of speech for purposes other than revealing truth. Derrida's term *logocentrism* seems a particularly apt description of the Western metaphysical tradition.

The term *logocentrism* also emphasizes the fact that deconstruction for Derrida is a *metaphysical* critique. To assume that it applies generally to the pragmatics of language use is to make a huge inferential leap without justification. Derrida is working within the Kantian tradition of questioning the conditions of the possibility of metaphysics; he is not doubting our ability to use language to get things done. According to Norris, "Deconstruction neither denies nor really affects the commonsense view that language exists to communicate meaning. It *suspends* that view for its own specific purpose of seeing what happens when the writs of convention no longer run."[30] Derrida himself employs the tools of classical Western metaphysics, such as the search for conditions of possibility, the syllogism, the principle of noncontradiction, and essence/appearance distinctions, among others.[31] Derrida acknowledges that he works within metaphysics:

> The movements of deconstruction do not destroy structures from the outside. They are not possible and effective, nor can they take accurate aim, except by inhabiting those structures. Inhabiting them *in a certain way*, because one always inhabits, and all the more when one does not suspect it. Operating necessarily from the inside, borrowing all the strategic and economic resources of subversion from the old structure, borrowing them structurally, that is to say without being able to isolate their elements and atoms, the enterprise of deconstruction always in a certain way falls prey to its own work. This is what the person who has begun the same work in another area of the same habitation does not fail to point out with zeal.[32]

The texts of deconstruction are themselves always subject to a deconstructive reading because they must use metaphysical language. One of the difficulties in reading Derrida is that he plays with his own text as he writes, showing its own deconstructive possibilities where it uses, as it must always use, metaphysical constructs.

Derrida uses the term "deconstruction" to translate the terms *Destruktion* and *Abbau* in Heidegger, where they meant the dismantling of the structure of metaphysics to see how it was constructed and to overcome it. As Schrift indicates, however, "Derridean *déconstruction* does not seek the overcoming of metaphysics; rather, convinced of the inescapable closure of metaphysical thinking, deconstructive reading seeks instead to circumvent the border between what is within the philosophical tradition as a metaphysics of presence, and what is external to that tradition."[33] Metaphysics privileges certain concepts and marginalizes others. Because metaphysics claims to be speaking of essences, such privileging and marginalizing become permanent within a given metaphysical tradition. Derrida insists that certain kinds of privileging and marginalizing are endemic to the entire Western tradition of metaphysics. His deconstructive reading attempts to bring out those marginalized meanings that have been suppressed in the text.

One of Derrida's best known, but least understood, challenges to privileged meanings is his questioning of the primacy of speech over writing. In the traditional model, speech signifies the presence of an idea in the mind. Writing is a supplemental signifier that signifies the signifier of speech. Therefore, speech is the primary sign system and writing is secondary. Derrida overturns this hierarchy. He argues that the basic character of the sign is better understood on the model of writing than on the model of speech. Speech misleads us into believing that the idea being signified is present. All signifiers stand for other signifiers, however; "the signified always already functions as a signifier. The secondarity that it seemed possible to ascribe to writing alone affects all signifieds in general, affects them always already, the moment they *enter the game.*"[34] Here Derrida seems to be very close to Peirce's semiotic theory, which I shall discuss in more detail in the next chapter. Peirce recognized that the process of interpretation was theoretically, but not practically, endless. A signifier (representamen) calls up a signified (interpretant) that is in turn a signifier for a new signified, ad infinitum. There is thus no transcendental signified standing as a guarantee of meaning. On these grounds, Derrida makes the startling claim "There is nothing outside of the text."[35] Our thinking cannot escape this ongoing process of semiosis, construed by Derrida as writing, or text.

All language use, then, partakes of the nature of writing in that it never directly signifies a present signified but defers meaning through the chain of signifiers. Furthermore, even in common usage, we use the term *writing* to mean more than marks on a page. We use it for the concept of inscription in general. "It is also in this sense that the contemporary biologist speaks of writing and *pro-gram* in relation to the most elementary processes of information within the living cell."[36] We can see that what Derrida means by "writing" is not literal writing:

If "writing" signifies inscription and especially the durable institution of a sign (and that is the only irreducible kernel of the concept of writing), writing in general covers the entire field of linguistic signs. In that field a certain sort of instituted signifiers may then appear, "graphic" in the narrow and derivative sense of the word, ordered by a certain relationship with other instituted—hence "written," even if they are "phonic"—signifiers. The very idea of institution—hence of the arbitrariness of the sign—is unthinkable before the possibility of writing and outside of its horizon. Quite simply, that is, outside of the horizon itself, outside the world as space of inscription, as the opening to the emission and to the spatial *distribution* of signs, to the *regulated play* of their differences, even if they are "phonic."[37]

Writing here is used figuratively as a synecdoche (species representing genus) for language in general. By *writing* he means an "arche-writing . . . which I continue to call writing only because it essentially communicates with the vulgar concept of writing."[38] Since an *archē* is a logical first principle, Derrida calls this figurative sense of writing that underlies the possibility of speech "arche-writing." Writing illustrates how language actually signifies and so is a more suitable synecdoche than the privileged synecdoche of the metaphysical tradition—speech. Writing shows its arbitrariness and its dependence on an instituted code. Speech hides these facts.

Derrida argues that the privileging of speech within the Western metaphysical tradition was a matter of logical necessity, not of chance.

The privilege of the *phonè* does not depend upon a choice that could have been avoided. It responds to a moment of *economy* (let us say of the "life" of "history" or of "being as self-relationship"). The system of "hearing (understanding)-oneself-speak" through the phonic substance—which *presents* itself as the nonexterior, nonmundane, therefore nonempirical or noncontingent signifier—has necessarily dominated the history of the world during an entire epoch, and has even produced the idea of the world, the idea of world-origin, that arises from the difference between the worldly and the non-worldly, the outside and the inside, ideality and nonideality, universal and nonuniversal, transcendental and empirical, etc.[39]

The metaphysics of presence requires the feeling of immediate contact with that which is signified. This feeling is achieved in listening to ourselves speak. The ideas we speak seem present to us. In fact, what was present and is now gone was the sound-image of a signifier. Nevertheless, the feeling of immediacy is sufficient to ground the metaphysics of presence. According to Derrida, metaphysics from Plato to Heidegger has relied upon the feeling of presence engendered by "hearing (understanding)-oneself-speak." The dualisms of metaphysics are a product of that system that constitutes *logos*—"the spoken/thought sense" whether finite or infinite (as in the logos of a creator God).[40] So for example, in Aristotle, the voice is the privileged signifier of mental experiences that are impressions or mirror images of things. These mental images form a kind of universal language, a logos. In medieval theology the logos is the mind of God. In both cases, spoken language is deemed to be closer to the universal truth of the logos.

This metaphysical tradition is the "metaphysics of presence" that is "logocentric" and hence the object of deconstruction. The key concept used by deconstruction is what Derrida calls *différance*. Différance is what Derrida puts in the place of origin, essence, and presence. Not a standard French word, *différance* is a neologism that illustrates its own meaning. When spoken, the *a* is phonemically identical to *e*; the difference between *différance* and *différence* is only apparent in writing. Therefore, to understand the play of difference between the words when spoken, we would have to be mindful of the written version. The neologism is also illustrative of the principle of undecidability in interpretation, because Derrida uses it to carry forward in noun form the ambiguity of the verb. The French verb *différer* includes both English meanings "to differ" and "to defer." This simple ambiguity is the key to the theory underlying deconstructive practice. Derrida uses the undecidability of the term to bring together linguistic structuralism and phenomenology in critique of each other.

From linguistic structuralism, Derrida has borrowed the notion that language is a structure of differences, at the levels of both signifier and signified. He uses this notion to critique the Husserlian demand that philosophy return "to the things themselves" and even the Heideggerian redirection of phenomenology toward Being itself. There is no fullness of an object (plenitude) present to the mind that can be reached through a phenomenological reduction. The phenomenological reduction leads back to the *trace*, a mark of difference that can suggest only that something might have passed this way. All it really shows is that a process of differing has taken place. This differing underlies all the essences of Husserlian phenomenology and also determines Heidegger's ontico-ontological difference:

The ontico-ontological difference and its ground [the transcendence of Das-ein] . . . are not absolutely originary. Differance by itself would be more "originary," but one would no longer be able to call it "origin" or "ground," those notions belonging essentially to the history of onto-theology, to the system functioning as the effacing of difference. It can, however, be thought of in the closest proximity to itself only on one condition: that one begins by determining it as the ontico-ontological difference before erasing that determination.[41]

Heidegger criticized his predecessors for effacing the ontico-ontological difference. For him, "the possibility of ontology, of philosophy as a science, stands and falls with the possibility of a sufficiently clear accomplishment of this differentiation between being and beings."[42] Derrida asserts that différance is the condition of possibility for the ontico-ontological difference itself.

Différance is not, however, some more originary metaphysical essence or first cause. It is neither pure being nor a being. As Caputo explains,

The namelessness of *différance* does not consist in being an unnameable being but in pointing to the differential matrix which generates names and concepts, in which they are produced as effects. Of course, as soon as it is coined, uttered, repeated, and entered into the lexicon of "post-structuralist" thinkers, *différance* becomes itself another nominal unity, one more effect of the differential matrix of which it means to be no more than indicator. But it would be a serious misunderstanding to think that it is some master name or kerygmatic announcement of a Being beyond Being, or of a presence which is so pure that it cannot itself appear and be present except by means of the finite and imperfect traces of itself which it leaves behind. Lacking all ontological profundity and mystical depth, *différance* stretches out laterally over the surface as the chain of substitutability, as the coded tracing, within which are generated all names, all the relatively stable nominal unities, including the name of God, including even the name *différance*.[43]

Thus, for Derrida, différance replaces the ultimate concepts of metaphysics but then must be regarded as erased, as leaving nothing in its place. Différance is used to show that the condition of possibility of all metaphysical concepts is the matrix of language itself, or as Derrida would say, arche-writing. The institution of a code of differences is logically prior to the understanding of essences or of the ontico-ontological difference. This code always deflects phenomenology from achieving its desire to return to the things themselves.

While using Saussurean structuralism to critique the claims of phenomenology, Derrida also finds the metaphysics of presence working in the heart of structuralism. Structuralism, despite its progress, "is plagued by a scientificist objectivism, that is to say by another unperceived or unconfessed metaphysics" because it fails to ask about the transcendental origin of the system itself.[44] Structuralism is a formalism that has not sufficiently considered the nature of form. An adequate consideration of form requires a phenomenological reduction, which would reveal the necessity of the *trace*. For difference to appear to us, we must retain "a minimal unit of temporal experience"; for "without a trace retaining the other as other in the same, no difference would do its work and no meaning would appear."[45] The sound-image of the phoneme *p* is meaningful, for example, only if we understand it in opposition to the sound-image of *b*. Therefore, a phenomenological reduction to the essence of *p* reveals the trace of *b* also, or else difference cannot be perceived. This is true as well of concepts: "it founds the metaphysical opposition between the sensible and the intelligible, then between signifier and signified, expression and content, etc."[46] The meaning of *intelligible* requires a trace of *sensible* as a ground of difference. Any meaningful term thus carries within itself the trace of its contradictory term. "The trace is in fact the absolute origin of sense in general. Which amounts to saying once again that there is no absolute origin of sense in general. The trace is the differance which opens appearance [*l'apparaître*] and signification."[47]

This play between contradictories is the source of meaning, including the meaning of "presence."

Differance is what makes the movement of signification possible only if each element that is said to be "present," appearing on the stage of presence, is related to something other than itself but retains the mark of a past element and already lets itself be hollowed out by the mark of its relation to a future element. This trace relates no less to what is called the future than to what is called the past, and it constitutes what is called the present by this very relation to what it is not, to what it absolutely is not.[48]

Most of the history of metaphysics has followed Aristotle in viewing time as a succession of nows. Evidence and truth are what is present to us in the here and now. What continues to be present to us, the eternally present, is isness, essence, *ousia*. This is the metaphysics of presence, to which even structuralism has fallen prey, in Derrida's view. For Derrida, *now* is a fiction, a construct to be deconstructed. According to Harvey, Derrida's approach is Husserlian, recognizing "a fundamental absence within the moment of the present. That is, with the movement of consciousness from retention to protention, and back again, we have a result that is synthetic which forms that which metaphysics calls the Now: the Present."[49] In our consciousness, the present is the play between remembering and anticipating. Consider the exercise of keeping a telephone number present in your mind while you dial it. You recite the number to yourself; that is, you repeatedly cast the number forward from memory into anticipation in order to keep it continually passing before the mind. Phenomenologically, the present is the pause (*epokhē*) between protention and retention. Through the play of opposition between recalling and anticipating, we create a space in which to construct the present. "The present is that from which we believe we are able to think time, effacing the inverse necessity to think the present from time as differance."[50] As Harvey notes, this metaphysical argument collapses metaphysics into mythology:

[T]he essence of immediate presence is that spacing which is absence itself— the distance from one moment to the next, which is incessantly on the move. Its mediation forms the essence of essence, which is to say, the sign as the detour on the way to truth, is precisely the truth of the truth. The metaphysics of metaphysics, if one prefers. But this is of course no longer metaphysics. Derrida's thought is focused on absence, on non-identity, on signifiers rather than signifieds-as-such, on "mythology" rather than "philosophy," and on the trace rather than the essence.[51]

Philosophy is discourse, and like any discourse it is susceptible to mythological and rhetorical analysis. The heart of metaphysics—presence—is a rhetorical figure, an oxymoron of protention-retention.

On the other hand, metaphysics inheres in all our forms of discourse, even our comic books. In *Animal Man*, Morrison's attempt to contact his mythical ideal of the Fox King is analogous to the philosopher's attempt to make essences evident. He remembers the torch signal from his childhood, and he repeats the signal, anticipating a response in the present that he has bracketed. The response is deferred to the future of that bracketed space of time, however; so Morrison leaves, despondent. We the readers see the returned signal, but even so, its meaning is deferred for us as well. The return signal, after all, is only another signifier in the infinite chain of signifiers. Yet the narrative suggests that Morrison would have gone on with his work if he had seen that signifier. Morrison was trying to ground his ethical decision in his myth. Because the light signal stood for his myth to him, the signifier would have sufficed. In the pragmatic world, signifiers and belief motivate action.

Deconstruction has little to say about ethics in practice. Bernasconi advises us not to ask what deconstruction has to offer as an ethic:

The demand that deconstruction provide *an* ethics betrays not only traditional presuppositions about the possibility of generating ethical systems, but also a miscomprehension about the nature of deconstruction, confusing it for one philosophy among others. Hence in the face of the demand for an ethics, deconstruction can reply, in the course of its reading of Levinas, that *the ethical relation is impossible and "the impossible has already occurred" at this very moment.* In other words, the ethical relation occurs in the face-to-face relation, as witnessed in the demand for an ethics itself, a demand which it is as impossible to satisfy as it is to refuse. To acknowledge this is to submit the demand for an ethics, not to instruction, but to deconstruction. And the *possibility* of ethics is referred, not to its actuality, but to its *impossibility* . This does not mean that writing ethical systems is impossible. Only that the attempt to do so is a denial of the ethical relation, though one which (fortunately) can never be complete; ontology denies the ethical relation when it presents its ethical system, but at the same time gives birth to it afresh in the saying of its said.[52]

Bernasconi's argument borrows Heidegger's notion of authenticity and applies it to Levinas's concept of the ethical relation. When an ethic is interpreted as rules, to develop an ethic is to be inauthentic and to deny the existential ethical relation. On the other hand, the demand for an ethic evidences the ethical relation in which we find ourselves. Unfortunately, deconstruction cannot help us decide what to do.

Still, Derrida expects us to know what is ethical within a pragmatic situation. He attacks dishonesty and errors in his critics. They should know better because they are operating within a relatively stable context of rules:

It constitutes the object of agreements sufficiently confirmed so that one might *count [tabler]* on ties that are stable, and hence demonstrable, linking words, concepts and things, as well as on the difference between the true and the false. And hence one is able, in this context, to denounce errors, and even dishonesty and confusions. This "pragmatics" . . . also entails de-ontological (or if you prefer, ethical-political) rules of discussion of which I remind my critics when I believe they have failed to observe them.[53]

Pragmatic situations determine probable meanings. Not just any meaning is acceptable. Without rules for understanding, the text itself would disappear. We should be aware of the rules for meaning when we are part of a continuing tradition, a relatively stable context for discussion.

Although Derrida expects us to know the rules, Bernasconi makes it clear that deconstruction will not provide them. Who is right?

They both are. Deconstruction cannot provide rules because it is not a constructive discourse. It is, as Caputo writes, parasitic:

> Deconstruction lies in wait for "discourse" to stake its claims and then it pounces on it, showing how much trouble this discourse has bought for itself by its boldness. . . . This is another way of saying that deconstruction itself has nothing to say, or better that there is no deconstruction "itself," that it is a parasitic practice, not a substantive position. In classical terms, the Being of deconstruction always exists *in alio*, by inhabiting the discourse of others, never *in se*, as something present in itself, as some form of *ousia*.[54]

Because it is skeptical and parasitic, deconstruction cannot offer values but only borrow those values that are extant, even the values of traditional humanism. According to Goodheart, deconstruction of the grounds of humanism is the privilege of skeptics in communities where humane values are generally accepted.

> It is inconceivable (at least to me) that a deconstructive attitude could exist in the time of the Spanish Civil War, World War II, or in Solzhenitsyn's Soviet Union. This is not to say that the skeptical intelligence could not direct a stream of fresh (even satiric) thought on the clichés that supported the Loyalist cause in Spain . . . or the Allied war effort or on Russian dissident thought. It is simply that skepticism never fully defined such an intelligence, that it remained rooted in convictions about truth, decency, and humanity, terms that it had no interest in deconstructing. Indeed, its concerns are with the moments when truth, decency, and humanity are betrayed by the right side.[55]

As Derrida's concern with ethics shows, today's chief skeptic also reaches beyond his skepticism to draw upon the values of the system he inhabits. Deconstruction cannot provide values, but it must draw upon other's values if it is to serve any purpose. An ecosystem made up wholly of parasites could not survive. That paragon of skepticism Hume himself argued that radical "Pyrrhonian" skepticism was ultimately useless:

> For here is the chief and most confounding objection to *excessive* skepticism, that no durable good can ever result from it while it remains in its full force and vigor. We need only ask such a skeptic, *What his meaning is? And what he proposes by all these curious researches?* He is immediately at a loss and knows not what to answer. A *Copernican* or *Ptolemaic* who supports each his different system of astronomy may hope to produce a conviction which will remain constant and durable with his audience. A *Stoic* or *Epicurean* displays principles which may not only be durable, but which have an effect on conduct and behavior. But a *Pyrrhonian* cannot expect that his philosophy will have any constant influence on the mind or, if it had, that its

influence would be beneficial to society. On the contrary, he must acknowledge, if he will acknowledge anything, that all human life must perish were his principles universally and steadily to prevail. All discourse, all action would immediately cease, and men remain in a total lethargy till the necessities of nature, unsatisfied, put an end to their miserable existence.[56]

The comic-book author Morrison illustrates the consequences of the excessive skepticism generated by postmodernism. His discourse has, indeed, ceased, even though the world of nature that he cared for remains in danger. In a deteriorating world, skeptical lethargy can be lethal.

Foucault and the Decline of Humanism

Strangely enough, man—the study of whom is supposed by the naive to be the oldest investigation since Socrates—is probably no more than a kind of rift in the order of things, or, in any case, a configuration whose outlines are determined by the new position he has so recently taken up in the field of knowledge. Whence all the chimeras of the new humanisms, all the facile solutions of an "anthropology" understood as a universal reflection on man, half-empirical, half-philosophical. It is comforting, however, and a source of profound relief to think that man is only a recent invention, a figure not yet two centuries old, a new wrinkle in our knowledge, and that he will disappear again as soon as that knowledge has discovered a new form.[57]

In this well-known quotation, Foucault offered reassurance to Lyotard, Derrida, and others who saw tyranny and violence in humanism; the end of "man" is approaching. Foucault did not mean that humanity is about to perish, of course, nor that the term *man* is soon going to be replaced by a less sexist term. What he meant is that man as the subject and object of knowledge will soon be replaced. Kant's solution to the problem of knowledge was based on a universalized subject of knowledge. Hume had divided knowledge into knowledge of existential facts and association of ideas. This division created the problem of moral skepticism: how is it possible to derive an *ought* conclusion (an association of ideas) from an *is* premise (an existential fact) and have it be anything other than an expression of individual sentiment? Kant's answer is that a priori knowledge involves more than habitual association of ideas; a priori knowledge involves necessary categories that are universal to all intellects—the laws of universal consciousness. Both empirical judgments and moral judgments rely on universal categories, not the haphazard association of ideas. The human subject, man, is the site of synthesis that makes knowledge possible.

The study of the possibility of knowledge thus becomes the study of the human subject. Man is then not only the subject of knowledge but the object. The Kantian critique emphasized the limitations, the finitude, of this subject. Human thought cannot avoid metaphysics because reason is unsatisfied with anything less than the perfection of immaterial being, but it must be critical of its own attempts to think "transcendental ideas." The dialectical extravagances of reason must be guarded against by effective critique.[58]

I doubt whether Kant had in mind critique as radical as Foucault offered. Foucault criticized the basic concept of a subject of knowledge. Instead of the Kantian approach to rational discourse in which a subject operating according to universal a priori laws of reason states the results of synthesis, Foucault's approach was that discourse in a given historical period constitutes rationality and the subject, as well as the object, of knowledge. Man was constituted subject and object when the modern system of discourse replaced the classical: "When natural history becomes biology, when the analysis of wealth becomes economics, when, above all, reflection upon language becomes philology, and Classical *discourse*, in which being and representation found their common locus, is eclipsed, then, in the profound upheaval of such an archaeological mutation, man appears in his ambiguous position as an object of knowledge and as a subject that knows."[59]

Whatever synthesis occurs is the result of discursive practices; so the site of synthesis is a particular system of discourse, not *man*. "Thus conceived, discourse is not the majestically unfolding manifestation of a thinking, knowing subject, but on the contrary, a totality, in which the dispersion of the subject and his discontinuity with himself may be determined."[60] Discourse comprises statements. Statements are groups of signs that contain a place for a subject. The subject is not the cause or origin of the statement; instead "it is a particular, vacant place that may in fact be filled by different individuals; but instead of being defined once and for all, and maintaining itself as such throughout a text, a book, or an *oeuvre*, this place varies—or rather it is variable enough to be able either to persevere, unchanging, through several sentences, or to alter with each one."[61] Because discourse requires subjects for its statements, discursive practices determine those variable subjects, as opposed to the subject determining the discourse. Foucault's approach to discourse had no need for a transcendental subject or even a psychological subject to account for statements.

At first glance, Foucault's approach may seem absurd, but he did not deny that a statement is stated by a speaker or author. What he claimed was that the speaker or author is not necessarily the subject of the statement and in any case not the guarantor of knowledge. Knowledge is determined by discursive practices that change from epoch to epoch. Some researchers may wish to examine variations between speakers in a given system of discourse; Foucault considered such research to be doxology, or the study of opinions. He himself, in contrast, was concerned only with how knowledge and its objects are determined by the discursive system. This is the study he called *archaeology*. The term suits his project in several senses: first, although he did not use the term *archai*, his search for the first principles of knowledge in a historical period is a fair use of Aristotle's term for the intuited first principles of science. Second, his orientation to knowledge makes use of the analogy of an archaeological dig. He follows Nietzsche in searching for hard documentary evidence— the "gray" method that Nietzsche contrasted with the method of "gazing around haphazardly in the blue after the English fashion."[62] Foucault studies documents as an archaeologist studies any artifact, looking for significant differences that show cultural change.

Foucault's insistence that the human science of an epoch is governed by common rules, by "historical *a priori*," is suggestive in its own way of the totalizing schema of Hegel, substituting discursive practices for the spirit of an age. Discursive rules determine knowledge for an entire epoch. "This *a priori* is what, in a given period, delimits in the totality of experience a field of knowledge, defines the mode of being of the objects that appear in that field, provides man's everyday perception with theoretical powers, and defines the conditions in which he can sustain a discourse about things that is recognized to be true."[63] He insisted that the body of rules for discourse were totalizing rules: "In any given culture and at any given moment, there is always only one *episteme* that defines the conditions of possibility of all knowledge, whether expressed in a theory or silently invested in a practice."[64] While presenting something like a spirit of knowledge for any given epoch, however, Foucault undermined the Hegelian concept of a developing spirit. For Foucault the rules defining knowledge were discontinuous from one age to another. In his early work, he referred to these separate sets of discursive practices that form knowledge as *epistemes*; he later preferred the term *discursive regime* because it indicated a relation between knowledge and power.[65]

What Foucault's argument does is reduce Kant's universal a priori categories to historical a priori rules. That reduction is accompanied by the loss of the knowing subject, whether construed as autonomous individual or transcendental spirit. Unlike the Hegelian historicism of dialectical development, Foucault's historical totalities are incommensurate with each other. His theory of truth is something like a systemic coherence theory; however, the coherence is with the rules of production of true discourse in a given era. Foucault offered no hope of progress toward a final truth at the end of inquiry. Truth remained entirely relative to the discursive regimes that seem to be random historical occurrences.

In his early work, Foucault radically relativized the notion of truth. Had he stopped there, he would have raised significant problems for communication ethics. His influence goes further, however. He subsequently emphasized the relation of knowledge and power. When he added analysis of power relations to his archaeological investigation, he called the result "genealogy," again following Nietzsche. Then, shortly before he died, he began to develop his own approach to ethics. Both his genealogical study and his ethical study extend his archaeological work.

Some readers treat Foucault's early work as though he were a structuralist. The *Oxford Companion to the English Language,* for example, lists Foucault as a structuralist historian.[66] In his preface to the English edition of *The Order of Things,* Foucault discounted that kind of interpretation in strong terms: "In France, certain half-witted 'commentators' persist in labelling me a 'structuralist.' I have been unable to get it into their tiny minds that I have used none of the methods, concepts, or key terms that characterize structural analysis."[67] The confusion arises because the episteme replaces the transcendent subject of knowledge in Foucault's analysis, just as the structure of semiotic codes or languages replaces the transcendent subject in structuralism. The term *episteme* seems to draw on the same structural paradigm as *morpheme* and *phoneme.* In structuralism, however, the structure itself is interpreted as a transcendental essence that produces knowledge. In Foucault's approach, no such fixed essence existed. Furthermore, the discursive system that he investigated was made up not of codes but of practices. The body of rules for discourse forms the subjects and objects that are encoded in language. The linguistic codes are merely the forms that discourse "has created and left behind." The task of the archaeologist "consists of not . . . treating discourses as groups of signs (signifying elements referring to contents or representations) but as practices that systematically form the objects of which they speak."[68] This emphasis on practices, or pragmatics, is typical of poststructural theory.

Nevertheless, Foucault's approach often has a feel of structuralism that goes beyond the minor similarity in terminology. His description of a body of practices gives it such rigidity that it appears to be an inescapable structure underlying all discourse in a given epoch. We are all familiar, of course, with continuing discourses that do not comply with the structure he defines. American fundamentalist discourse, for example, continues for the most part within the tradition that Foucault defined as the Renaissance episteme. Foucault was aware of differing discourses; he summarily dismissed strands of thought that disagreed with his totalized summary of the discursive regime: "There are themes with scientific pretensions that one may encounter at the level of opinion and that are not (or are no longer) part of a culture's epistemological network: from the seventeenth century, for example, natural magic ceased to belong to the Western *episteme*, but it persisted for a long time in the interaction of beliefs and affective valorizations."[69] Because he dismissed such strands of thought as "opinion," his analysis of an episteme should not be taken to stand for a society as a whole. His analysis actually was limited to a narrower range of discourse in an academic-scientific milieu. This body of discourse is important and authoritative in Western societies, but it does not have the totalizing effect his writing often suggests.

This totalizing aspect of his analysis becomes more significant in his focus on the analysis of power in genealogical studies. Foucault's concept of power is not only subjectless; it is global and polymorphous. Traditional power had to be displayed in order to be effective; modern disciplinary power is invisible. Disciplinary power works by imposing visibility on those whom it subjects. "Their visibility assures the hold of the power that is exercised over them."[70] The manifestation of power is no longer the appearance of the sovereign but the examination of the subject. The subject is the object of subjection by means of observation and documentation. Individuals are individualized, classified, and normalized by the discursive regime.

Such classification could be interpreted semiotically, but Foucault rejects this interpretation. The analogy underlying his system is not language but war: "The history which bears and determines us has the form of a war rather than that of a language: relations of power, not relations of meaning."[71] The Nietzschean will to power shows itself in a "microphysics of power" exercised in the smallest details of discipline of the body, and this microphysics should be "conceived not as a property, but as a strategy."[72] Foucault's emphasis on power as "exercised rather than possessed" eliminated the etymological connection of power with potential. In doing so, he further blurred the distinction between power and force. He also developed a strange concept of strategy without a *stratēgos*, that is, a military leader. Foucault personified power as though it were able to manage a battle using global strategy while denying any agent behind that strategy.

In our search for a communicative ethic, Foucault's concept of power leaves us with serious problems. A Foucauldian approach logically leads to the anomie that paralyzed the comic-book rhetor Morrison. How can one resist strategic deployments of power that have no source? In his own critique of Foucault, Taylor noted that "purposefulness without purpose requires a certain kind of explanation to be intelligible. . . . A strategic pattern cannot just be left hanging, unrelated to our conscious ends and projects." Not that "all patterns issue from conscious action, but all patterns have to be made *intelligible* in relation to conscious action."[73] Why? Because that is the only way we can plan our conscious action to achieve our ends. If the strategy of power has gone awry, what are we to do? Resist? How could we know our resistance wasn't simply another manifestation of the strategy of domination?

Consider the problem briefly from the viewpoint of a woman in American culture. Let us suppose this woman comes to view the current strategy of power with alarm. She recognizes that traditional discursive practices have unfairly subjected women and minorities to systemic sources of power. What is she to do? On the basis of Foucauldian theory, it doesn't matter. She is not responsible for the current discursive regime no matter how she acts. Any action she does take is simply going to be a manifestation of the current regime. If power is not a property or possession but a line of force within the discursive regime, she cannot gain it and use it to help others. The modes of power and resistance blur. She cannot draw upon moral argument to influence any men to share power. These men cannot share power because they do not possess it either. If moral suasion is merely another manifestation of the discursive regime, these privileged men might just as well enjoy the power that happens to flow their way, accepting it as their fate to have been born into this particular discursive regime. Nietzsche would agree that the men have no choice because the will to power will lead any animal (even the philosopher) to "expend all its strength and achieve its maximal feeling of power."[74] Nietzsche's solution was to develop *amor fati*—not mere acceptance but love of one's destiny. By this reasoning, if it is the fate of men in our discursive regime to be privileged and the fate of women to resist, each should learn to love that fate.

Learning to love one's fate fits with what Biesecker expects of a critical rhetoric in her interpretation of Foucauldian resistance. She calls for a rhetoric of pleasure that explores "the power of pleasure to incite ourselves and others to action."[75] Like Lyotard, she reduces deliberation to libidinal drives because she sees no possibility of reasoned choice in a Foucauldian interpretation of power and resistance. The resistor is not an autonomous subject but is created by the discursive regime. "As is the case with power, the individual who resists is an effect of force relations." Resistance occurs because the practices of making sense within a given discursive regime contain "virtual breaks or structures of excess." The subject who inhabits that rupture is simply the means by which resistance becomes a practice. Deliberate choice seems impossible because "those practices that we will call 'resistant' are, quite simply or nominalistically speaking, those practices that do not make sense within the available lines of intelligibility or discernment. That is, they do not signify (which is to say, make meaning) because they cannot be referenced within the field."[76] Finally, even the practice of freedom is no longer connected with deliberate choice. According to Biesecker, Foucault's aesthetic ethic constitutes "the substantive practice of freedom (which always already takes the form of resistance)."[77] This is a strange conception of freedom that does not allow deliberate choice of whether or not to resist. Apparently, to be free is to be compelled to resist by the nature of the discursive regime.

Said's friendly criticism of Foucault addresses this loss of deliberate choice to resist in Foucauldian theory:

> Many of the people who admire and have learned from Foucault, including myself, have commented on the undifferentiated power he seemed to ascribe to modern society. With this profoundly pessimistic view went also a singular lack of interest in the force of effective resistance to it, in choosing particular sites of intensity, choices which, we see from the evidence on all sides, always exist and are often successful in impeding, if not actually stopping, the progress of tyrannical power. Moreover Foucault seemed to have been confused between the power of institutions to subjugate individuals, and the fact that individual behavior in society is frequently a matter of following rules and conventions.[78]

Said offers a fair criticism of Foucault's theory but not Foucault's practice. In practice Foucault had little problem determining appropriate sites of resistance and distinguishing useful conventions from domination. He was very active in prison reform in France; but he did not attempt to undo the practice of giving examinations in school, even though he relates incarceration and examination as disciplinary practices in his theory ("At the heart of all disciplinary systems functions a small penal mechanism").[79] In practice, he could distinguish between legitimate and illegitimate uses of power. He called for intellectuals to participate in local resistance against the illegitimate uses of power. Unfortunately, his own theoretical perspective limited his ability to give good reasons in support of such resistance. Instead, all he offered was what Grumley called a "restless *will to change.*"[80]

In his final work, a study of sexuality and ethics, Foucault began to address the problem of a grounds for ethical action. Those grounds turned out ultimately to be aesthetic. For Foucault, ethics was a problem of the self relating to itself. He derives his understanding of ethics from his interpretation of Greek practice, in which "the principal work of art which one has to take care of, the main area to which one must apply aesthetic values, is oneself, one's life, one's existence."[81] In his analysis of ethics, Foucault draws a useful distinction between morality and ethics. *Morality* has two different meanings. First, it may mean the moral code, which is often supported by an institution such as the family, church, or school. The second meaning of morality is the actual behavior of individuals compared with these encoded values and rules. Apart from rules, however, there is the additional *ethical* question of "the manner in which one ought to form oneself as an ethical subject acting in reference to the prescriptive elements that make up the code."[82]

Clearly, even for Foucault, ethics requires a subject. The idea of forming oneself as a subject suggests Kant's autonomous subject. As Foucault himself asserted, however, the Foucauldian subject is much more limited than the Kantian subject:

I do indeed believe that there is no sovereign, founding subject, a universal form of subject to be found everywhere. I am very sceptical of this view of the subject and very hostile to it. I believe, on the contrary, that the subject is constituted through practices of subjection, or, in a more autonomous way, through practices of liberation, of liberty, as in Antiquity, on the basis, of course, of a number of rules, styles, inventions to be found in the cultural environment.[83]

Foucault never developed the implications of this argument. If certain discursive regimes constitute more autonomous subjects than other regimes do, then the quality of an ethical life is related not only to the self but to the discursive regime within which the self exists. In the Greek model that Foucault drew upon, the art of ethics was not removed from the art of politics. The possibility of improving the discursive regime as well as the quality of one's own life could provide a framework for ethical judgments, but Foucault never fully develops the relationship. As a result, his ethical concepts remain arbitrary and wholly subjective.

On the other hand, however, Foucault's actual practice suggests a richer perspective than that provided in his theorizing. Foucault placed himself under a morality of academic discourse that encouraged dialogue rather than polemic. An acknowledged follower of Nietzsche whose theory, like Nietzsche's, was based on a war analogy, Foucault disavowed the polemic form (*ta polemika*—warlike exercises) that Nietzsche loved. In an interview conducted shortly before he died, Foucault showed that he acted according to a cooperative ethic of communication:

It's true that I don't like to get involved in polemics. . . . That's not my way of doing things; I don't belong to the world of people who do things that way. I insist on this difference as something essential: a whole morality is at stake, the morality that concerns the search for the truth and the relation to the other.

In the serious play of questions and answers, in the work of reciprocal elucidation, the rights of each person are in some sense immanent in the discussion. They depend only on the dialogue situation. The person asking the questions is merely exercising the right that has been given him: to remain unconvinced, to perceive a contradiction, to require more information, to emphasize different postulates, to point out faulty reasoning, etc. As for the person answering the questions, he too exercises a right that does not go beyond the discussion itself; by the logic of his own discourse he is tied to what he has said earlier, and by the acceptance of dialogue he is tied to the questioning of the other. Questions and answers depend on a game—a game that is at once pleasant and difficult—in which each of the two partners takes pains to use only the rights given him by the other and by the accepted form of the dialogue.[84]

This is not the communicative ethic of a besieged subject at war but of a subject with rights achieved through a particular discursive regime. The rights are not "immanent" in a given discussion; they exist because a traditional system of practices supports them. In his support of the morality of dialogue, Foucault is defining himself as an ethical subject in relation to his own autonomy as a speaker and in relation to the discursive system that supports his autonomy and his partner's as well. More than aesthetics is involved in such an ethic.

Foucault was quite a remarkable man. His archaeological, genealogical, and ethical works offer important insights that should affect the ethical judgments we make. Nevertheless, his explicit theory is insufficient for motivating ethical action. Foucault believed that modernism was inherently incapable of formulating a morality.[85] He also believed that we were still within the modern episteme. If so, it would follow that we could not expect to develop effective guides to action until we enter a new, still unknown episteme. That would be the discursive regime in which, he was willing to wager, "man would be erased, like a face drawn in sand at the edge of the sea."[86] Blair and Cooper argue that Foucault's desire is not antihumanist but is compatible with the traditional humanistic emphasis on freedom and choice.[87] I do not disagree that Foucault draws upon traditional humanistic values. Underlying Foucault's later theory and practice we can discern at least a modified concept of a subject of ethical action. The problem is that his theoretical work has deconstructed the traditional support for humanistic values without reconstructing an alternative view. I don't believe we can wait for the dawning of a new era to begin reconstruction. Without theoretical support, our humanistic values are being eroded. We must, whether it seems pleasurable or not, reconstruct a discursive regime that encourages the autonomy of its subjects in their pursuit of a happy life.

Reconstructing Ethics

We have taken this detour into the theories of postmodernism and the travails of a comic-book author because there is more to postmodernism and poststructuralism than the excessive skepticism that may result. Hume points out that a "mitigated skepticism" that is "corrected by common sense and reflection" could be "both durable and useful."[88] Skepticism is most useful for countering our natural tendency to dogmatism, arising out of our discomfort with uncertainty. A healthy skepticism opens us to new ideas, new vocabularies for coping with our world. Let us grant that all our communicative systems are imperfect. The important question is: are some systems better or worse than other systems? The art of ethics is the art of making practical decisions, even when—Aristotle would say, *especially* when—those decisions cannot be certain. A theory of ethics offering a vocabulary that better identifies the ethical problems in most communication situations will improve our communicative practice. This is the project of the present book.

The vocabulary I offer is drawn from ecology and various aspects of communication theory. I will also draw upon the insights of the American pragmatists, Peirce and Dewey, in addressing the problems raised by the postmodernists. Peirce called pragmatism "critical common-sensism";[89] pragmatism mitigates skepticism with common sense, as Hume suggests. Of course, common sense itself is open to criticism, as the postmodernists have shown; so pragmatism attempts to walk the difficult path between dogmatism and excessive skepticism by using common sense to criticize itself. The key is never to wander very far from lived experience. Concepts are always related to possible experience.

Like the poststructuralist, the pragmatist also looks at semiotics in practice, that is, in communication or thought, rather than in the abstract, as the structural linguist does. The Peircean semiotic is triadic, as opposed to the dyadic model of Saussurean structuralism. Some of the problems of meaning raised by deconstruction are as trivial for practical communication as Heisenberg's uncertainty principle is for our day-to-day encounters with the physical world. Both Derrida and Heisenberg indicate the limits of our understanding, not the impossibility of understanding at all. In practice we are able to get quite a bit of cooperative work done with our communication. Considering all the problems, our sign systems are amazingly effective.

The pragmatic approach also unites reason and emotion. We use reason to govern emotion, but we do so ultimately in the service of emotion by transforming emotions into attainable desires. We do not need to reverse the traditional hierarchy and place the libido over reason. We "individuals" comprise subsystems of various kinds, some of which are unknown to us. In practice we integrate these systems as we meet our needs and desires, sometimes well, sometimes poorly. Reasoning is a way of mentally experimenting with outcomes. If we deliberate well, we have a greater likelihood of satisfying our wants (I assume here the universe is not total chaos). Deliberation can itself be enjoyable and may even be practiced for its own sake. Puzzles are published for their entertainment value. The bifurcation of reason and emotion may be analytically useful at times, but it does not reflect the nature of our experience as a whole. What our experience does indicate is that we often have conflicting goals and desires as well as conflicting beliefs. When we deliberate as "individuals" within our own minds, we are more like a community of subordinate systems than a single, transcendent will. As Lyne put it, in this pragmatic semiotic approach, "even the 'person' incorporates an audience."[90]

If we apply Derrida's theory to the problem of the individual versus community, we find the concepts mutually interdependent; the meaning of each depends upon the other. An individual is not absolutely indivisible (literally, an atom) but is considered so only in relation to a larger system of which it is part. A community is a community only insofar as it is a system of individuals. Each term requires the *trace* of the other for its meaning. Neither is primary. Individualism privileges the single human being as the basic term, while communitarianism privileges the social group; but an ecological perspective takes both as necessary terms. Postmodernism has effectively attacked the primacy of the subject in humanism. The deconstruction of the a priori subject of metaphysics does not entail the loss of the a posteriori subject of practical action, however, as Foucault acknowledges. An attenuated, less arrogant humanism remains possible if the individual is considered to be a system made up of subordinate systems, existing alongside parallel systems, within superordinate systems. Individualism and communitarianism are then just different levels of analysis of the ecosystem.

From the pragmatic perspective to be presented in this book, both the individual self and the community are achievements of semiosis.

Semiosis is communicative practice, not merely linguistic codes. The uniqueness of the human system is a matter of degree of semiotic capability and hence deliberative ability. Reasoning, construed semiotically as deliberation, is not unnatural but a development within nature. For better or worse, reasoning is our human way of coping, both as individuals and as groups. The pragmatic truth of our reasoning is measured not by correspondence to an antecedent originary object but by our effectiveness in coping with our environment. This effectiveness, in turn, can be measured only by testimony and consensus because the individual cannot test all relevant hypotheses and survive. We are interdependent in our knowledge.

The systemic effects of communication, however, are not limited to the epistemic aspects of testimony. Our communication patterns constitute the patterns of our social systems. Communication interconnects matter with symbols in practical action that is part of the semiotic process. From a pragmatic perspective, the resulting relations are real. Communication is, therefore, ontical in its creation of social ways of being; and an ecological theory of communication ethics requires ontological as well as epistemological analyses of consequences. In what follows, I will discuss both of these aspects of communication ethics in general theory and in more specific contexts.

The book is divided into two parts. This first part is a discussion of the general theory of an ecological ethic of communication. In chapter 2 I will show how pragmatism offers an alternative to dogmatic metaphysics and excessive skepticism. In subsequent chapters I will discuss how communication is involved in the development of communities and individuals, and I will offer a pragmatic theory of communicative virtue, including the virtue of practical wisdom. The second part of the book will draw out some implications of that theory within various common contexts of communication occurring at different levels of community. I will discuss the problem of ethics in interpersonal communication, organizational communication, and political communication. My purpose will be not to develop a code of ethics for each of these areas but to show how an ecological approach illuminates ethical problems in these contexts.

Throughout these discussions, I will be using a model of communication ethics based on a socially ecological perspective. Whether we want to or not, we fill a niche and so perform a function in our social ecosystem just as we do in our physical ecosystem. In the language of existentialism, you could say that we are cast into this interdependent world. We may or may not function well within the ecosystem, and the ecosystem may or may not function well in supporting us. Ethical responsibility is reciprocal. The basic principle of my theory of communication ethics is that the individual should support the communicative ecosystem that supports the individual. Supporting the ecosystem, however, does not mean blind loyalty to the way things are but includes building, maintaining, and remodeling the system. In extreme circumstances the remodeling may be radical. Support of the individual does not mean dictating the good to the individual but enabling the individual to pursue the good according to that individual's own life narrative. The system's interest in socialization of the individual is limited to inculcating ecologically practical wisdom.

This broad principle allows for the fragmentation and diversity that postmodernism illustrates while insisting upon the possibility of community. Incommensurability should not itself become a totalizing term. Some degree of mutual interest exists between fragmented subsystems. Neither the part nor the whole should be privileged a priori. Derridean deconstruction draws our attention to those contradictions that underlie an assumed homogeneity in the metaphysical discourse about community, but deconstruction does not preclude creating community in practice. So long as *community* and *social ecosystem* are interpreted pragmatically, they are useful terms for our attempts to create an environment that better supports our individual quests for the good. In chapter 2 I will explain what I mean by interpreting *pragmatically*.

2

The Pragmatic Alternative

[Hegel] has committed the trifling oversight of forgetting that there is a real world with real actions and reactions.

—C. S. Peirce

The "trifling oversight" of forgetting the real world also underlies postmodernism's inability to develop a theory of practical action.[1] Drawing upon linguistic theory, the poststructuralists have repeated the structuralist error of confusing a code function with a sign function. In doing so, they leave out the connection with reality. If communication is not connected with reality, then an art of communicative ethics is irrelevant. The postmodernists act as if ethics were important, but they are unable to offer reasons that go beyond individual whim.

The problem begins with Saussure: not with his emphasis on speech, which engages Derrida's attention, but with his elimination of *parole*—the act of communicating. By eliminating communication, Saussure was able to focus his attention on his object, the codes of language. From this focus he was able to develop very useful hypotheses about the formal requirements of codes, abstracted from their use in actual acts of signifying. Saussurean semiology is the structural study of codes and code functions. All of this abstraction and reduction is appropriate for his study of language per se. The problem arises when others apply this linguistic theory to acts of communication as though it explained the act of communicating.

The consequence of such abuse of Saussure's theory is a dyadic theory of the sign. Abstracted from use, a sign comprises a signifier and signified. Derrida argues effectively that the two are not different categories but different cases of the same type of object. Every signifier must be a signified if it is to be understood as a type. Every signified is also a signifier whose signified is always deferred. Nevertheless, the sign remains a dyad because each signifier functions differently. Eco, following Hjelmslev, refers to this conjunction of signifiers as a sign function. Eco, however, specifically limits semiotics to the study of codes; so his sign function is really a code function.[2] Eco's separation of codes from their production, his division of semiotic and factual judgments, and his bracketing of conditions of truth from conditions of signification all lead to a narrow, linguistic view of semiotics. His project is to delineate a discipline of semiotics with boundaries that eliminate the object. As a result, he collapses the Peircean object into the interpretant to make Peirce's approach seem more compatible with Saussure's. Eco himself does not discount the importance of reference, but he removes it from the field of semiotics. Like Ramus, who sought to improve the disciplinary boundaries of rhetoric and logic by removing invention and arrangement from rhetoric, Eco's bracketing of reference has unintended consequences for the study of communication. Communication loses its grounding in the realities of everyday life.

In distinguishing between a code function and a sign function, I am agreeing with Peirce's position that signs in practice are irreducibly triadic. A sign function occurs when a signifier is related to an object in such a way that it gives rise to another signifier (its interpretant). The signifier *man*, for example, functions as a sign because it connects its interpretant, *male human being*, with the same object that it is related to, a gendered class of a species of animal. My point is that when we use codes we relate them to objects, real or fancied, and that relationship to an object is necessary for the code to function as a sign. Otherwise, we could never lie or make a mistake with our signs: a signifier would simply generate a signified that, in turn, is a signifier to another signified, ad infinitum. Error, or for that matter, truth, can only occur when the signifier and signified are related to a third element. The dyadic model, if it is taken to be complete, is irrelevant to the problem of coping with a real world.

Postmodernism in general and poststructuralism in particular have grown out of the dyadic perspective, and they are both susceptible to the critique of being irrelevant to the real problems of our world. When they are not irrelevant, they have smuggled in an object to recreate the triad. Foucault's discussion of "power relations" involves some very complex interpretants, but it also seems to stand for some reality in society. We can argue whether the term is appropriate, whether it gives rise to good interpretants of that object in the real world he is suggesting. If it were not taken to stand for a real object, however, Foucault's text would be a meaningless academic exercise, full of sound and fury, signifying nothing. Science, too, would then become an empty academic exercise. Lyotard's discussion of the legitimation of science limits it to the ability to "generate ideas, in other words, new statements."[3] This dyadic viewpoint cannot distinguish science from science fiction, which generates plenty of ideas. Derrida's claim that there is nothing outside the text requires that reality be somehow incorporated in the text; otherwise, there is nothing inside the text either. Furthermore, for his statement to make sense, the word *text* must be taken to refer to some object.

The dyadic model ultimately disables communicative ethics because reality never enters in. How can we talk about the consequences of a communicative act if those consequences can never be known? To say an act has consequences is to make a claim about a future reality that we expect to encounter. If no reality is ever encountered in our semiotic processes, talk of consequences is trivial. Deliberation would be a fruitless exercise; rationality, an empty concept. In a dyadic model, the interpretation of any sign must be either random or behaviorally determined. One could not say that both signifier and signified stand for the same thing—a triadic notion—therefore, the association of signifier and signified is either conditioned or random. The idea of reasonable deliberation is lost in either case. Herein also lies the fear of fascism in claims of truth: if signification is purely dyadic, then a community consensus is simply a total determination of meaning and a loss of freedom. The only opposition to fascism is randomness, diversity for its own sake, the celebration of incommensurability, and paralogy. Because the dyadic model does, in fact, represent an aspect of communication—the necessary code function—postmodernism alerts us to some real dangers. If the dyadic model of linguistics is taken to be a complete model of semiotic praxis, however, no communicative ethic is possible. We must look elsewhere for a theory that can accommodate the warnings of postmodernism and still grant us the power to deliberate and act rationally, at least on occasion. In short, we are looking for a theory that better explains how the postmodernists themselves actually do communicate when they argue for their beliefs.

Peircean Realism

Peircean realism is a version of scholastic realism. The term *real* was itself invented in the thirteenth century, according to Peirce.[4] It means that which exists regardless of whether or not someone thinks it exists. "Objects are divided into figments, dreams, etc., on the one hand, and realities on the other. The former are those which exist only inasmuch as you or I or some man imagines them; the latter are those which have an existence independent of your mind or mine or that of any number of persons. The real is that which is not whatever we happen to think it, but is unaffected by what we may think of it."[5] Reality constrains our opinions. "There is something, therefore, which influences our thoughts, and is not created by them."[6] Scholastic realism claimed that universals could be real. Before addressing that question, however, we must refine the meaning of *real* to understand what it means pragmatically.

American pragmatism is based on the pragmatic maxim of meaning, which Peirce enunciated in his well-known article "How to Make Our Ideas Clear." The article is a critique of Cartesian metaphysics and its reliance on clear and distinct ideas supposedly present to the consciousness. Long before Derrida attacked the metaphysics of presence, Peirce argued that thought is always mediated and so never immediately present. A sensation or feeling may be immediately present, but thought comprises a series of such sensations. "Thought is a thread of melody running through the succession of our sensations."[7] Thought is a process of attaining belief, which, for Peirce, is a habit or rule for action. The *logical* outcome of thought is an appropriate rule for action. Therefore, his maxim for clarifying thought addresses possible differences in praxis: "[C]onsider what effects, which might conceivably have practical bearings, we conceive the object of our conception to have. Then, our conception of these effects is the whole of our conception of the object."[8] In terms of his semiotic theory, the concept is the sign. Its meaning comprises all of the possible interpretants related to the object, but its *logical* meaning is limited to those interpretants that would account for a possible difference in practice, that is, in our experience of the object. Logical interpretation of the concept as a sign amounts to a kind of mental experimentation with it to determine how it might affect our experience of the object. This process allows for the possibility that the object itself may influence our understanding of it through our semiotic interaction with it.

Reality is a concept, and all concepts are signs, so this pragmatic maxim should apply to the sign *reality* as well. In practice, the concept of reality serves to test the beliefs of those who are willing to put their beliefs to the test. The practical effect of *reality* is to correct false beliefs and affirm true beliefs for those who have a "scientific attitude," that is, the willingness to test their beliefs against facts.[9] Scientific inquiry in the long run tends toward the truth because it allows itself to be corrected by reality. Therefore, by the pragmatic maxim, "the opinion which is fated to be ultimately agreed to by all who investigate is what we mean by truth, and the object represented in this opinion is the real."[10] Truth depends upon a consensus of scientific minds at the end of inquiry, but this consensus is determined by reality and thus represents reality.

Peirce is careful to identify this pragmatic interpretation of truth and reality as the consensus that *would* result at the end of inquiry, not any actual consensus that exists. Although a lifelong friend of William James, he disagreed with James and Schiller who reinterpreted truth as an actual consensus. An actual consensus is what we live by, but it is not the same as the Truth that "*would* ultimately be found if the inquiry were pushed to its ultimate and indefeasible issue."[11] The distinction is meaningful because it requires us to hold all of our actual beliefs provisionally, in case new information should require us to correct that belief. Scientific fallibilism also leads to a corollary that I take to be an ethical principle for the community: "Do not block the way of inquiry."[12]

Today's neopragmatists, most notably Richard Rorty, depart from the pragmatic realism of Peirce. Rorty rejects the notion that truth is some third thing (tertium quid) between meanings of words and the way the world is.[13] Using Davidson's analysis of language based on field linguistics, Rorty argues that the internal and external cannot be combined: "We still have beliefs, but they will be seen from the outside as the field linguist sees them (as causal interactions with the environment) or from the inside as the pre-epistemological native sees them (as rules for action). To abjure *tertia* is to abjure the possibility of a third way of seeing them—one which somehow combines the outside view and the inside view, the descriptive and the normative attitudes."[14] Rorty is here denying the triadicity of semiotics, choosing instead to view the sign situation as two separate dyads: one, an external interaction with the environment; the other, a signifier-interpretant relation (a code function). Code functions are determined by linguistic communities; and so, for Rorty, community is all that matters:

Pragmatists would like to replace the desire for objectivity—the desire to be in touch with a reality which is more than some community with which we identify ourselves—with the desire for solidarity with that community. They think that the habits of relying on persuasion rather than force, of respect for the opinions of colleagues, of curiosity and eagerness for new data and ideas, are the *only* virtues which scientists have. They do not think that there is an intellectual virtue called "rationality" over and above these moral virtues.[15]

By this logic, moral virtues, too, simply reflect the codes of the community. From inside, no critique of those values could base its claim on anything other than coherence within the communal code.

As in many observations from a dyadic perspective, there is a good deal of truth in Rorty's argument. "Rationality" in practice does depend upon virtues of inquiry. In saying so, however, I am claiming not merely that his argument agrees with the generally nominalist tendency of our postmodern community but also that his analysis gives rise to interpretants I believe applicable to the real semiotic situation. As Horne points out in her essay on the relationship between Rorty's neopragmatism and the field of rhetoric, knowledge is discursive and intersubjective.[16] I find his analysis incomplete, however, and I worry about the implications of his position. Doesn't Rorty's position make the virtues of science simply a matter of fashion in our particular community? If so, then from a Peircean perspective, postmodern neopragmatism is a retrogression to a nonscientific method of fixing belief.

In his article "The Fixation of Belief," Peirce describes four methods that humans have typically used to fix their beliefs, a belief being a habit of thought that will determine our actions.[17] Doubt, in contrast to belief, is an irritant that serves as a stimulus until it is laid to rest by belief. "The irritation of doubt causes a struggle to attain a state of belief. I shall term this struggle *inquiry*, though it must be admitted that this is sometimes not a very apt designation."[18] *Inquiry* is certainly not an apt term for the first method of settling opinions that he discusses: the method of *tenacity*. Tenacity is the method whereby an individual continually seeks reinforcement for a belief and avoids conflicting information. Tenacity is very common. We use techniques of selective perception and selective retention to avoid the discomfort of doubt. Tenacity accounts for the natural conservatism reflected in the statement, "This is the way I've always done it." We do not like our habits of thought or action disrupted. The method of tenacity is ineffective in the long run, however, because humans live in community. We will begin to doubt our beliefs when we find that others whose opinions we respect believe differently from us. "Unless we make ourselves hermits, we shall necessarily influence each other's opinions; so that the problem becomes how to fix belief, not in the individual merely, but in the community."[19]

Community beliefs are stabilized in three different ways: the authoritative method, the a priori method, and the scientific method. The method of authority is the method of tenacity raised to the level of community. Some institution in the community serves "to keep correct doctrines before the attention of the people, to reiterate them perpetually, and to teach them to the young; having at the same time power to prevent contrary doctrines from being taught, advocated, or expressed."[20] Inquiry in the authoritative method amounts to inquisition into deviations from orthodoxy. This method is completely compatible with Rorty's criterion of "solidarity." Peirce finds the authoritative method somewhat effective but problematic:

[W]herever there is a priesthood—and no religion has been without one—this method has been more or less made use of. Wherever there is aristocracy, or a guild, or any association of a class of men whose interests depend or are supposed to depend on certain propositions, there will be inevitably found some traces of this natural product of social feeling. Cruelties always accompany this system; and when it is consistently carried out, they become atrocities of the most horrible kind in the eyes of any rational man. Nor should this occasion surprise, for the officer of a society does not feel justified in surrendering the interests of that society for the sake of mercy, as he might his own private interests. It is natural, therefore, that sympathy and fellowship should thus produce a most ruthless power.[21]

Rorty would certainly object that this form of solidarity is fascist, whereas the version he subscribes to is liberal and democratic. He writes that "our best chance for transcending our acculturation is to be brought up in a culture which prides itself on *not* being monolithic—on its tolerance for a plurality of subcultures and its willingness to listen to neighboring cultures."[22] Clearly, he believes not in solidarity alone but in a solidarity built around some basic principles that prevent the natural cruelties of the authoritative method. Rorty seems to be drawing upon some sort of a priori principles.

The metaphysical practice of the a priori method is a form of fixing belief that Peirce also critiques. In this method free discourse is allowed so that, by means of disputation, the community will reach agreement. "Systems of this sort have not usually rested upon observed facts, at least not in any great degree. They have been chiefly adopted because their fundamental propositions seemed 'agreeable to reason.' " In practice, however, the quality of being agreeable to reason does not result in the settlement of doubt. "It makes of inquiry something similar to the development of taste; but taste, unfortunately, is always more or less a matter of fashion, and accordingly, metaphysicians have never come to any fixed agreement."[23] So in fact, metaphysics turns out to be a form of ethnocentric a priori method. Peirce gives the example of the Christian belief in monogamy, which the Hindus interpreted as immoral treatment of women. The a priori method is like the authoritative method in its inability to settle a conflict in the facts of experience, which tell us that these are two equally developed systems of metaphysics that contradict each other. Our belief in one turns out to be a matter of chance. So also is Rorty's belief in democratic liberalism; he happens to have been brought up in a culture that teaches the value of tolerance. Tolerance is, therefore, a fashion of the times, or as Foucault would say, a historical a priori of this discursive regime. In terms of inquiry, it matters little whether such a priori rules are enforced by traditional authority or by diffused forms of power within society.

In contrast with this approach that depends on chance fashion, Peirce looks for a method by which our beliefs may be caused by something external to any actual consensus, something not affected by fads of thought. The method is one in which all rational inquirers would agree on the ultimate conclusion. According to Horne, Rorty's appeal to solidarity is drawn from Peirce when he argues that "we can make no sense of the notion that the view which can survive all objections might be false."[24] This ultimate agreement that survives *all* objections, however, is not merely ethnocentric, as Rorty's position claims; for Peirce this ultimate agreement is just what we mean by correspondence with reality. So Peirce argues for a method in which reality influences our opinions. This, of course, is the scientific method. For it to succeed, there must be some degree of regularity in reality. If there is, then we should be able to perceive this reality, because it will have regular effects on us. We would naturally adapt our behaviors, including our communicative behavior, to these regular effects.

Reconsidering Davidson and Rorty's example, this adaptation to reality is what the field linguist observes as causal interactions with the environment. What the native speaker takes to be rules of action are the result of a natural scientific method. As Peirce points out, "Everybody uses the scientific method about a great many things, and only ceases to use it when he does not know how to apply it."[25] If the native language were not related to the objects in the environment, the field linguist could not learn the language. The native language certainly seems to mediate between its interpretants (rules of action) and the regular objects in the environment. This triadic model of signifier-interpretant-object underlies the possibility of the scientific method.

The possibility of the scientific method is also the source of optimism in pragmatism, opposing the dour skepticism of postmodernism. Real agreement is possible, if not probable. If our signs are related to our real environment, then we are not trapped in incommensurable language games. As Lyne argued, "Framed in contemporary language, it might be said that any socially constructed reality can be penetrated from without."[26] We can communicate about the practical objects in our environment. Since metaphysical language uses metaphors drawn from practical language, we should also be able to gain some understanding of other metaphysical perspectives. I do not mean to underestimate the difficulty involved, but difficulty is not impossibility. Communication and community remain real possibilities. Not believing in these possibilities, of course, can be a self-fulfilling prophecy.

Rorty also objects to the notion of truth at the end of inquiry because he does not believe that the end of inquiry has any pragmatic meaning. He claims we have no way of recognizing the end of inquiry in practice.[27] But this objection seems to be another confusion of the would-be and the will-be. Many of our current beliefs may be true in the sense that they would never be contradicted by an unlimited community of inquirers. We will never know whether this is true, just as we will never know whether an infinite number of tosses of a coin will actually end up half heads and half tails. Gambling houses believe in the statistical hypothesis, and they generally take the money of those gamblers who do not believe. Peirce's truth at the end of inquiry is like the statistical hypothesis that serves as a guide to practical action. For Peirce, it justifies the whole process of synthetic inference, which includes statistical hypotheses.[28] The end-of-inquiry also serves as a practical denial of excessive skepticism. Because the conception of an end of inquiry means that our settled beliefs could be true in the absolute sense, we are required to have a reason for doubting a well-supported hypothesis. Cartesian doubt is unjustified; the fact that we can entertain a doubt is not enough reason to doubt our beliefs. All of our beliefs are fallible, but well-supported beliefs deserve our allegiance. Since it has the practical effect of requiring both doubt and belief to be open to criticism, the idea of truth at the end of inquiry certainly has practical consequences. At the very least, like Peirce's argument about belief in God, it results in a "hypothesis of the highest Plausibility, whose ultimate test must lie in its value in the self-controlled growth of man's conduct of life."[29]

In any case, the belief that true statements are possible within the scientific method does not entail that any particular method in use is the correct method of science. It is the critical attitude of testing hypotheses against experience that constitutes the general method that Peirce calls scientific. Particular methods can only be justified by their results. In addition, we should not confuse science as general method with science as a body of knowledge or as a particular cultural practice. The claims in any body of knowledge are fallible, influenced by cultural a priori beliefs, and certainly susceptible to the kind of critique Foucault offered. Scientists in our culture are often anointed with priestly status, further confounding the method of science with the method of authority. When scientists have a personal interest at stake, such as the preservation of high status, they can no longer make valid inductive inferences. Self-interest may be a fertile ground for the generation of hypotheses, but it tends to bias the inductive testing of those hypotheses. The principle of induction requires that all facts be treated equally in order that probable arguments should ultimately lead to truth. "What follows? That logic rigidly requires, before all else, that no determinate fact, nothing which can happen to a man's self, should be of more consequence to him than everything else. He who would not sacrifice his own soul to save the whole world, is illogical in all his inferences, collectively. So the social principle is rooted intrinsically in logic."[30]

Logical induction requires us to sacrifice self-interest on behalf of the inquiring community. Logic presumes community spirit; but because none of us completely escapes problems of self-interest, our inferences are likely to be flawed. The flawed arguments by nineteenth century white scientists that claimed to prove scientifically the inferiority of the Negro race are striking examples of the failure of inference due to self-interest.[31] A less obvious example is the popularity of postmodern theory among literary theorists and rhetoricians, or for that matter, the popularity of positivism among empiricists. In both cases, professional interest encourages not counting certain types of evidence. The corrective can only be by means of a community that is itself *as a whole* disinterested. The ultimate truth, then, would have to be cross-cultural and perhaps even cross-species in its consensus. In other words, the community of inquiry must be a wide open community whose only criterion of membership is the willingness to submit ideas to the test of their consequences in experience. More relevant than the possibility of an end of inquiry is the question of how such a community could be developed. This question of the importance of developing better communities is one on which pragmatists like Peirce, Dewey, and Rorty have not disagreed.

A problem remains, however. Are we not presuming the reality of community? *Community* signifies a general concept that is admittedly vague. Even if we grant the reality of individuals, could we not consider *community* to be simply the name of an aggregation of individuals who alone are real? This position reflects the nominalism of Ockham, who argued that only singular things have existence. He denied that relations exist as realities different from the things related. If only singular things exist, then terms relating singulars exist only as names (*nomina*) in the mind. In the mind such a name may exist as a singular mental concept, but the external communality it claims to represent can have no real existence.[32] This nominalistic argument, further developed by Hobbes, underlies the atomistic individualism of the Enlightenment. Its rhetorical appeal is understandable because it supported the Protestant liberation argument against the authoritative Roman Catholic method of fixing belief. As a result, nominalism became the fashion of modernism. It seems unsatisfactory in several respects, however.

Consider a group of individuals standing and waiting for a streetcar. Even though they have a common purpose, that communality is merely an aggregate of their individual purposes. Nominalism adequately accounts for this situation. But now suppose that a car stalls on the streetcar tracks, preventing the streetcar from arriving where the group is waiting. One person in the group tries to push the car out of the way but fails. Another tries and fails, then a third, and so on. After a bit of deliberation, the group decides to synchronize their pushing of the car. Together they push the car clear of the tracks. The interaction of their efforts, coordinated through their communication, was more than an aggregate of their individual efforts. Once united to accomplish a purpose that could only be achieved through conjoint action, the group was a different entity. Granted, it was an entity with a short life span; nevertheless, considered in terms of its pragmatic effects, the united group was different from the group of individuals. The difference depended upon a change in their relations accomplished through communication.

Consider also what scientific inquiry has revealed about the nature of atomistic individuals. The term is actually redundant, based on Greek (*atomos*) and Latin (*individuus*) words that both mean *indivisible*. Indivisible objects would constitute ideal singulars for nominalistic metaphysics. The idea of indivisibility exploded at Los Alamos in 1942, however, when the atomic bomb proved that atoms could be split. Atoms turn out to be regular interactions of subatomic particles, such as protons, neutrons, electrons, muons, neutrinos, positrons, and so on. These are called "elementary particles," but who knows how they themselves are constituted? At any rate, human beings cannot qualify as nominalistic singulars. Even our ability to digest food depends upon colonies of other life forms in our intestines. We are systems of systems of systems of . . . systems of elementary (?) particles. Since the average life of these particles is much less than a second, nominalism has a hard time explaining how we humans can exist as "individuals." If you are nothing but an aggregate of your parts, then you have changed identity some million times in the last second. All of us have. Yet isn't there some continuity in form that we recognize as real? The transcendent subject, so attacked by post-modernists, was a nominalistic attempt to create a unitary, singular subject out of the multitude of experiences that constitute an "individual."

The postmodern nominalist solves this problem by dropping reality out completely and reducing semiosis to a dyad. If atomic facts cannot be known, then all we know is our system of "naming." Hence for a postmodern theorist like McKerrow, there is no distinction between reality and "social reality" or knowledge and opinion.[33] Rorty tells us to "think of human minds as webs of beliefs and desires. . . . Do not ask where the new beliefs and desires come from." This web is "a self-reweaving mechanism" that also "produces movements in the organism's muscles—movements which kick the organism itself into action. These actions, by shoving items in the environment around, produce new beliefs to be woven in, which in turn produce new actions, and so on for as long as the organism survives."[34]

Peirce would agree in part with Rorty that our webs of beliefs are habits of action. Peirce's triadic semiotic, however, explains the connection between our semiotic web and those "items in the environment" we shove around. When we shove them around, we perceive the consequences and adjust our beliefs accordingly if we are using the natural method of science. Peirce would also point out that our difficulty in affirming our own identity arises from our nominalistic metaphysics, not from our experience. Experience teaches us that both regularity and chance occur in nature. Our identity is one of those regularities of nature that is mixed with elements of chance. The elementary particles that constitute us operate according to principles that we could regard as habits of nature. These habits of nature are as real as our own beliefs and affect the environment as well; that is, "General principles are really operative in nature. That is the doctrine of scholastic realism."[35]

[T]hough it makes the truth of whatever is true of the law [of inertia, as an example] to depend upon thought in general, [the doctrine] does not make it depend upon the thought of any particular person or any particular group of persons. So if you believe that modern science has made any general discovery at all, you believe that general so discovered to be real, and so you *are a scholastic realist* whether you are aware of it or not. Not only does all *science* hang upon the decision but so do Truth and Righteousness! Nominalism and all its ways are devices of the Devil if devil there be. And in particular it is the disease which almost drove poor John Mill mad—the dreary outlook upon a world in which all that can be loved, or admired, or understood, is figment.[36]

This question of realism involves more than the principles of science because, as Lyne pointed out, for Peirce "such general ideas [as truth and righteousness] form a semiotic matrix *to* which humans adapt their behavior—not by brute necessity . . . but by force of attraction."[37] The reality of these general concepts lies in their ability to affect concrete behavior. Failure to believe in realities like truth and justice leads to the bleak world we saw in the comic-book author Morrison. Peirce's depiction of nominalistic modernism applies as well to postmodernism, which reacts against but grows out of the nominalism of modernism.

Our own reality as individuals and communities is also at stake. We as individuals are real systems because we comprise habitual interactions of subsystems that include more than language. We semiotically interact with our various subsystems that connect us with our environment. That pattern of interaction is our form. In the same way, social systems are real because they comprise regular patterns of interaction between their subsystems within a larger environment. Community is a type of social system in which the members see their communality of purpose and act together to achieve it. The recognition of communality and the coordination of action are functions of communication. Therefore, the real existence of communities depends upon the nature of the communication within the respective social systems. The effects of communication are real, and they involve both ontical and epistemic aspects. The chief requirement for an effective community is belief in that community by its members. The epistemic belief will shape the ontical community that results.

In practice, however, the beliefs about community, like those of justice and righteousness, seem to be vague. Can something so vague be real? Vagueness is a type of indeterminacy. If a signifier were completely determinate, it would allow "no latitude of interpretation" for either the utterer or the interpreter of the sign.[38] One type of indeterminacy results from the nature of the sign as *general*. A general sign leaves the determination of the specific case to the interpreter. If I write, "Human beings are mortal," you as interpreter might conclude that you yourself are mortal, your parents are mortal, or anyone else you consider human is mortal. This is the purpose of a general sign, to stand for the principle abstracted from all those cases. On the other hand, a sign is *vague* when it "reserves for some other possible sign or experience the function of completing the determination."[39] Today's horoscope, for example, claims that "assertiveness pays off."

The determination of the interpretation of this statement depends upon the reader's experience and how that experience is interpreted. Both the subject *assertiveness* and the predicate *pays off* are vague. *Assertiveness* is vague because it is a matter of degree on a continuum between meek and aggressive and "wherever degree or any other possibility of continuous variation subsists, absolute precision is impossible."[40] Peirce's logic of vagueness seems to be the precursor of fuzzy logic, which is proving to be important in the development of artificial intelligence. In this case of the horoscope, the difference between *assertiveness* and *aggressiveness* is difficult to determine beforehand, especially in those fuzzy boundary areas where the extremes meet. *Payoff* is vague because of individual differences of feeling. What I take to be a payoff depends upon my idea of reward, which depends upon my idea of what is good. *Good* is a very vague term. Suppose I were assertive and lost my job as a result because my boss did not value assertiveness. Eventually, I would get another job. If I ended up with a boss who appreciated my honest opinion, I might then interpret the results as *good*. If I did not improve my situation, I would have learned from my experience, and that learning would be good if I came to value it. The horoscope is vague enough that any subsequent experience could be taken to confirm it; horoscopes are so vague that they are useless because they signify no real difference in practice.

Not only horoscopes are vague, however. Some degree of vagueness is inherent in all communication. "Even in our most intellectual conceptions, the more we strive to be precise, the more unattainable precision seems," Peirce observed, long before Heisenberg discovered the uncertainty principle.[41] Nevertheless, vagueness does not render understanding impossible as deconstruction seems to imply. One reason is that indeterminacy is limited by the context and purpose of communication or thought. The example Peirce uses is of two Englishmen conversing on a train:

If one mentions Charles the Second, the other need not consider what possible Charles the Second is meant. It is no doubt the English Charles Second. Charles the Second of England was quite a different man on different days; and it might be said that without further specification the subject is not identified. But the two Englishmen have no purpose of splitting hairs in their talk; and the latitude of interpretation which constitutes the indeterminacy of a sign must be understood as a latitude which might affect the achievement of a purpose. For two signs whose meanings are for all possible purposes equivalent are absolutely equivalent. This, to be sure, is rank pragmaticism; for a purpose is an affection of action.

What has been said of subjects is as true of predicates. Suppose the chat of our pair of Englishmen had fallen upon the color of Charles II's hair. Now that colors are seen quite differently by different retinas is known. That the chromatic sense is much more varied than it is positively known to be is quite likely. It is very unlikely that either of the travelers is trained to observe colors or is a master of their nomenclature. But if one says that Charles II had dark auburn hair, the other will understand him quite precisely enough for all their possible purposes; and it will be a determinate predication.[42]

Signs that are practically determinate may not be metaphysically determinate, so practical determination does not refute the deconstructive arguments of Derrida when they are applied to metaphysics. Practical determination does, however, undermine the claims of those deconstructionists who misapply Derrida's method to questions of practical import.

Vagueness can also stimulate the growth of understanding, what we could call the hermeneutic process. Signs can be living things, growing and changing in their implications. Peirce illustrates this conception in discussing the hypothesis of God (a hypothesis being a type of sign): "The hypothesis of God is a peculiar one, in that it supposes an infinitely incomprehensible object, although every hypothesis, as such, supposes its object to be truly conceived in the hypothesis. This leaves the hypothesis but one way of understanding itself; namely, as vague yet as true so far as it is definite, and as continually tending to define itself more and more, and without limit."[43] The hypothesis of God is an extreme example of vagueness encouraging hermeneutic inquiry. This is also an area in which inquiry is commonly blocked by the authoritarian method. The same principle applies to concepts such as a constitution, however. Consider how the American Constitution has been developed by extended interpretation through the years. The original terms were vague and so allowed for new applications. Even without amendments, the Constitution demonstrates the principle of growth of signs. A strong argument can be made, for example, that the Equal Rights Amendment would be redundant because those rights are guaranteed by the Constitution as it has grown. Decide for yourself. Read section 1 of the Fourteenth Amendment in light of the current meaning of "equal rights under the law," that is, considering all of the possible differences in current practice the phrase would require. A conservative Supreme Court, of course, may interpret the Constitution according to earlier meanings, just as parents may interpret their adult offspring as juveniles. In both cases the authoritative interpreters ignore significant changes in practice that should affect the meaning. Peirce's approach views vague signs, like constitutions, as processes of development.

Closely allied with his notion of living signs is his concept of gradual induction. A logically universal hypothesis is supported by what Peirce calls crude induction. Peirce cites the example of eighteenth-century scientific opinion that no stones fall from the sky. One counterexample disproved it. The contradictory hypothesis that some stones fall from the sky, however, is indeterminate. Gradual induction helps determine such hypotheses by making "a new estimate of the proportion of truth in the hypothesis with every new instance."[44] The indeterminate hypothesis thus becomes more and more determinate as inquiry progresses. To continue Peirce's example, we are now able to predict some meteor showers. Gradual induction can be either qualitative or quantitative. The statistical methods employed in the many branches of science today are examples of quantitative gradual induction. The inclusion of blacks, women, and homosexuals under the label "persons" in the Constitution is an example of qualitative induction.

Given these various implications of vagueness, I take the term *community* to be an admittedly vague sign of what is real, as real as our own selves (another vague sign). The vagueness is in part due to where we are in our inquiry. We have not yet developed sufficient interpretants through qualitative induction. We must first develop the hypothetical terms that will enable us to pay attention to the relevant facts of our experience that apply. We will continue to do so through the remainder of this chapter and, indeed, through the remainder of this book in a hermeneutic of the human communicative ecosystem. From our discoveries so far, we can see that communicative ethics requires a hermeneutic of our ecosystem and of ourselves to determine wise action in the vagueness of our situation. This hermeneutic will also reveal, however, that some degree of indeterminacy is part of the reality of social systems in general. Social systems are open systems with fuzzy boundaries, because the system's structure is the regularity of interaction and that is a matter of degree. The regularity also is general but not universal, involving some order but not total order. Furthermore, our communication can increase or decrease the order that exists. The way we signify our social system affects the way we act, which in turn affects the structure of that social system. Changing the structure of our social system is an ontical consequence of communication that is usually neglected in studies of communicative ethics. As Aristotle suggested long ago, politics, ethics, and rhetoric are intertwined.

The next step in the hermeneutic of our ethical situation will be to discuss triadic semiotics in greater depth. I have glossed over some difficulties involved in the signification of reality that require better explication. Peirce's scholastic realism is not the authoritative realism of the Middle Ages but a sophisticated semiotic approach that anticipates much of the poststructural critique of language yet refuses to yield to skepticism. In order to understand the pragmatic conceptualization of community and public, we need to understand triadic semiotic theory and, briefly, the phenomenology behind it.

Triadic Semiotic Theory

On the basis of the preceding discussion, I find reasonable and well supported the hypothesis that our signs engage us with reality. Our understanding of reality may be vague; the reality itself may be indeterminate to some degree. These problems illustrate the need of continuing inquiry. Nevertheless, the hypothesis that much of our knowledge is adequate is supported by the fact that we as a species have survived through changing environmental conditions. The means of our survival has been semiosis, the "peculiar action of signs."[45] We exist ecologically as semiotic creatures. Any thorough semiotic theory must include an explanation of how we know our environment. Dyadic semiotic theories have not been up to this task. For this reason poststructuralism and postmodernism, in general, have led to excessive skepticism. The result is that many valuable insights of the postmodernists have not reached much beyond those academic professionals whose interests are benefited by the emphasis on symbols and the neglect of reality. I recently attended a seminar by a theorist of public policy who was attempting to develop a postmodern model of policymaking. The problem was that his model never led to a decision; it multiplied the diversity of discussion endlessly. Managers in practice are not likely to have much patience with such a theory. Peirce's theory, however, provides the basis for a model that we can use to incorporate the valid insights of postmodernism without paralyzing practical action.

Peirce's theory of signs draws upon his phenomenology. Phenomenology, or phaneroscopy, as Peirce also called it, is the study of what appears to the mind. Based upon his observation of what appears to the mind, Peirce developed three categories of being: "My view is that there are three modes of being. I hold that we can directly observe them in elements of whatever is at any time before the mind in any way. They are the being of positive qualitative possibility, the being of actual fact, and the being of law that will govern facts in the future."[46] He labels these categories Firstness, Secondness, and Thirdness. By using ordinal numbers, he indicates that they exist in relation to each other: "they are so inextricably mixed together that no one can be isolated, yet it is manifest that their characters are quite disparate."[47] At times, however, his usage of the concepts changes and he writes as if they existed independently. Greenlee suggests that we think of the categories as tools for analysis, whether they stand for phenomena or factors of phenomena.[48]

Firstness is the category of feeling, "the passive consciousness of quality, without recognition or analysis." This is quality abstracted from existence, for example, the feeling that redness is appearing. Quality separate from existence is possibility. Redness considered apart from any red thing, that is, related only to itself, consists in the potential to be red. The realm of possibility is the realm of freedom. When we speak of opportunity cost, we illustrate how enactment limits freedom. Actualization is Secondness, a dyadic relation, "[c]onsciousness of an interruption into the field of consciousness, sense of resistance, of an external fact, of another something."[49] "Actuality is something *brute*. There is no reason in it."[50] Secondness is a relation between two things, an effort and a resistance. We know other things exist by their brute effect on us, so Secondness is the mode of existence. Stimulus-response and signifier-signified are examples of Secondness.

Thirdness is closely connected with Peirce's scholastic realism. It is a general tendency, rule, or habit. Phenomenologically, it is "synthetic consciousness binding time together, sense of learning, thought."[51] Thirdness is illustrated in our necessary ability to make predictions based on relations between objects. The accuracy of our predictions varies greatly, of course, showing the various degrees of indeterminacy involved. Nevertheless, we can make many predictions with astounding accuracy. As I write this, it is summer here in Louisiana. I predict that tomorrow will be hot and humid. This virtually certain prediction is based not on my experience of heat and humidity today—a kind of Secondness—but on the continuity of my experience across several Louisiana summers, in short, on induction. Induction confirms general rules that are predictions.

If the prediction has a tendency to be fulfilled, it must be that future events have a tendency to conform to a general rule. "Oh," but say the nominalists, "this general rule is nothing but a mere word or couple of words!" I reply, "Nobody ever dreamed of denying that what is general is of the nature of a general sign; but the question is whether future events will conform to it or not. If they will, your adjective 'mere' seems to be ill-placed." A rule to which future events have a tendency to conform is *ipso facto* an important thing, an important element in the happening of those events. This mode of being which *consists*, mind my word if you please, the mode of being which *consists* in the fact that future facts of Secondness will take on a determinate general character, I call a Thirdness.[52]

All three modes of being involve realities, because each can be an object represented in true sentences. The true representation itself, however, must be a Thirdness, because in asserting its truth it predicts that no further facts will disprove what it states. In pragmatic terms, claims of truth, even if about some Secondness in the past, always point to the future.

Peirce insists that Thirdness is irreducible; it cannot be broken down into relations of Secondness. He offers two examples of this irreducibility. The first is the act of giving: if A gives B to C, that act is not reducible to A losing B and C gaining B. My giving you a dollar involves more than my losing a dollar and your gaining a dollar. Giving is by its nature a synthesis and, thus, triadic. Another example involves forked versus straight roads. A straight road is dyadic; it joins two terminal points. I could extend it by adding segments to each end, but it would still just connect two terminal points. A forked road connects three terminal points and so is triadic; those three points stand in a new and different relation to each other. By combining forked roads, we can create complex networks of roads that connect an indefinite number of terminal points. The network is logically reducible to triads but not dyads.[53] The logical concept of synthesis or mediation is like the forked road that joins three points. Multiple plural relations can be built up from it. A recent study by Burch in formal logic confirms Peirce's thesis that triadic relations are not reducible to dyadic relations.[54]

Peirce points out that Thirdness is necessary to the concept of learning as well. This aspect of Thirdness is illustrated by a maxim about pilots. Some pilots have 2,000 hours of flying experience; others have 1 hour of experience repeated 2,000 times. The point is that each hour is an event that could be either learned from or simply repeated. One pilot might synthesize her hours: she develops hypotheses, tests them inductively, and builds up a repertoire of predictive rules for flying. The hypotheses she formulates are Thirds that mediate between the hour experiences, which were Seconds. Another pilot might simply repeat the experience of Secondness over and over again. Without Thirdness, without mediation, there is no learning. Thirdness makes it possible for us to represent our experiences in their relationship to each other and to make inferences on the basis of that representation.

The epitome of Thirdness is semiosis. "A *Sign*, or *Representamen*, is a First which stands in such a genuine triadic relation to a Second, called its *Object*, as to be capable of determining a Third, called its *Interpretant*, to assume the same triadic relation to its Object in which it stands itself to the same Object. The triadic relation is *genuine*, that is its three members are bound together by it in a way that does not consist in any complexus of dyadic relations."[55] The sign is determined by its object, and the interpretant is determined by the sign, so that the interpretant is mediately determined by the object. Take as an example the natural sign of fire: smoke. If an animal experiences the uncomfortable heat of a fire while smelling smoke, the smoke will come to represent the object fire. The animal has a new triadic relation to fire. In the future, smoke will determine the interpretant—the experience of uncomfortable heat—as a sign of fire considered as uncomfortable heat. The physical object *fire* mediately determines the uncomfortable experience through the mediation of the sign *smoke*. But the semiosis does not stop here. The interpretant of discomfort also is a sign, whose object is the correlation of smoke and fire, and whose interpretant is a feeling of fear. The interpretant of fear is, in turn, a sign of the correlation of discomfort and smoke-fire; and so it determines a further interpretant, the muscular motion of fleeing. This is an example of zoosemiosis, semiosis at the animal level that underlies anthroposemiosis.[56] It also illustrates that semiosis is a continual process; the triadic model merely represents a step in that process. In addition, the example shows that interpretants can be logical, emotive, and/or energetic (causing exertion).

The method of determination of the sign in this case is a kind of secondness. Smoke stands for fire because smoke is physically connected with fire. Peirce calls such a sign an *indexical* sign, which represents its object "because it is in dynamical (including spatial) connection both with the individual object, on the one hand, and with the senses or memory of the person for whom it serves as a sign, on the other hand."[57] In an *iconic* sign, the relation of object to sign is one of resemblance. In a *symbolic* sign, the relation is determined by a rule or convention. For semiosis in general, this is a useful division of signs. As Greenlee points out, however, in human semiosis, some degree of symbolism is involved in each of the other types of signs. A weathervane, for example, points toward the wind because it is acted upon by the wind; but the interpretant of the weathervane is also determined by convention.[58] That convention arose, of course, from the indexical nature of the weathervane as sign.

The common symbolic aspect of human signs has misled structuralists and poststructuralists, who base their analysis of signs on language and ignore the underlying zoosemiosis, which is our primary contact with our environment. Peirce analyzed perceptive judgments as semiotic processes, even though they are subconscious and, hence, uncritical processes. Our perceptions are interpretants of signs that are in turn interpretants of more basic signs. By logical analysis, this is an infinite sequence of signs.[59] On this type of analysis, Derrida bases his argument that originary meaning is always deferred in the movement of différance. For the critique of metaphysics, he makes an important point; the essence of any real thing cannot be made present to us through dialectical or logical analysis of our language. All that analysis can show are our inferences, which are interpretants, and never the origin of those inferences. It does not follow, however, that we do not know the objects of our environment because all we know are signs. When we consider ourselves trapped in our prison house of signs, we are, as Peirce points out, letting ourselves become confused by a version of Zeno's paradox.

Zeno of Elea wrote a book in the middle of the fifth century B.C. that used paradox to argue against plurality and motion. The paradox is an apparent contradiction used to undermine the findings of common sense. Aristotle discusses Zeno's paradoxes of motion in the *Physics* (239b). Peirce uses the paradox of Achilles and the Tortoise to illustrate why our analysis of signs seems to contradict common sense. Achilles was a great runner, but according to Zeno he could not have overtaken a tortoise if the tortoise was given any amount of head start. Let's say Achilles is at point A and the tortoise is some distance ahead at point B. While Achilles runs to point B, the tortoise also moves ahead to point C. If Achilles runs ten times as fast as the tortoise, point C will only be one-tenth of the distance away from B that A was, but it will be some finite distance. Next Achilles runs from B to C, but the tortoise moves from C to D (a distance 1/100 of the original distance). Achilles must now run from C to D; but of course the tortoise has moved to E (1/1000 of AB). Each time Achilles covers the distance to the next point, the tortoise moves another distance away. In order to overtake the tortoise, Achilles would have to run an infinite number of intervals of a finite distance in a finite amount of time. Since it is clearly impossible for Achilles to run an infinite number of such intervals, he will never arrive at the same point as the tortoise at the same time. So no matter how fast he is, Achilles cannot catch the tortoise.

Zeno's paradox is an interesting exercise in logic, but we know from our experience that faster runners pass slower runners. The problem in the paradox is caused by the confusion of a continuum with discrete points. In fact, Achilles runs continuously, not in ever-decreasing intervals. The fact that a line can be divided into an infinite number of points does not mean that the line is infinitely long. The line does not comprise the points as parts but is simply the continuum between two points.[60] Perceptual semiosis is also a continuum, and the infinite regress fails to represent what actually happens for the same reason that Zeno's paradox fails to represent an actual run. "Namely, just as Achilles does not have to make the series of distinct endeavours which he is represented as making, so this process of forming the perceptual judgment, because it is subconscious and so not amenable to logical criticism, does not have to make separate acts of inference, but performs its act in one continuous process."[61] Logical analysis breaks semiosis down into steps so that the relation of the interpretant to the object can be criticized, but semiosis itself is a continual process that begins with the physical object and results in the perceptual judgment. This inability to observe in no way affects the fallibility of the process. At the subconscious level, our perceptions are fallible but not correctible.

Humans, like other animals, exist in a world of perceptions that are subconscious semiotic acts. Because semiotic systems such as sense organs, nervous systems, and brains vary between different species, each species lives in what von Uexküll labeled an *Umwelt*. As Deely explains, "The environment selectively reconstituted and organized according to the specific needs and interests of the individual organism constitutes an Umwelt." Human semiosis is unique because it continues semiosis far beyond simple perception and immediate use of objects in the environment. The uniqueness consists in our ability to reflect on our own semiotic acts. This special feature of anthroposemiosis, which Deely calls *textuality*, leads to a "specifically human Umwelt, the Lebenswelt, as it is [some]times called, [which] is a uniquely malleable Umwelt open in ways no other Umwelt on this planet is open to reconstitution along alternative lines of objectification, both within itself and in its relations with the external environment physical as such."[62] In short, perceptions are determined by the interaction of organism and environment; therefore, the objects known are not simply the objects as they exist in themselves apart from the process of semiosis. The difference here is between the known and unknown (but not necessarily unknowable, as in Kant) aspects of the object. The Umwelt is a partial world compared with the real world, but it has represented the real world adequately for survival of the species, an achievement that goes beyond mere solidarity. Humans, once semiotically aware of the limits of their Umwelt, seek to bring it into agreement with the physical world. That is the project of science, of knowledge in general, made possible by the growth of anthroposemiosis into forms of language. Language allows us to share our perceptions, correcting and enlarging the world of our experience.

Peirce distinguished between the semiotic object, "the object as it is represented," and the "dynamic object," which is the object that partially determines the sign. He acknowledges that we live in an Umwelt: "It is perfectly true that we can never attain a knowledge of things as they are. We can only know their human aspect. But that is all the universe is for us."[63] Signs are relational; we can only know dynamic objects insofar as they act upon us and become semiotic objects. To speak of an object without relation to us is to speak of an object that has no meaning for us. That is a restatement of the pragmatic maxim; our concepts can refer only to possible experience. The possibility of knowing reality and making true statements is not meant in a way that transcends our human limits. We are capable of limited but true knowledge, sufficiently determinate for all of our practical purposes. We do not know what our human limits are; technology regularly extends our possibilities of semiosis. Reality itself is the ultimate end limit of the possibilities of human knowledge through semiosis.

Deely distinguishes between an "object" in representation and a "physical object," which besides being an object is also a thing. Physical objects are not limited to material objects but include any reality that exists apart from our thought; so the term *physical* as Deely uses it is congruent with scholastic realism.

Objects are *not* what things are in a being prior to and independent of experience. Objects *are* what the things become once experienced—that is, once they take on the existence proper to experience. But objects *are* not only things experienced. Objects are more than things, even when—which is not always the case—they are also things. Objects always involve a "relation to an observer," so to speak, or, more exactly, to an organism experiencing. Things only sometimes involve such a relation.[64]

Deely's use of "object" returns to the pre-Kantian use that is also reflected in Heidegger's discussion of Dasein's comportment toward beings.[65] The object is a product of semiosis because it is the physical thing as known in experience. All signs have objects, but not all objects have corresponding physical objects. If I ask, order, or promise, the object of my sign is a future possibility, not a present thing. If I ask you, for example, to close the door, the object of the sign is the future possibility of the door being closed, related to the interpretant of your closing the door. If I tell you about my dream, the signs within the dream stand for fictional objects, but the fact that I dreamed is an object that is also a physical thing—a reality. Herein lies the explanation of "social reality." The objects signified within a "social reality," a Lebenswelt, may or may not be real things; however, the fact that they are acted upon as if real is, itself, a reality that is physical in the scholastic sense. An example is the sign *race* in American culture, which stands for no coherent physical object but as an objective social reality has profound consequences for society.

The sign always represents an object because signs are essentially relational, something standing for something else. Considered as signifier, or sign vehicle, a sign is often thought of as an object. The sign itself, however, is not the object but the relation brought about when the object is interpreted as standing for another object. Once the sign is interpreted as standing for an object, the triadic relation is real, *whether or not the physical object exists*. To illustrate the nature of this kind of relation, Deely raises the question: "In what sense is the parent of a dead child still a parent?"[66] Parenthood, like signification, is a relative form of being. In its common form, parenthood as a relation results from the dyadic action of sex between female and male, but it is not the same as that dyadic relation. Nor is being a parent a property of an individual, such as the color of one's eyes. "In short, the characteristic of being a parent rests not on the dynamic interaction of sexual activity alone but on that taken together with, coordinated with, a certain outcome that exists precisely as a trajectory independent of either parent in his or her individual being."[67] In one sense, the relation is permanent; that is, within the order of understanding, this child will always be the child of these parents. This relation holds true whether or not the physical nurturing relationship continues. The individual parent is not understood as an individual unless she or he is understood as parent of that child, and the child is not understood as an individual unless she or he is understood as the child of those parents.

Here we have the first and the most general sense in which being is relative: according to the requirements of understanding. Within experience, every individual exists in such a way as to require being thought of in terms of things the individual is not, in order to be understood for what the individual is. This requirement transcends the independent aspect of the individual existent and in fact reveals that independent aspect to be itself dependent upon other factors, some present and still essential (like the atmosphere and gravity, for example) and others past and essential no longer to the individual existing before us (like the dead parents, say, or the prehistoric organisms that began the process of establishing an oxidizing atmosphere).[68]

Deely, following the usage of Duns Scotus, refers to this aspect of relation pertaining to an individual as the "transcendental relation."

In addition to its importance for the understanding of sign relations, the transcendental relation of individuals is a key concept in my ecological theory of communication ethics. An individual cannot simply be understood atomistically as a whole unto itself but must be understood also in its relations to its environment. To be is to be related to an ecosystem with a past and a future. In other words, our relations are part of our identity. Atomistic individualism is a denial of some of the most important aspects of our identity. We will never come to understand ourselves if we do not include our relations to others. Admittedly, Derrida has shown that we are not immediately present to ourselves as subjects. From a Peircean perspective, however, we can still come to know ourselves in a limited way; that is, we know ourselves not directly in the manner of the Cartesian *cogito* but indirectly as signs in the process of developing.[69] The hermeneutic of ourselves must include our transcendental, ecological relations if we expect to attain happiness.

Moreover, the triadic relation is real in its own right apart from the subjective aspect of transcendental relations. Real relations exist between things that are not in things. Deely calls the relation per se the *ontological relation*. It is the Thirdness, the pattern of relation considered in itself. This relation can exist whether one is aware of it or not. If an egg and sperm were combined in a petri dish, for example, the parents might be unaware of their parenthood relation; nevertheless a real, physical relation exists. The child's genetic code will be a synthesis of the father's and mother's codes. In this case, the relation is physical but not objective because the relation is not an object of knowledge. A relation could be objective but not physical, as when a couple has sexual relations for the purpose of having a child. The child is known (vaguely) as an object but does not yet exist physically; but the relation really exists between that nonphysical object and the couple. The third case of ontological relation is the case in which the relation exists objectively and physically; the parents are aware of their parenthood, and their child really exists at the time.[70]

Well, then, what is the answer to the question about parenthood when the child has died? "The parent remains a parent at the level of transcendental relation, while ceasing to be a parent at the level of physical relation, although this physical relation continues to exist objectively to the extent that the parent or anyone else thinks about it. The same relation formed now only in thought formerly existed also physically, and it is by virtue of that same relation that the parent is a parent."[71] The ontological relation is, in a sense, indifferent to the real existence of the objects that are the ground of its being. The same pattern or relation exists as long as its elements exist objectively and/or physically. An assertion about the relation will be true, of course, only if the relation exists physically as asserted, allowing for the modality of the assertion.

This explanation of ontological relations is important for two reasons. First, because a sign is an ontological relation, the process of signification occurs whether or not the object signified also exists physically—that is, in Peirce's terminology, exists as a dynamic object. This explains error, deception, and the questionable "positivities" Foucault claimed were the product of discursive regimes. As we shall see in chapter 4, honesty is a relation of discourse to semiotic objects; truth is a relation of discourse to dynamic objects—reality. Second, the indifference of the ontological relation can account for the organization of chaos into community. A relation between objects that are not physical may result in a physical object. The purely objective relation of parenthood involving a couple who have sexual relations in order to have a baby, for example, is very likely to result in their physical parenthood. Consider a family to be an example of a small community. A community exists when the members are aware of their communality; that is, when the communal relation exists objectively in the understanding. The members will then act on the basis of that relation and in doing so will develop into a community. On the other hand, a communal relation that does not exist objectively, even if it exists physically, will soon dissolve into chaos because it will not be reinforced in action. Communication is the means whereby communality is made objectively known to the members of the social ecosystem. Like the individual, the community must be made aware of its own relational being. The actual community is the result of the semiotic interpretation of the objective community.

Basic perception, zoosemiosis, uncritically presumes the object experienced to be a physical object. The survival of a species depends upon the semiotic correlation being a generally true correlation. Nothing about semiosis in itself guarantees that the correlation is true; as an ontological relation a sign is indifferent to the physical existence of its object. Therefore, what is necessary for any species to survive is that physical objects are capable of representing themselves as objects of experience to that species. Physical objects may be unknown, but they cannot be unknowable. The capability, or potential, of self-representation is a dyadic aspect of a sign. This dyadic aspect of representation is a source of great confusion, according to Deely. A sign is always a kind of representation, but not all representations are signs because not all are triadic. When I vote, that action is a self-representation. My political opinion indexically determines my vote. My vote is not a sign of my political opinion, however, until someone (myself even) interprets the vote as representing my opinion. Self-representation is a transcendental relation; that is, my opinion cannot be understood as the kind of entity it is unless it is understood as able to represent itself indexically. The ability of my political opinion to represent itself indexically by means of the vote is the ground of the ontological relation that is a true sign. The election of my *representative* is the result of semiosis wherein all the votes cast are interpreted as standing for the opinion of the electorate. This difference between a sign and self-representation at the level of community underlies several ethical problems in political communication, which I will discuss in chapter 7. Suffice to say here that political consensus is not dyadic self-representation but the triadic result of political deliberation.

Confusion exists in our political discourse because this particular confusion underlies much of our popular metaphysics since Descartes, as Deely points out:

> The confusion of signs as such with representations has been, historically, perhaps the most common cause of misunderstanding of the role of signs in experience. This confusion is what led Descartes and Locke to posit ideas as the objects of our awareness and then to trouble themselves mightily with the problem of figuring out how these self-representations might or might not be causally connected with or resemblant of the assumed (but not directly experienced) existence of extramental things. Once it is understood, however, that objects as such are always representations but representations as such are never signs, it becomes clear that, to whatever extent ideas are signs, they are differentiated from, rather than identified with, the objects of our awareness here and now. The distinction between representation and sign, in what concerns semiotics, is the distinction between object and sign.[72]

Our sensations are like votes: they are objectively sensible signifiers determined by physical things that are capable of representing some aspect of themselves as experienced objects. So a red thing, for example, is able to represent its redness as an object to us by means of our sensation of red. But neither the sensation nor the experienced object is a sign. The sign is the ontological relation that occurs when the sensation red is interpreted to stand for the physical object in its aspect of redness. The self-represented object is the ground of the relation that is the sign, but the ground is not the sign. "[I]n the case of a sign, what is fundamental (the representation grounding and founding the relation of signification) and what is formal (the relation of signification itself) never coincide."[73] Ideas, considered semiotically, are the signs as formal relations, not the objects of the signs. Derrida was right; différance is essential to the sign. This very difference, however, is what enables us to truly to perceive when our sensations are inferred to stand for the physical objects that do indeed determine them in self-representation.

Because the ontological relation is formal, the existence of illusory objects does not make the sign unreal. A dream really signifies its objects, even though those objects are not real. All signs really represent objects, whether physical things or not. Therefore semiotic analysis is itself a signification of real, physical objects—the signs being analyzed. For Peirce, logic is one form of semiotic analysis.

Grammar and rhetoric are others.[74] Most of Peirce's emphasis is on the logical aspects of signs; the pragmatic maxim is primarily a logical maxim. He is concerned with the pursuit of knowledge for its own sake, and so he focuses on the truth-value of semiosis. This is not a narrow, technical study, however, because for Peirce "logic is only an application of morality." He regards "Logic as the Ethics of the Intellect—that is, in the sense in which Ethics is the science of the method of bringing Self-Control to bear to gain our satisfactions."[75] Logic is the art of self-controlled reasoning. This art, along with the companion arts of grammar and rhetoric, is possible only for the animal that is capable of semiosis to the extent that it can signify the process of signification itself—that is, the human animal. With this capability of being critical of our own habits of signification comes special responsibility. Apel notes that Peirce saw a performative aspect in logical assertion and an ethical responsibility for the performance:

Peirce bases his thesis that all meaningful statements have a relationship to the future on the interesting observation, made in 1902, that whoever asserts or claims that a proposition is true thereby assumes responsibility for it, that is, for the conditioned predictions it entails (5.543). Peirce further develops this point of view by means of linguistic analysis, first in his 1903 lecture on Pragmatism (5.29ff.) and then, most of all, in a fragment from 1908 (5.546–47). Ceremonious statements that explicitly take responsibility for their content, such as an oath before a court, merely make visible, as through a magnifying glass, the willful, morally relevant, active aspect that is inherent in every assertion of the truth of a proposition. For Peirce there is therefore a continuum between "performative" and "constative" utterances, which in modern linguistic analysis, following Austin, are sharply distinguished. Not just the oath as a legal act, but every assertion that implicitly claims truth is an action by which the one making the assertion enters into reality in a causal, dynamic way and becomes engaged morally in the communication community.[76]

Apel's interpretation of Austin may be arguable, but he accurately represents the confluence of ethical and logical elements in Peirce's thinking.

Peirce's emphasis on logic, however, still falls short of the full ecological impact of communication on the community. Lyotard's libidinal economy, for example, is insufficient but nevertheless necessary for an adequate theory of communication ethics. Logic focuses on truth value, but other values must be considered as well. In the final section of this chapter, I will draw upon the insights of Dewey and other pragmatists who have broadened the general approach of Peirce.

I will interpret these extensions, however, in the light of the triadic semiotic perspective to which Peirce contributed so much.

Individual and Community Values

Peirce has shown the importance of the community of inquiry to the production of truth. Deely has shown that we cannot understand the meaning of an individual without taking into account its relations to other elements in its ecosystem. The corollary deserves more attention than Peirce gives it; a social system must also be understood in terms of its relations to its parts and to other social and physical systems. These understandings lead to what I call the *ecological* approach to communication ethics. I take ethics to be the practical art of making good decisions. When applied practically, the pragmatic maxim leads to Mead's formulation of *intelligence* as "conscious foresight of consequences."[77] Peirce's logic can certainly help in the application of intelligence to our decision making, but it gives only a partial answer to the question of what would be *good* in the way of consequences. Truth would be a good outcome; but in Peirce's system, one can only work toward the truth without knowing whether one has achieved final truth. When the desired consequence exists in the indefinite future, proximate consequences are increasingly important. In other words, on the road of infinite inquiry, it pays to stop and smell the flowers.

Dewey's pragmatic approach concerns itself with a variety of ends. In fact, he subordinates the quest for knowledge to more immediate purposes of fulfillment:

What is sometimes termed "applied" science, may then be more truly science than is what is conventionally called pure science. For it is directly concerned with not just instrumentalities, but instrumentalities at work in effecting modifications of existence in behalf of conclusions that are reflectively preferred. Thus conceived the characteristic subject-matter of knowledge consists of fulfilling objects, which as fulfillments are connected with a history to which they give character. Thus conceived, knowledge exists in engineering, medicine and the social arts more adequately than it does in mathematics, and physics. Thus conceived, history and anthropology are scientific in a sense in which bodies of information that stop short with general formulae are not.[78]

His use of the term *fulfilling objects* treats objectivity similarly to the way we used it in the previous section. In this context, however, Dewey limits objects to the products of semiosis in human communication, in which "events turn into objects, things with a meaning."[79] Even introspection depends on communication; it is soliloquy, and soliloquy is "product and reflex of converse with others."[80]

Following Peirce and Mead, at least in the context of anthroposemiosis, Dewey sees signification as dependent upon communication. Signification makes possible the understanding of purpose and agency that is not possible in things as mere things:

What a physical event immediately is, and what it *can* do or its relationship are distinct and incommensurable. But when an event has meaning, its potential consequences become its integral and funded feature. When the potential consequences are important and repeated, they form the very nature and essence of a thing, its defining, identifying, and distinguishing form. To recognize the thing is to grasp its definition. Thus we become capable of perceiving things instead of merely feeling and having them. To *perceive* is to acknowledge unattained possibilities; it is to refer the present to consequences, apparition to issue, and thereby to behave in deference to the *connections* of events.[81]

In Peirce's terms, the immediate feeling of an event is a Firstness, the event itself is a Secondness, and the connection of an event to its consequences is Thirdness. The nature of semiosis as Thirdness is what makes the connection of feelings and events possible. This semiotic perception of the relation between feelings and events is the source of values.

Values exist because Firstness, the feeling of quality, exists in immediate sensation:

Empirically, the existence of objects of direct grasp, possession, use and enjoyment cannot be denied. Empirically, things are poignant, tragic, beautiful, humourous, settled, disturbed, comfortable, annoying, barren, harsh, consoling, splendid, fearful; are such immediately and in their own right and behalf. . . . [E]sthetic quality, immediate, final, or self-enclosed, indubitably characterizes natural situations as they empirically occur. These traits stand in themselves on precisely the same level as colors, sounds, qualities of contact, taste and smell. Any criterion that finds the latter to be ultimate and "hard" data will, impartially applied, come to the same conclusion about the former.[82]

Values, however, are not these qualities as Firstness, which would be as purely experienced, but as Thirdness, that is, as related to the events that produce them.

This Thirdness is why Lyotard's libidinal economy is insufficient for a theory of valuation. Dewey agrees that the "vital impulse," equivalent to Lyotard's use of libido, is a nonrational factor in valuation. The reason is simply that in itself it is a pure existent, a Secondness; all existents considered in themselves are nonrational. Thus one could truly say that "values *spring from* the immediate and inexplicable reaction of vital impulse and from the irrational part of our nature."

But the sentence cited is often interpreted to mean that vital impulses *are* valuations—an interpretation which is incompatible with the view which connects valuations with desires and interests, and which, by parity of logic, would justify the statement that trees are seeds since they "spring from" seeds. Vital impulses are doubtless conditions *sine qua non* for the existence of desires and interests. But the latter include foreseen consequences along with ideas in the form of signs of the measures (involving expenditure of energy) required to bring the ends into existence.[83]

The libido may be the source of the feelings experienced in an object, however, libido alone cannot explain valuation.

When we value something, we do so in one of two ways, according to Dewey. To value is either to *prize* or to *appraise*. When we prize something, we care for it. The act of prizing or caring for something occurs only when we perceive a lack of something or a danger to something within a specific context. In this sense of prizing, which is related to desiring, we do not value what we take for granted until it is gone or threatened. Value as prizing is thus related to possible courses of action to obtain or preserve what is valued as an end. Value as appraisal on the other hand is connected with standards; it shows itself in statements of what should happen according to some norm. Moral rules are norms for appraisals but merely one species in a broad genus. "Every recurrent form of activity, in the arts and professions, develops rules as to the best way in which to accomplish the ends in view. Such rules are used as criteria or 'norms' for judging the value of proposed modes of behavior."[84] Appraisal is thus concerned with valuation of means.

These aspects of valuation are normally treated as separate, as in the commonplace "the end does not justify the means." Dewey argues, however, that the separation of end and means, prizing and appraisal, is an error. "For what is deliberation except weighing of various alternative desires (and hence end-values) in terms of the conditions that are the means of their execution, and which, as means, determine the consequences actually arrived at?"[85] We may simply act out of habit or impulse, but when we act with purpose, with an end in view, we are hypothesizing that some means will bring about that objective. If we deliberate well in accordance with the pragmatic maxim, we will consider all of the possible consequences of those means and evaluate the end in light of those consequences. Good deliberation addresses the problem that the commonplace about ends and means only vaguely points toward.

Valuation is a semiotic mediation of ends and means, a Thirdness that synthesizes prizing and appraisal. Like all semiosis, valuation is theoretically endless. The ends-means distinction is a distinction between points on a continuum:

[T]he distinction between ends and means is temporal and relational. Every condition that has to be brought into existence in order to serve as means is, *in that connection,* an object of desire and an end-in-view, while the end actually reached is a means to future ends as well as a test of valuations previously made. Since the end attained is a condition of further existential occurrences, it must be appraised as a potential obstacle and potential resource. If the notion of some objects as ends-in-themselves were abandoned, not merely in words but in all practical implications, human beings would for the first time in history be in a position to frame ends-in-view and form desires on the basis of empirically grounded propositions of the temporal relations of events to one another.[86]

As in Peirce's semiotic continuum, the process may have apparent resting points that appear as episodes; however, these are merely points of revaluation that continue the process even if in a different direction.

Dewey's method of valuation parallels Peirce's explanation of the scientific method of belief. The actual values extant in a society, evidenced by its actions, including communicative action, are products of the method of tenacity, authority, a priori metaphysics, or a mixture of the various methods. These values may, at times, reflect the accumulated experience of a community in relating ends to means, and so it would be pragmatically unwise to devalue traditions without evidence of undesirable consequences ensuing from the tradition. Furthermore, any critique of traditional values necessarily draws upon other values in showing the undesirability of probable outcomes. By restoring rational deliberation to valuation, however, we can increase the likelihood of obtaining the ends we actually seek in the situation we are actually in. Values, like truths, should be treated as hypotheses that are still undergoing testing. Legitimate doubt should cause inquiry into the particular value doubted just as it should lead to scientific inquiry in the case of facts. As with scientific inquiry into truth, inquiry into values is useful only if semiosis allows a probable knowledge of reality.

In any given social system, deliberative valuation is the quintessential *public* act. But what type of object is the public? For Dewey, the public is not some a priori entity discovered by metaphysical dialectic but an a posteriori object discovered by experience. Our experience teaches us that "conjoint, combined, associated action is a universal trait of the behavior of things" and that "such action has results."[87] When the consequences of human action are perceived as semiotic objects, they become the source of plans and strategies to gain some consequences and avoid others. These consequences fall roughly into two classes, the public and the private. If the important consequences of interaction are confined to those involved, the interaction is private. According to this distinction, for example, under most circumstances sexual acts of consenting adults are considered private. On the other hand, some acts affect others who are not directly involved. The same sexual acts during an epidemic of sexually transmitted diseases can have important consequences on others not directly involved. Those indirectly affected need some means of indirect influence over those actions that affect them. Public rhetoric encouraging "safe sex" is an example of such indirect influence.

A social system exists simply as a pattern of associations, whether it is known objectively or not. A community comes into being when we reflect on the relationship itself, on the Thirdness, as an object deserving attention. We then begin to plan our behavior in light of that relationship, and a community develops. In Deely's terms, community is the ontological relation between individuals when it is objectively known. Dewey offers an analogy: "The planets in a constellation would form a community if they were aware of the connections of the activities of each with those of the others and could use this knowledge to direct behavior."[88] Communities and publics exist, at least potentially, at all levels of our ecosystem. A couple can form a community when they come to recognize the nature of their relationship. Families, neighborhoods—any association of individuals or groups capable of perceiving their relationship as an object affected by their actions can form a community. Because Thirdness is observed empirically by seeing the connections in events and appreciating the changed quality of experience, the development of community begins in local, face-to-face interactions. Our homes and neighborhoods are nurseries for the development of community.

Even in Dewey's time, however, the breakdown of community was evident. "The machine age in developing the Great [i.e., massive] Society has invaded and partially disintegrated the small communities of former times without generating a Great Community."[89] Mass commerce and mass communication have attained some integration of society; but "in spite of attained integration, or rather perhaps because of its nature, the Public seems to be lost; it is certainly bewildered."[90]

The local face-to-face community has been invaded by forces so vast, so remote in initiation, so far-reaching in scope and so complexly indirect in operation, that they are, from the standpoint of the members of local social units, unknown. . . . An inchoate public is capable of organization only when indirect consequences are perceived, and when it is possible to project agencies which order their occurrence. At present, many consequences are felt rather than perceived; they are suffered, but they cannot be said to be known, for they are not, by those who experience them, referred to their origins. It goes, then, without saying that agencies are not established which canalize the streams of social action and thereby regulate them. Hence the publics are amorphous and unarticulated.[91]

In bemoaning the loss of public deliberation, Dewey here sounds like Habermas, who articulated the loss of the liberal bourgeois model of a public sphere for deliberation in the late twentieth century.[92] At times, Dewey's notion of a space for public deliberation seems based on that model, especially as instantiated in New England town meetings. The Deweyan conception of a public, however, requires a revised conception of the public sphere from the more limited model described by Habermas. As a symbol of a complex Thirdness, the "public sphere" must grow by incorporating the results of inductive testing if it is to describe an ethical ideal to be made concrete in practice.

In the Deweyan conception of public, there are many publics; therefore, there must be many public spheres. Fraser's reconceptualization of the public sphere is more compatible with this pragmatic a posteriori understanding of community than is Habermas's.[93] Recognizing that the Habermasian public sphere excluded many social groups, she points out that these "subaltern publics" have developed their own discursive arenas. These subaltern publics, however, do not merely talk among themselves but seek to affect the larger public, of which they are also members. Her approach to the problem of the public sphere can be translated ecologically into the concept of multiply layered communicative ecosystems involving contestation as well as cooperation. Effective interaction between these publics requires an improvement in the actual conditions of equality, not merely the bracketing of inequality. Furthermore, we cannot determine a priori which issues are public rather than private. Recognizing relationships to indirect consequences is the result of communal deliberation, as Dewey points out. Therefore, as Fraser argues, "there is no warrant for putting any strictures on what sorts of topics, interests, and views are admissible in deliberation."[94] Finally, an adequate conceptualization of the public sphere cannot arbitrarily separate the workings of civil society and the state. Fraser calls those publics that lack decision-making authority "weak publics," in contrast to the "strong publics" with administrative power. A pragmatic, ecological model of the public sphere must consider the interrelationship between these publics and the inequalities of power relations between the many levels of publics.

The problem is not that the Habermasian notion of a "public sphere" is a counterfactual ideal. A well-developed ideal can be a force for the betterment of society. Our understanding of that ideal must grow inductively, however, as we incorporate the experiences of all. Fraser's modification of the ideal is a contribution to the qualitative induction that corrects our understanding. The Secondness of experience is allowed to change the meaning of the symbol "public sphere." From a pragmatic perspective, this is real progress toward truth and justice. Of course, we have a long way to go. We exist in a social ecosystem, but we lack ecological understanding of its relationships. From the dyadic, nominalistic, postmodern perspective, we are doomed. We are simply caught in a chain of signifiers that can lead to no ecological truths because concepts like "public sphere" are mere fictions. Our semiotic codes shape us, manipulate us, and write our destiny. All that remains for us is to choose either the role of Sisyphus or of Narcissus in playing out our doom.

As a pragmatic realist following the line of argument presented in this chapter, I deny those claims. Yes, we are trapped in semiotic codes that hinder our ability to address the real problems that press us. But semiosis is not immune to reality; it is triadic and partially determined by reality as long as we are open to correction by experience. We can semiotically discover real objects, including that elusive object of communality and the virtues that accompany it—not infallibly but much better than we do now. We can work toward creating better opportunities for public discourse at all levels of the ecosystem. Criticism should improve practice by comparing our practice to our possibilities—that is, our ideals. Deconstructive criticism that does not eventually lead to reconstructive practice is a waste of time. We may not be able to get back to the origins of our semiotic usage, but we are surely going to face the consequences of that usage. From the pragmatic perspective, consequences are the guide to practice and the corrective for our semiotic errors. We are the semiotic animal that can criticize and improve its own semiotic practice. To do so, we must improve our communication throughout our social ecosystem. For both individuals and communities, communication offers the possibility for ecological awareness or ecological ignorance. Etymologically derived from the Greek word *oikos*, which means *home*, our *ecosystem* is the network of relations constituting our home. For better or worse, we will live in this home that is built in part upon our communicative practices. A pragmatic ecological ethic suggests that we aim for the better by taking responsibility for the public consequences of our communicative actions. That responsibility is based on the reasonable hope that we really can do better in living up to and further developing our ideals.

3

From the Archaic to the Ecological

The contrast between a pragmatic, ecological approach and the postmodern approach should be clearer at this point. The postmodernists have many valid points to make about the difficulty of relating our signs to an antecedent, pristine reality or to a pure, rational essence that is somehow removed from power relations. Their critiques, however, have lost sight of the fact that, regardless of the difficulty, our semiotic systems enable us to cope with our environment. In short, they seem to have gotten themselves trapped in Zeno's paradox, forgetting that Achilles will beat the tortoise and that we do interact with our environment. The problem is not whether we cope but rather how we can improve our coping. An ecological approach avoids the synecdochic error of identifying semiotic with language. To be ecological is to recognize that language is just one semiotic system among many that constitute our multifaceted relationship to the overall ecosystem that is our life support system. The importance of our linguistic system derives from its being a major part of our communicative system, which in turn plays a major role in our semiotic relationship with our environment, both social and physical. The communicative system has ethical implications because it affects our overall quality of life.

Although a communicative system is a subsystem of the total ecosystem, it can be considered an ecosystem itself because it nurtures the individuals within it in their quest for the good. Admittedly, there are many different ways an ecosystem could develop and still nurture its individual members; no given system can serve as a transcendental model for communicative ecosystems. But the general principle that a functioning ecosystem supports its constituent members and that its functioning members fill niches in the ecosystem provides a reciprocal ideal that transcends cultures while avoiding a dogmatic a priori definition of what should constitute the good for the individual or for the culture in any given case. This underlying principle of the ecological ethic serves only to provide a model for investigation into what constitutes the good in a given case of communication.

Besides its base in Peircean pragmatism, the approach I propose here also draws upon the functional approach to morals contained in Aristotelian ethics, especially as further developed by Alasdair MacIntyre. I offer a non-Foucauldian *archaeology* of sorts: I suggest we reconsider a more *archaic* concept of ethics. The *archai*, or first principles, proposed here, however, also reflect a synthesis with modern and postmodern concepts reinterpreted pragmatically. From this perspective, communal relations are real. Just as we must live in a biological ecosystem, we must *necessarily* communicate in a communicative ecosystem. However symbolism and communication may have arisen, they must have arisen out of a relationship between people. As communication developed, the nature of that relationship was altered forever; but the fact that communication must take place within a system of relationships has not changed. Each of us learned to communicate within a system of relationships, most often, a family. As in the biological ecosystem, the particular form or culture of the communicative ecosystem is contingent upon historical circumstances. The Aristotelian version of ethics is based in a particular subculture of Athenian aristocrats. As a result, while suggesting a profitable overall approach to ethics, Aristotle's ethics lack the authority of true archai in a multicultural society. His particular ethics are elitist and sexist, but they suggest possibilities that could transcend elitism and sexism.

The archai of an ecological ethic consist of a reinterpretation of key concepts in ethical theory—virtue (*aretē*), the end (telos) of an individual life, practice (praxis), and the mean (*meson*)—in light of the functional properties of communicative ecosystems. From these functional properties I will hypothesize a foundation for communicative ethics based in a dialectical balance between the telos of the individual and the telos of the system. The telos of individual as used here takes into account the transcendental and ontological relations that support the narrative quest for the good. The telos of the system is public in the Deweyan sense that it is based in our communal interest in maintaining and improving the communicative ecosystem.

The narrative quest for the good of the individual and the communal interest are united by means of communication. Classical Aristotelian rhetoric and more recent rhetorical theories illustrate the potential for community building in communication. Our communicative systems are not merely mechanistic systems connecting cybernetic controllers but complex networks of mechanical and symbolic functions. Both systems theory and rhetorical theory can help us interpret our complex ecosystem. In the discussion that follows, I will analyze the ontical and epistemic functions of communication in building or destroying communities and individuals.

Community, Virtue, and Truth

Because I must reclaim the original functional sense of the ethical terms used, I will begin by examining Aristotle and MacIntyre's contributions to our understanding of these terms before developing them further in light of the ecological model. Aristotle's theory of ethics is based in aretē, often translated as *virtue*. Many translators prefer to render the term as *excellence*, however, because in Greek usage *aretē* was a functional concept. Virtue in this sense is excellence in carrying out a purpose or role. We use the word *virtue* in the Greek sense of *aretē* when we say, "This computer has the virtue of compatibility with the most popular software programs." Virtue is not a chance excellence in functioning but a disposition to function well over time; that is to say, Aristotelian virtue is Peircean Thirdness. In humans, virtue is a habit of regularly functioning well in a particular role, that role being determined by the needs of the community—the polis. The highest value for the individual human being is happiness, which Aristotle defines as an activity of the soul in conformity with virtue throughout a complete life.[1] So for Aristotle, the happiness of the individual is ultimately determined by that individual's functioning within the community and by the community's ability to create the conditions of possibility for happiness.

MacIntyre's major contribution to the Aristotelian ethic is anchoring the telos of the individual in that person's own narrative of her life and anchoring the meaning of virtue in practices that arise out of community life. The fragmentation of postmodern thought makes it difficult to visualize the human life as a unity. But in MacIntyre's concept of selfhood, the unity of the self "resides in the unity of a narrative which links birth to life to death as narrative beginning to middle to end."[2] According to MacIntyre, human actions in general are "enacted narratives."[3] What MacIntyre has added to Aristotle's ethical theory is a dramatistic view of human action, similar to Kenneth Burke's (which, in turn, relies heavily on implications in Aristotle's metaphysics). MacIntyre is often specifically dramatistic, and his dramatism contains an awareness of systemic constraints:

Now I must emphasize that what the agent is able to do and say intelligibly as an actor is deeply affected by the fact that we are never more (and sometimes less) than the co-authors of our own narratives. . . . We enter upon a stage which we did not design and we find ourselves part of an action that was not of our making. Each of us being a main character in his own drama plays subordinate parts in the dramas of others, and each drama constrains the others. . . . Each of our dramas exerts constraints on each other's, making the whole different from the parts, but still dramatic.[4]

The *telos*, or final purpose, of the narrative is the quest for good. "The unity of a human life is the unity of a narrative quest" for the good.[5] Virtues are those dispositions or habits that

not only sustain practices and enable us to achieve the goods internal to practices, but which will also sustain us in the relevant kind of quest for the good, by enabling us to overcome the harms, dangers, temptations and distractions which we encounter, and which will furnish us with increasing self-knowledge and increasing knowledge of the good. The catalogue of the virtues will therefore include the virtues required to sustain the kind of households and the kind of political communities in which men and women can seek for the good together and the virtues necessary for philosophical enquiry about the character of the good. We have then arrived at a provisional conclusion about the good life for man: the good life for man is the life spent in seeking for the good life for man, and the virtues necessary for the seeking are those which will enable us to understand what more and what else the good life for man is.[6]

If happiness is the summum bonum, then happiness consists in the life spent on the quest for the good.

Another key element in MacIntyre's ethics is the concept of a *practice* because practice, which depends upon community, is a source of goods. By *practice* MacIntyre means

any coherent and complex form of socially established cooperative human activity through which goods internal to that form of activity are realized in the course of trying to achieve those standards of excellence which are appropriate to, and partially definitive of, that form of activity, with the result that human powers to achieve excellence, and human conceptions of the ends and goods involved, are systematically extended.[7]

MacIntyre is here extending and developing Aristotle's notion of praxis as the actualizing (*energeia*) of a potential (*dunamis*) purely for the sake of actualizing rather than for the sake of achieving a productive result (*ergon*) from that actualizing.[8] Notice that the achievement of internal goods requires a "socially established" and "cooperative" activity. In other words, practice can only take place within a communicative system, even though it involves more than communication. A good example of the distinction between practice and production in contemporary affairs can be found in the way we talk about the Olympics. Athletic artistry performed for its own sake is a practice within a community of athletes that develops norms of excellence; so it is praxis in MacIntyre's and Aristotle's sense. I recall an interview a few years ago with a U.S. skier who was glowingly proud of her sixth-place finish because she had achieved such a high level of artistry in the actual performance of the event. The ranking was simply her community's symbolizing of the excellence she had achieved. The medal counters, however, who at that time were continually comparing the total medals achieved by the United States, the Soviet Union, East Germany, and the other Cold War powers, were measuring success by a productive result. In the reasoning of the medal counters, the ergon of Olympic athletics is to gain a gold medal; they were not concerned with the practice for its own sake. The medal counters were interpreting Olympic athletics as poiēsis, a productive art resulting in the achievement of goods extrinsic to the performance itself. In both MacIntyre's and Aristotle's theories, however, practices are concerned with intrinsic, not extrinsic, goods.

In reality, of course, practices are not so easily distinguished from productive activities. A person engaged in any given activity may aim for goods that are both intrinsic and extrinsic. One may take up skiing, for example, purely for its own sake or to gain business contacts or for a mixture of the two reasons. The productive aspect of sport often dominates the praxis as the financial stakes get higher. A striking example of how far production overcomes praxis occurred in a more recent Winter Olympics when thugs injured the knee of a figure skater so that another skater would win the competition. The financial rewards for a winning figure skater may be immense, but under these conditions they would represent not excellence of practice but the product of thuggery.

Regularly repeated activities are most likely to be hybrid practices, offering both intrinsic and extrinsic rewards. This mixing of practice and production makes the distinction between the two a case of more or less. The categories are fuzzy categories. For this reason MacIntyre takes portrait painting to be a practice, whereas Aristotle considered it not a praxis but a poiēsis, a productive art. MacIntyre departs from Aristotle in considering the product as part of the practice. The excellence of the finished painting is a result of the excellence of the practice of painting. Actually, whether portrait painting is praxis or poiēsis depends on the purpose of the painter. If the painter's purpose was to make a product to sell, then the act of painting was poiēsis. If the painter created the painting as the byproduct of an act of painting whose purpose was to paint as well as possible, then the act was clearly praxis. Most likely it was a mixture of the two.

As MacIntyre points out, "in the ancient and medieval worlds the creation and sustaining of human communities—of households, cities, nations—is generally taken to be a practice."[9] Since from a pragmatic perspective, the act of creating and sustaining community is a communicative semiotic act, I would adapt MacIntyre's statement to the ecological model by simply saying that the building, maintaining, and revising of communicative ecosystems is a practice in MacIntyre's sense. Community is not a fixed product serving some external end but a complex of continuing communicative acts between individuals and subgroups. Communication thus serves an ontological function in the practice of creating and destroying communities. As Farrell has pointed out, "rhetoric in the classical sense provides an important inventional capacity for the conventions, emotions, and cognitions necessary for affiliation in a community of civic life."[10] Following MacIntyre's definition of virtue in relation to practice, virtues of communication would be acquired habits that tend to enable communicators to achieve those goods which are internal to the practice of communication and the lack of which effectively prevents them from achieving any such goods.[11] Because the ontological function is intrinsic to communication, virtues enable communicators to achieve intrinsic goods by maintaining and improving the functioning of the communicative ecosystem.

Furthermore, since the telos of a human life is the quest for the good rather than the production of any specific good, human life is more praxis than poiēsis.[12] Happiness is not a product but the state that accompanies the active practice of seeking the good. Individual acts of production are part of a continuum of ends-means that constitutes the practice. So an individual, for example, has a job to produce income in order to seek the good. At the same time, certain income-producing activities that are hybrid production-practices retain in their performance the characteristic of offering intrinsic rewards. The portrait painter may earn an income from painting even while achieving the intrinsic good of excellence in artistry. Only at the extreme of drudgery does an act of production not retain any aspects of practice.

Communication itself is a fuzzy hybrid of poiēsis and praxis. An episode of communication that contained no elements of attempts to influence would be rare. Although Farrell treats conversation and rhetoric as two separate genres of communication, he also notes that rhetoric often emerges within conversations.[13] One might begin a conversation simply for the sake of conversing, but during the course of the conversation opportunities to influence the other are likely to arise, to be perceived, and to be acted upon. In addition, communicative acts have consequences, whether they are consciously intended or not; so communication as praxis may turn out to be productive in effect. One might unintentionally persuade someone else not to commit suicide, for instance, by engaging the other in seemingly unrelated conversation that happened to have the effect of confirming the other's personhood.

Communication as productive activity—that is, as rhetoric—must answer to general theories of ethics incorporating more encompassing views of the ecosystem than offered here. If one knowingly persuades another to perform a given action, say, to murder somebody, one is responsible for the effects of that action. Baruch Goldstein, a disciple of the late Rabbi Meir Kahane, for example, murdered at least forty Muslims worshiping at a mosque inside the Tomb of the Patriarchs.[14] To the extent that Kahane's rhetoric called for such acts of violence, the rhetoric is as unethical as the act that ensued. Obviously, rhetoric is unethical if its intended product is unethical. Since rhetoric can be a means leading to almost any possible action, the universe of possible actions and effects that could result from a rhetorical act is beyond the scope of this study. Rhetoric in such cases can be considered part of the action that should be addressed under a general theory of ethics. Even if the intended product of a rhetorical act is neutral or benign, however, the rhetoric may have negative consequences for the communicative ecosystem that makes rhetoric possible. One example would be a lie that deceives someone into performing a good act. This study is especially concerned with the effects of communicative acts on the potential for future communicative acts within the communicative ecosystem. Communicative ethics, to return to our previous example, is concerned with the many seemingly innocuous acts of communication that set the stage for violent discourse by people like Rabbi Kahane. It is these subtler types of communicative consequences that call for a special theory of ethics for communication.

Communication as a practice is a source of goods such as self-expression and development of identity that contribute to the individual's quest for good. In addition, communication is the means of building, maintaining, and transforming the various communicative ecosystems within which communication as both praxis and poiēsis take place. The total communicative ecosystem in existence includes any given social system or community—for example, Aristotle's polis, which in his conceptualization includes many more functions than our limited concept of state. The polis was the ultimate level of community for Aristotle. From an ecological perspective, the polis would better be seen as one level of communicative system within the larger ecosystem. An ethics of communication must consider effects on the various levels of systems within the communicative ecosystem. Among these levels that are built, maintained, and transformed is the individual—a complex system unified by its narrative. Here is where the Foucauldian ethic comes into play: the individual must address the question of how she forms herself as an ethical subject within community practices that provide opportunities for excellence.

Because individuals must develop their ethics through membership in communities and because the value of a practice can only be assessed by situating it in a larger framework, MacIntyre also anchors his theory of ethics in the requirement for a continuing tradition— a tradition that is, in fact, a continuing argument about what is to be considered good within that tradition.[15] This concept of a discourse tradition is narrower than the general concept of communicative ecosystem, but it is broader than the concept of polis because it extends across time and into other cultures through translation. On this point MacIntyre's argument has been challenged as relativistic. For if the nature of the good depends upon a particular tradition's definition of the good, and that tradition's definition is not commensurable with another tradition's, how would one choose between them? MacIntyre points out that one can engage traditions in a dialectical examination of specific problems. One tradition may provide better answers than another.[16] But a more serious problem seems hidden by the question of cultural relativism: how can a continuing tradition criticize itself? On what grounds beyond the tradition could such criticism take place? A tradition that attains hegemony may not have to contest with rival traditions. No doubt such a tradition will enforce its own definition of the good; but should that definition be accepted?

As Dewey and Tufts pointed out, the art of ethics cannot be confined to group or tribal standards. Group morality is for the most part unconsciously habitual, favoring a fixed order rather than progress. A theory of ethics must address two collisions that take place in the development of society:

1. The collision between the authority and interests of the group and the independence and private interests of the individual.

2. The collision between order and progress, between habit and reconstruction or reformation.[17]

MacIntyre's discussion of this problem of collisions is incomplete, but it points in the direction of Peirce's theory of truth and reality. MacIntyre distinguishes between a rational tradition and an irrational tradition. The very rationality of the tradition depends upon its openness to these kinds of collisions. Drawing upon Peirce's discussion of the fixation of belief, we could extend this to say that the collisions are a condition for the entire question of truth and falsity. As a community conducts inquiry, discrepancies arise between beliefs. A core of shared beliefs survives, but other beliefs are transformed. Members of the community can then contrast their new beliefs with their old beliefs. "Between those older beliefs and the world as they now understand it there is a radical discrepancy to be perceived. It is this lack of correspondence, between what the mind then judged and believed and reality as now perceived, classified, and understood, which is ascribed when those earlier judgments and beliefs are called *false*."[18] MacIntyre presents truth as the adequacy of mind to the thing in the scholastic tradition (*adequatio mentis ad rem*). His conceptualization requires a Peircean, not a Cartesian, view of mind:

It is [a conception] . . . of mind as activity, of mind engaging with the natural and social world in such activities as identification, reidentification, collecting, separating, classifying, and naming and all this by touching, grasping, pointing, breaking down, building up, calling to, answering to, and so on. The mind is adequate to its objects insofar as the expectations which it frames on the basis of these activities are not liable to disappointment and the remembering which it engages in enables it to return to and recover what it had encountered previously. . . . Representation is not as such picturing, but re-presentation.[19]

MacIntyre's conception of mind is compatible with Peirce's notion of mind as the process of semiosis. The expectations are the immediate objects of semiosis, which in turn are either adequate or inadequate to the semiotic encounter with physical, dynamic objects. MacIntyre's formulation is fully in accord with Peirce's pragmatic maxim, and his concept of truth sounds remarkably like Peirce's concept of truth as that which survives to the end of inquiry:

To claim truth for one's present mindset and the judgments which are its expression is to claim that this kind of inadequacy, this kind of discrepancy, will never appear in any possible future situation, no matter how searching the enquiry, no matter how much evidence is provided, no matter what developments in rational enquiry may occur. The test for truth in the present, therefore, is always to summon up as many questions and as many objections of the greatest strength possible; what can be justifiably claimed as true is what has sufficiently withstood such dialectical questioning and framing of objections.[20]

What MacIntyre calls a tradition is a community of inquiry extending through time, a closely coupled communicative system, because the implications for ethical practices are often worked out to a remarkable degree of precision. But even a more loosely coupled system requires a similar concept of truth in inquiry. In the last chapter we saw Peirce insisting that logical inquiry depended on the openness of the community of inquiry to all challenges. The rationality of deliberation requires communicative openness. Given such openness, to say that something is true is to say more than that it is warranted and assertible within a given language game. A closed fascistic system may include warranted and assertible statements that can never be falsified because the system precludes confrontation with others. The stronger definition of the meaning of truth offered by MacIntyre, when he is given a Peircean reading, gives us grounds for denying that such communities are rational. It also gives us grounds for critiquing hidden hegemony within our own communities.

At the same time, both MacIntyre and Peirce recognize that rational deliberation can take place only within a community with its semiotic structures that make advanced inquiry possible. If we truly begin with a tabula rasa or by doubting everything, we will get nowhere. The Enlightenment attempt to empty ourselves of all that is not universal has led to the anomie of postmodernism. According to MacIntyre, Durkheim saw anomie as the condition of normlessness arising from the breakdown in norms in the late nineteenth century. This tendency toward fragmentation in postmodern culture has since, as we've seen, been embraced by postmodern theorists.

Anomie, as Durkheim characterized it, was a form of deprivation, of a loss of membership in those social institutions and modes in which norms, including the norms of tradition-constituted rationality, are embodied. What Durkheim did not foresee was a time when the same condition of anomie would be assigned the status of an achievement by and a reward for the self, which had, by separating itself from the social relationships of traditions, succeeded, so it believed, in emancipating itself. This self-defined success becomes in different versions the freedom from bad faith of the Sartrian individual who rejects determinate social roles, the homelessness of Deleuze's nomadic thinker, and the presupposition of Derrida's choice between remaining "within," although a stranger to, the already constructed social and intellectual edifice, but only in order to deconstruct it from within, or brutally placing oneself outside in a condition of rupture and discontinuity. What Durkheim saw as social pathology is now presented wearing the masks of philosophical pretension.[21]

The postmodern thinker can borrow rationality only from living traditions. By attempting to stand outside all discourse traditions, relativism and perspectivism lack a grounding for rationality, which requires continuity and correction in dealing with the objects of the environment.

Nietzsche came to understand this very well. The perspectivist must not engage in dialectical argument with Socrates, for that way would lie what from our point of view would be involvement in a tradition of rational enquiry, and from Nietzsche's point of view subjection to the tyranny of reason. Socrates is not to be argued with; he is to be mocked for his ugliness and his bad manners. . . . And the use of aphorism is itself instructive. An aphorism is not an argument. Gilles Deleuze has called it "a play of forces" . . . , something by means of which energy is transmitted rather than conclusions reached.[22]

What rationality exists is parasitic upon a community of inquiry from which the postmodernist remains estranged. Because the Kantian ideal of sensus communis as a universal sense common to all rational beings has proved illusory, the postmodernist finds rationality illusory, instead of recognizing the rationality of sensus communis as the critical common sense of a community interacting with its environment and communicating a tradition of beliefs and values that is open to testing. The postmodern disillusion follows from the modern illusion that a universal language of abstract reason could exist apart from the lived languages of real communities.

Rationality is a virtue that is an excellence in the practice of critically examining and applying one's own beliefs and values to daily life. So rationality, as MacIntyre uses the term, is the intellectual virtue of *phronēsis*, practical wisdom, which I shall discuss more thoroughly in chapter 5. Like other virtues, it has meaning only within a given historical community, engaged with its world. Rationality is a virtue of symbol use, and human symbol systems are community matrixes that reflect community experience with the objects of its world. Even our internal arguments depend upon the semiotic codes we have learned through our relations with our communities. As Kenneth Burke has pointed out,

even the most arrant individualistic American writer is involved in cooperative enterprises—for if we were accurate, we should certainly designate as collaborators all the other poets and critics by whom a writer, no matter how subjective his concerns, was induced to write as he does—and particularly among his collaborators are the masters whose "line of thought" he carries on. Or by pursuing this same analysis, we can recognize that even the most thoroughly romantic poet was always deeply involved with "collective" productive forces, since he was using the most collective implement of all, the corpus of linguistic symbols amassed by the group. For this reason, though he went to a desert island and wrote there, he would not be conducting a strictly "private enterprise," his every concept taking him back to the social unit out of which it arose.[23]

While agreeing in part with the postmodernists that our rationality can work only within a given symbol system, we should recognize that the principles of rationality and truth cut across these systems. Since a belief is a habit of action, we must acknowledge that the various traditions share a common meaning for truth that is stronger than warranted assertibility. Warranted assertibility merely places a statement within a system of such statements. In doing so, truth is interpreted dyadically and nominalistically as goodness of fit. This aspect of truth—the dyadic coding—is very important to meaning; but it is not sufficient. We act on objects with purposes in mind. Our actions indicate that we believe our conceptualizations of objects to be adequate re-presentations of the physical, dynamic objects, not just well fitted to our semiotic codes. If we are reasonable, we will want our codes to be corrected so that they are more adequate to our environment. None of this requires the "presence" of pristine objects but merely adequate re-presentations that stand for objects. Even the postmodernists act according to a belief in the codes (the *nomina* of nominalism) as objects to be re-presented. My argument is that their re-presentation of signification as merely dyadic codes is not adequate to the object. In fact (*factum*, deed), we all appear to use a stronger meaning of truth. This stronger meaning of truth involves ethical considerations of truth-telling and of tolerance of diversity. Such virtues contribute to the building and reforming of communicative systems at all levels. Better communities, in turn, result in stronger epistemological claims.

The concept of communicative ecosystem is broader than the concept of continuing tradition for several reasons. As Foucault has shown, the discursive regime includes power relations that limit the possibilities of discourse. We are often unaware of the fact that our habitual practices create a systemic power distribution that prevents the open conflict of ideas and so weakens our truth claims. Our common sense is not then the critical common sense that Peirce called for. In addition, most of us no longer live in a closely coupled community tied to a particular definition of good. The broader communicative ecosystem comprises diverse loosely coupled communities with differing conceptions of the good. The telos of the ecosystem is the nurturing of all the individuals and other subsystems, such as discourse traditions, living within it. Since the telos of a human life is the quest for the good, a communicative ecosystem's virtues are those that enable its constituent members to seek in their own way for the good.

A continuing tradition is very likely to constitute a large part of the individual's definition of good, but the tradition itself can be evaluated on the basis of its consequences for the communicative ecosystem. So a given oligarchic continuing tradition could be criticized on the basis of its failure to nurture the practice of communication among all its members. Or a benevolent oligarchy may be accepted as a necessary step in a cultural ecosystem's development but may also be criticized as unable to sustain and improve that ecosystem as the constituent members develop. Perhaps this is why children must leave home to continue their development; the oligarchy of parents is unable to adapt to adult patterns of communication with the children. At any rate, the ability to criticize a given cultural pattern on the basis of the telos of the communicative ecosystem takes into account both the collision between group and individual and the collision between order and progress.

MacIntyre points out that differing traditions can communicate on some shared grounds, but he insists that "there is no set of independent standards of rational justification by appeal to which the issues between contending traditions can be decided."[24] While agreeing with MacIntyre that all of us must argue from a tradition, I believe that consideration of the system that enables argument is a ground upon which the different traditions can meet. The commonplace that two people have agreed to disagree implies an acceptance of diversity on a common ground of supporting the communicative system that makes argument possible. As I have shown, MacIntyre's own discussion of truth and rationality in traditions is compatible with a broader conception of acceptance of diversity as a necessary condition of truth and rationality in any given system.

In the archaeology thus far presented here, I have agreed with Aristotle and MacIntyre that the individual human has a telos of seeking the good within a given social system and that social practices are a source of goods. I agree that virtue for the individual is defined functionally by the role played within that system. I further agree that virtue in its application requires practical wisdom (phronēsis). I have extended these earlier theories in the addition of a functional systemic telos to the individual narrative telos as a general model of the ethical situation for human communication.

A communicative ecosystem has a telos because it is a human institution. The universe may at times appear to be as absurd as Nietzsche and others have claimed, but it demonstrates regularities as well. Setting aside the interesting metaphysical question of whether the universe has a telos, our experience teaches us that zoosemiotic creatures have ends in view for their actions. Furthermore, as Dewey pointed out, through conjoint, deliberate action, humans may impose additional order and purpose upon their environment. Social systems have the telos of nurturing the individuals within them because that is the purpose for which we have instituted them. All individuals have an equal claim to systemic support because no individual can justify an a priori claim to greater or lesser support. The ideal communicative system supports all of its parts equally, and the parts in turn support the communicative system. The practice of supporting the system is a source of goods for the individual and thus complements the individual telos considered as a quest for the good.

The idea of a communicative ecosystem that serves its members equally is counterfactual—an ahistorical model by which historical ecosystems may be assessed. Because no historical system will meet the ideal, the individual quest for the good will also involve transformation of the existing system based on possibilities within the historical situation. Knee-jerk support for the existing system is not inherently virtuous. The telos of the individual and the telos of the larger system are interrelated, and both must be taken into account in the making of ethical decisions. Virtue is the habitual disposition to take both into account. The practice of living ethically will include the practice of system building and system transforming.

A Rhetorical Perspective on Systems

I have been arguing that the notion of ecosystem gives ethical theory the needed concept with which to critique a particular set of cultural values. The key to my argument is the fact that we as communicators must operate within communicative ecosystems, and that fact forms the basis of our communicative ethics. Human communication is a practice that constitutes a major part of the individual human pursuit of the good, but this individual pursuit must operate within the boundaries of the functional requirements of the ecosystem. Since the principle of functional reciprocity—that the ecosystem should support its constituent parts and the constituent parts should support the ecosystem—is clearly the hingepin of my ethical theory, the purpose of this section is to explain further the concept of communicative ecosystem upon which my argument is based.

An ecosystem is simply a system within which we live—a system that nurtures and supports us; a communicative ecosystem is a system that nurtures and supports our practice of communication. A system, in turn, is a "complex of elements in interaction, these interactions being of an ordered (non-random) nature."[25] Even a mechanistic notion of system as an organized complexity stands opposed to the atomistic individualism of the Enlightenment scholars. It is also opposed to the nominalism of neopragmatists like Rorty who treat terms like *system* as mere choices of vocabulary, even though their own analysis presumes the real existence of systems. My contention is that we really exist as systems within systems, not as unitary atoms within an aggregate of atoms, and that this fact of existence is the basis for ethics.

The nature of society as a communicative system is a continuing theme in sociological and political studies. The sociologists Peter Berger and Thomas Luckmann suggest the complex systemic nature of society by noting that modern societies have "a shared core universe, taken for granted as such, and different partial universes coexisting in a state of mutual accommodation."[26] More recently, the sociologist Richard Harvey Brown has observed that social structure emerges from the practice of discourse.[27] Political philosophy, as well, has begun to take notice of the dependence of the concept of polity on communication. The political theorist Fred Dallmayr has attempted to synthesize various communicative and hermeneutic theories into the study of politics. Politics is seen as closely related to concepts of friendship and communication, conceived of as both conversation and discursive argument. Following Michael Oakeshott's lead, Dallmayr is concerned with achieving linkages between the different voices in the polity.[28] It is becoming clear to many contemporary theorists, as it was to Aristotle, that what constitutes social or political systems as systems is the process of communication that links the various parts into a larger whole.

The discipline of general systems theory attempts to derive universal principles of how systems operate, regardless of their sphere of operation. Ludwig von Bertalanffy pioneered the search for what he called "isomorphisms" or structural similarities that transcend fields such as physics, chemistry, biology, sociology, and communication.[29] My objective in employing systems theory is not to return to the old metaphor of society as organism, which Fascism exploited, nor to reduce society to a mechanistic definition of system, but rather from observation of societies and organisms as systems to attempt to discover the similarities that they share by virtue of being systems. In this way, I hope to explain the general characteristics of systems better.

There are, at least in theory, two main types of systems—open and closed. An open system imports and exports either energy or information by means of its interactions with other systems. A closed system does not interact with other systems and so can neither import nor export. Although the model of a closed system is often used in laboratory experiments, it does not seem to exist in a pure form in nature (with the possible exception of the universe itself). The dyadic model of linguistics also results in a theoretically closed system. In nature, however, systems tend to be more or less open, to allow a greater or lesser exchange of energy-matter or information. Systems are thus continually in process.

Social systems, like all systems, must achieve some measure of stability before the parts can be considered to be a whole. The relationship between the parts must approach a steady state before we as observers would perceive the system as a semiotic object. From a systems point of view, what we perceive as "substance" is a steady state of the system and consists of a relatively stable pattern of interactions between the parts rather than any notion of fixed matter. Substance, that which stands under the parts to unify them into a whole, is Peircean Thirdness. Consider the substance of our bodies: We are made up of many smaller systems (cells, molecules, atoms, etc.) that are constantly being replaced in the larger system of the body through the intake of energy. Despite the continuous processes of import and export, the body maintains a more or less steady state of composition.[30] Likewise in a social system, such as a school, the steady state is achieved through the constancy of the structure of relationships despite the continual change in the elements that compose it. Although students, teachers, and principals change, the pattern of communicative interactions is stable enough for us to recognize the pattern as substantially constituting a school.

Any given system maintains a state of balance between the whole and its parts. Using a physical analogy, that state of balance could be described as an equilibrium between centripetal force and centrifugal force. Centripetal force is the tendency of the system to collapse upon its center; centrifugal force is the tendency of the parts to scatter away from the center. Because an ecosystem exists through space-time, an ecosystem cannot be tied to a static notion of balance such as that contained in the term *homeostasis*, which is a uniformity of position as though the system could remain in the same state. Balance in an ecosystem is not a fixed point but a regularity through time—a "perpetual transaction." This conceptualization of equilibrium is captured in the term *homeorhesis,* which is relative uniformity of movement through time.[31] Homeorhesis is an equilibrium between the centrifugal force of the group and the centripetal force of the individual, but in addition it is an equilibrium that is sustained by means of systemic adaptation to an external environment through time. Thus homeorhesis accounts for both collisions listed by Dewey and Tufts: the individual versus the group, and progress versus order. In Peircean terms, homeorhesis is a complex Thirdness accounting for stability within change.

This complex Thirdness is the reason an ecological model for communication ethics is based in virtues rather than laws. A legalistic ethical code assumes homeostasis rather than homeorhesis. The code presumes that the system will remain the same so that a stipulated action today will continue to be appropriate into the indefinite future. But virtue in the Aristotelian sense is the disposition to find the changing point of equilibrium—the mean (meson)—in a complex relationship.[32] Aristotle, for example, points out that the appropriate amount of food for Milo the wrestler to eat would be excessive for the average person. One might develop rules of thumb based on past experiences, but the actual application in a given case requires the exercise of practical wisdom (phronēsis).[33] Aristotle's basing of virtue in a flexible mean is correct in principle because it recognizes the complexity of the calculus involved. As we shall see in the next chapter, practical wisdom involves multivalued logic and fuzzy categories. Aristotle, however, subordinated this kind of reasoning to pure theoretical wisdom (sophia) and certain knowledge (epistēmē) in his overall scheme. Philosophy thus tended toward the Cartesian understanding of rationality and aimed for certainty through a system of laws.

From an ecological perspective, the mean cannot be predetermined because it is a point of equilibrium between many different systems, all of which are in process. Even Milo's food requirements must vary with changes in his own physical system and changes in his environment. Virtue disposes a person to seek the mean, and practical wisdom consists of the ability to find it, at least roughly, acknowledging Peircean vagueness. Whereas a system of laws derived through formal logic is beyond critique, an ethic based on virtue and practical wisdom requires a regular reappraisal of the adequacy of the existing state of affairs. When the definition of virtue is limited to a continuing tradition or culture, however, it suffers to a degree from the same liability as a codified ethic. No standard external to the tradition would be available with which to critique the tradition itself. Thus such a system favors order over progress and so cannot remain viable over changing conditions. Individual virtues are defined within the constraints of the system without considering what the virtues of the system should be. Both legalistic codes and cultural traditions treat the system as a closed system.

On the other hand, it is obvious that actual systems—whether human bodies or schools—change over time. Cybernetic theories of negative feedback can be used to model the achievement of steady state within a system but cannot account for change such as evolution and learning.[34] In the cybernetic model negative feedback results in a system response that attempts to nullify the deviation and so achieve the steady state. An automobile's cruise control, for example, relies on negative feedback to maintain a set speed. If the speed is set for fifty-five miles per hour and the controller notes a deviation in a positive direction (e.g., +2 m.p.h.), it applies a correction in a negative direction (reducing the fuel-air supply), thus seeking to nullify the deviation. Negative feedback results in an input of opposite sign in order to return to the steady state.

In a social situation, negative feedback is opposition to change through counteraction in the opposite direction. Rhetoric in favor of social change will be met by rhetoric attempting to reestablish the status quo. Order attempts to assert itself against progress. All else being equal, the two cancel each other and the steady state is maintained. So, for example, students on a college campus are routinely bombarded with appeals to join or support different causes. Most of them are not affected at all; they provide their own counterarguments to maintain the status quo ("Perhaps after I graduate I'll look into that, but right now I don't have time").

Nevertheless, sometimes the rhetoric works, and lives are changed. Change in a system comes about through amplification of a deviation, and it is achieved through positive feedback. Consider again the cruise control: suppose that the controller were programmed to correct in the same direction as the deviation. If the feedback indicated +2 m.p.h. fast, the controller would then add fuel-air, thus increasing the speed even more, causing the controller to add even more fuel-air. The car would continually accelerate until it was affected by some other input, such as the driver's disconnecting the cruise control. Let us return to the case of the students on campus. The state of their own minds may be such as to give positive feedback to the rhetoric they hear. So the student who feels she has just failed exams may provide positive feedback to her mental controller as it assesses the rhetoric of the depravity of human nature as spoken by the campus evangelist. Further positive feedback could be provided by memories of childhood Sunday schools. The positive feedback can amplify the initial deviation from the status quo resulting in a conversion experience. In an actual case, of course, the complex of feedback would involve both positive and negative elements. At the point where the negative reasserts itself, a new steady state would be achieved. The student, for example, may decide that she doesn't want to be a "religious fanatic," but she might just go to church with her parents during the summer.

These same operations apply in the processes of evolution and learning. Given a need to adapt to the environment, a species or a social system can evolve by means of what Maruyama calls the second cybernetics of deviation amplification through positive feedback. The trend in evolution of a system is toward increased organization and complexity giving a greater ability to cope with more varied environmental situations. A price is paid, however, in the decreased stability of the system.[35] For cognitive systems, the process of adaptive self-organization is the process of learning. Given a system of constructs, reflective self-consciousness must compare that system with its experiences of the environment. Negative feedback will attempt to eliminate discrepancies by correcting the input: to some degree we as individuals and as societies can selectively perceive. But a large number of anomalies caused by the system's poor adaptation to its environment will eventually result in a reorganization of constructs, assuming that the environment cannot be changed to match the constructs. Thus, "the learning process results in the construction of increasingly functional mappings of relevant states of the environment, permitting a greater degree of predictability of future inputs."[36] The learning process accomplishes for the individual and for the group as cognitive systems what the evolutionary process accomplishes for the species. In this way, systemic adaptation corresponds to the concept of rationality discussed earlier, requiring adequacy of mind (semiosis) to the object. Both adaptability and rationality depend upon openness to correction.

As Lyotard pointed out, systems theory has tended toward a mechanistic, production model of society. This tendency, however, does not seem inherent in the concept of system. Kim, for example, has developed a more complex theory of feedback that recognizes the complexity of interactions between subsystems.[37] Measures of deviation have often been limited to comparison of goal and output or of change in input versus final output. A third criterion sometimes used has been the deviation between the output of one subsystem and another, such as the rich and poor classes of a country. In all of these cases, the emphasis is on production (poiēsis) and output (ergon), not the practice (praxis) of building communities. Kim, however, introduces a fourth criterion of degrees of negentropy (or organization and structure of the system). Deviation then could be measured in terms of effects on the structure of the system, that is, negentropy-maintaining, negentropy-decreasing, or negentropy-increasing. Even maintaining or decreasing the level of organization, however, requires generating structure because structure is continually being lost through entropy. "Morphostasis indeed is a kind of *morphogenesis!*"[38]

Systems theory helps explain the collision between order and progress that Dewey and Tufts observed in the moral development of society.[39] Broadly conceived, order is maintained by society through the cybernetic process of negative feedback; progress is achieved through the cybernetic process of positive feedback. Foucault's concepts of power and resistances throughout a discursive regime can just as well be represented as cybernetic processes, but the picture becomes less totalizing. To a degree, order can be maintained by ignoring environmental needs or by manipulating the environment within the possibilities of the status quo. But eventually progress—that is, adaptation through reorganization—will be required. Rhetoric is used in support of both order and progress. Communication in general is the means of organization for social groups; rhetoric is used morphogenetically to change or to fight change. In either case, rhetoric relies on the perception of the social system as a shared substance. Rhetoric, however, is more than communication regarded as a medium for systemic feedback in a mechanical model. Rhetoric uses symbols to create the sense of community. Rhetoricians may have neglected the role of systems, or "discursive regimes," in controlling change; but systems theorists have tended to take a simplistic view of communication as transfer of information. As Hugh Dalziel Duncan pointed out, communication is rhetorical because it does more than transfer information with its use of symbols: "We use such symbolic expressions not to 'define' or 'celebrate' already existing social bonds, but to create them. . . . Without the arts of social presentation there would be no community because the sentiments, attitudes, and values necessary to consensus could not be created without them."[40] Rhetoric can make an inchoate public into a community by using symbols that give rise to interpretants of common substance. The substance of a system is especially susceptible to symbolic manipulation because of the vagueness in the symbols and the continuous nature of systems.

The concept of substance depends upon the "holon-property" of a system.[41] The holon-property is the sense of wholeness in a system (*to holon*, the whole) from which we derive the notion of substance through discernment of the boundaries of that substance. Wholeness is not self-evident in an open system, however. In a closed system, the boundaries of the whole are clear because no interaction takes place beyond those boundaries; but in an open system, information and energy are imported and exported, and so the boundaries are less clear. Wholeness in this sense is functional: a system that organizes and stabilizes itself in its environment is a whole. At the same time, that system constitutes part of a larger hierarchy of systems. This characteristic of systems is sometimes called the Janus-faced nature of systems because Janus was the Roman god of the gate who looked in two directions simultaneously. An atom as a whole, for example, is a system of smaller parts that are organized and stabilized; at the same time, the atom constitutes a part of a larger system that is the molecule, which in turn constitutes part of a larger system such as a crystal. In the same way, an individual is a cognitive system made up of interacting component systems. The individual is a part of a family, communicative ecosystem$_1$ that is itself part of a neighborhood, communicative ecosystem$_2$ that is part of a community, communicative ecosystem$_3$ that is a part of larger associations up to the limits of regularized communicative interactions—the communicative universe. From this perspective, open systems are wholes at one level and parts on another level of the hierarchy of systems.[42] Thus the holon-property is a function of the level of analysis. As we shall see, rhetors seek to help us develop an "appropriate" level of analysis.

Holon-properties of systems are problematic in both epistemological and ontological terms. The epistemological problem is the problem of knowing: how do we know systems as wholes? How do we perceive boundaries of systems, for example? The ontological problem is concerned with the existence of systems when those systems are social systems: how do social systems come into and out of being? If we fail to perceive the holon property of a given social system, will that system atrophy? The way we talk about systems illustrates the problem of vagueness, discussed in the last chapter. Systems are vague epistemologically because our semiotic codes for the systems we inhabit have a large latitude of interpretation. Systems are vague ontologically because they are open, with fuzzy boundaries and changing parts. That is why the Enlightenment nominalism of the individual fails. Both the epistemological and ontological problems with vagueness are, in fact, ethical problems for communication in general and rhetoric in particular. From an ecological perspective, communication has both epistemological and ontological consequences that must be taken into account.

One would expect that if a social system exists, it exists whether or not it is included in a particular rhetor's ontology. But rhetoric can have a self-fulfilling effect in the social sphere. Social systems are systems primarily through their communicative channels. A system is defined by its pattern of interactions, and the interactions are for the most part communicative. If a rhetor convinces an audience that a given social system does not exist, the audience may tend to ignore communications at the level of that social system, thus weakening the system of interactions. A system that exists and benefits it constituent members, however, is unlikely to be totally abolished by rhetoric; a counterrhetoric is eventually likely to arise on behalf of the system. Dyadic theories cannot account for such resistances as other than randomness, but a triadic theory can. Despite its vagueness, the system exists as a dynamic object that is able to represent itself semiotically to human awareness and become an immediate object of semiosis. I mean to say not that it cannot be ignored but rather that it always has the potential to provoke a conterrhetoric to the nihilistic rhetoric that would destroy its dynamic existence. This counterrhetoric serves as negative feedback to maintain the steady state of the system or at least to reduce the amount of change in the system.

The change that does take place in the system is a change in the coupling between elements. If the superordinate system is seen to be less important, fewer interactions take place and the subordinate elements become more independent. Fewer variables within these elements are affected by interaction. As long as there is some interaction, the elements remain coupled; but the degree of interaction determines whether the system is loosely coupled or tightly coupled.[43] In systems theory, then, centrifugal and centripetal forces within a system are seen to operate on the coupling of the system. Centrifugal forces loosen the coupling, and centripetal forces tighten the coupling. Tightly coupled systems are less vague and more easily observed; so we tend to recognize tightly coupled systems as real and not notice loosely coupled systems that may be more important to our welfare. We may also represent our communicative ecosystems with signifiers, such as the ghastly metaphor of the "melting pot," that impose tighter coupling on the system as the immediate object of our understanding than exists in the dynamic object. Our desire for clarity over vagueness makes our semiotic re-presentation inadequate to the physical object.

The ecological model offers no a priori ideal for coupling in a system because the coupling should vary with the nature of the parts being coupled and the larger environment in which the system must function. What the ecological model of an ideal system does stipulate is that all parts are equal because no part has an a priori greater right to seek the good by means of the system. In actual systems observed by systems theorists, however, the parts are not equal in their influence on the system.[44] Those elements that have greater effect on the state of the system are called leading parts. The brain and the heart, for example, are leading parts within the physical system of the body. Within our communicative system, opinion leaders function as leading parts. Whether a leading part deserves to play the role of leading part is, then, another important ethical question for the ecological model of rhetorical ethics. As Farrell has argued, the "norm of authority" regards "authority as itself a form of argument."[45] Lacking a priori justification, privileged positions in the communicative system must be based on a posteriori analysis of consequences on the ecosystem involving both stability and adaptability.

From the preceding discussion of systems theory, it should be clear how ambiguous the notion of "substance" is. This ambiguity of substance is compatible with both ancient and contemporary rhetorical theory because the art of rhetoric has always concerned itself with problems of community. One of the purposes of this book, however, is to show how all areas of communication are involved with some level of community and so are rhetorical in effect. Furthermore, recognition of the ambiguity of substance is not a denial of the importance of substance or its reality. We need only consider the importance of the steady state of our bodies to recognize that substance as steady state is important to our nurture. Substance is the stability that allows the constituent elements to adapt well to the system of which they are a part. Yet too much stability results in a dinosaur system that cannot survive as the historical circumstances change. Thus the golden mean regains its importance to ethical theory when renewed by an ecological perspective.

An Ecological Perspective on Rhetoric

In Aristotelian ethical theory, to seek the golden mean is to seek an ideal point between two extremes. The mean is sought in an ecological theory of ethics because an ecosystem faces destruction at its extremes—collapse into unity and dispersal into entropy. Centripetal force leads toward unity, and centrifugal force leads toward entropy. In a system tending toward collapse, the ecosystem no longer fulfills its telos of supporting the individual members; instead, the members become merely supports of the system, which seems to exist for its own sake. In a collapsing communicative ecosystem, all diversity is seen as the vice of deviance. Uniformity becomes the ideal, and so redundancy occupies the channels of communication. Eventually, the lack of information makes the system unable to evolve to meet new challenges. As the system dies, its surviving components are taken over by new systems.

In a system tending toward dispersal, the individual elements in the system draw upon the system but do not support it. The individuals become unaware of their interdependence and drift further apart. As the links between the individuals atrophy, the system's support of the individuals and the individual's support of the system become weaker. In a communicative ecosystem, much information is available in the individual elements, but it cannot be synthesized because of a lack of channels and insufficient redundancy to make the information understandable. As the system disappears, the individuals are soon unable to communicate with each other. This threat to the survival of a communicative system is captured in the myth of the tower of Babel.[46] In order to communicate, the individuals must reattach themselves to other systems. The members of a dispersing system may be especially tempted to attach themselves to a collapsing system as they sense the need for increased unity.

The cycle of dispersal and collapse is at the heart of Kenneth Burke's analysis of Hitler's successful rhetoric. The parliament of the declining Habsburg Empire was a "babel"—"the wrangle of men representing interests lying awkwardly on the bias across one another, sometimes opposing, sometimes vaguely divergent."[47] After the First World War the disarray worsened as the intentional dismemberment of German unity by the Allies, particularly France, was coupled with the international economic depression, which itself reflected the lack of order in the capitalism of atomistic individualism. The German people, caught in a disintegrating system, yearned for unity. Hitler's rhetoric offered that unity: "the wrangle of the parliamentary is to be stilled by the giving of *one* voice to the whole people, this to be the 'inner voice' of Hitler, made uniform throughout the German boundaries, as leader and people were completely identified with each other."[48] To counter the centrifugal force of the disintegrating Weimar Republic, Hitler offered the centripetal force of fascism—a unification achieved by the creation of an enemy to rally against, the Jew. Hitler temporarily succeeded in building a new system out of the remains of the old, but eventually his Third Reich collapsed on itself because of its blind dependence on the "inner voice" of Hitler.

What Burke's analysis of Hitler's rhetoric displays is rhetoric's potential for system building and system destroying. It is this potential to which I refer when I claim that rhetoric has an ontological function in changing the "substance" of the systems in which we dwell by changing our knowledge of those systems. Epistemology and ontology are thus intertwined. We live in a hierarchy of communicative systems, but we are not always aware of the holon-properties of these systems. Rhetoric operates by changing our awareness of our relationship to various systems.

For Aristotle, the polis was made up of other communities, subsystems made up of patterns of association (*koinōniai*). Each community, down to the basic level of friendship between two people, is based in the perception of common interest (*to sumpheron*).[49] Burke develops this notion further in his concept of "consubstantiality." "To call a man a friend or brother is to proclaim him consubstantial with oneself, one's values or purposes."[50] Consubstantiality is created through the process of identification, which is the province of rhetoric.[51] From the ecological point of view, the rhetorical potential for creating consubstantiality through identification constitutes a centripetal force in that particular communicative ecosystem.

Burke's understanding of the unifying power of rhetoric complements and clarifies Aristotle's theory of rhetoric. Aristotle's rhetoric builds upon the basic appeals, or sources of persuasion (*pisteis*),[52] which are potentially found in the character of the one speaking (ethos), in the disposition of the audience (pathos), and in the lines of argument of the speech itself (logos) as it re-presents the objects of concern (pragmata).[53] Each of these pisteis is an area in which consubstantiality with the audience must be developed by the rhetor. Aristotle's rhetorical theory is very much audience-centered and so tends to unify speaker and audience in relation to the subject.[54]

The actual character of the speaker is not the rhetorical issue but rather how the listeners perceive the speaker's relationship to them.[55] In Peircean terms, although the actual character of the speaker is the dynamic object that is signified, the art of rhetoric concerns itself with how symbols can be selected to give rise to interpretants that will determine some aspect of the speaker's character as the semiotic object for the interpreters. The semiotic object, the persona, created by the speech may be only loosely connected with the dynamic object of the speaker's actual character, or personality. Vagueness is a property of both the object signified and the symbols used to signify, and this vagueness is exploited in rhetoric.

According to Aristotle, the three qualities in a speaker that lead an audience to be persuaded are practical wisdom (phronēsis), virtue (aretē), and goodwill (*eunoia*). In determining what is considered virtuous and wise, the speaker must take into account what the audience counts as virtuous. Scythians, Spartans, and philosophers emphasize different virtues; the speaker must at least begin with what the audience esteems as virtue.[56] In other words, the speaker must identify with the audience's definition of virtue, or, in more contemporary terms, with the audience's value system in order to display virtue and wisdom. Goodwill is an expression of friendship that, as Burke pointed out, is based in consubstantiality. Aristotle's discussion supports Burke's approach: A friend shares joy in the good times and sadness in the bad. Friends have the same idea of what is good and what is bad; they have the same friends and enemies. Friends necessarily wish for the same things.[57] In sum, the appeal based on the speaker's character depends upon the creation of the appearance of consubstantiality with the audience. This identification, of course, is a centripetal force within communicative ecosystems.

On the other hand, rhetoric may have a centrifugal effect when the speaker attacks the ethos of the opposition. Aristotle pointed out that if one can demonstrate friendship, one can demonstrate enmity, depending on the speaker's purpose.[58] A later author, the unknown Roman who wrote *Ad Herennium,* amplified this point to show that a speaker can gain the appearance of goodwill by making the adversary hated and unpopular.[59] This is the strategy employed in modern political mudslinging: one candidate hopes to gain some measure of consubstantiality with the electorate by showing that the other candidate is further removed from the thinking of the audience.[60] These attempts to build consubstantiality can become very convoluted. A controversial issue in the 1994 mayoral campaign in New Orleans illustrates these convolutions. Anonymous, sleazy flyers attacking various candidates were circulated during that campaign. Partisan investigators claimed to have discovered several links between the distribution of the flyers and one candidate's campaign organization. Allegedly, this candidate's organization was involved in distributing a flyer that viciously attacked a "Negro loving Jew" who was running. What complicates the charge is the fact that the accused candidate was also the Jew under attack. His opponents accused him of circulating material attacking himself. He, in turn, accused his opponents of infiltrating his campaign and framing him.[61]

Whether true or not, the charges are not ridiculous in light of the principle of consubstantiality in rhetoric. This Jewish candidate used the flyers in mailings to Jewish organizations around the country, appealing for funds to fight the vicious opposition he was facing in New Orleans. Jews in other areas would have been sensitized to the dangers of anti-Semitism in Louisiana by the previous publicity accorded to the campaigns of David Duke and his association with neo-Nazi causes. The threat of anti-Semitism would increase the bonds between this candidate and Jews around the country, who would then contribute financially to his campaign. Furthermore, to be attacked as a Negro-loving Jew would not hurt him in New Orleans. With a majority black population and a large Jewish community, New Orleans had soundly trounced David Duke. The white anti-Semitic vote was not likely to affect the election. To win in New Orleans, however, this candidate needed black votes. In attacking him as a Negro-loving Jew, this flyer also increased his consubstantiality with blacks, reminding them that both still suffered from discrimination and that this candidate had long been active in civil rights campaigns. So whether or not this candidate was actually involved, the charge that he had something to gain makes sense.

On the other hand, most of those who made the charges were associated with the campaign of the other leading candidate, an African-American who was the son of a former mayor. This candidate's father had been involved in divisive political rivalries and had created much opposition within the black community. Therefore, this candidate had a need to increase his own consubstantiality with the black community and prevent black voters from crossing over to the Jewish candidate. By charging the Jewish candidate with such machinations, the black candidate could subtly reinvigorate the recurring image of the Jewish exploiter of blacks. Malcolm X provided a fairly moderate view of that image in his autobiography:

[I]n every black ghetto, Jews own the major businesses. Every night the owners of those businesses go home with that black community's money, which helps the ghetto to stay poor. But I doubt that I have ever uttered this absolute truth before an audience without being hotly challenged, and accused by a Jew of anti-Semitism. . . . I have told them that if I tell the simple truth, it doesn't mean that I am anti-Semitic; it means merely that I am anti-exploitation.[62]

By alluding to the Jewish candidate's cunning in manipulating black voters, the African-American candidate could build greater consubstantiality between himself and other blacks, limit black crossover votes, and perhaps even divide the white liberal vote. So he, too, had something to gain by rhetorically exploiting the issue.

Regardless of who is responsible for the distribution of the flyers, all those involved are responsible for the consequences of their rhetoric about the flyers. By using the flyers to build consubstantiality with Jews around the country, the Jewish candidate presented New Orleans as inhospitable to Jews. The result was an increase in the division between those Jews in other states and the New Orleans community. That division will ultimately be reflected in writings about New Orleans and in discussions about which cities are good sites for business expansion. New Orleans has many real problems. Exaggerating neo-Nazi influence exacerbates those problems. So does increasing the division between the Jewish and African-American communities with portrayals of the wily Jew exploiting innocent blacks. Such stereotypes make it more difficult to deal with actual cases of exploitation. Insofar as rhetoric makes categorical claims about Jews, it creates a defensive reaction that resists considering whether one particular person, who happens to be Jewish, is exploiting some blacks in some way. As a result, someone who is exploiting rentals, for example, could justify her actions to herself and to her own community by claiming to be a victim of anti-Semitism. If she identifies with her community in the postmodern mode as incommensurable with the black community, she will act in accordance with that identification. She will be immune to moral argument on behalf of the larger New Orleans community.

The point is that rhetors draw upon consubstantiality in attempting to build their own credibility and rhetorical power. In attempting to unify at one level, rhetors often divide at another level. Rhetors are responsible for the ontical effects of their appeal to ethos on the various communicative systems that support them. The situation is analogous to other forms of production. The producer may or may not sustain the ecosystem that makes production possible. Since the *pistis* of ethos is often called the "ethical appeal" by rhetoricians, the irony is that the ethical appeal may well be ecologically unethical.

The pistis of pathos also involves consubstantiality because it requires the speaker to adopt the emotional frame of reference of the audience, to perceive the subject from the listener's point of view. Aristotle's discussion of pathos, while primitive, is an apparent attempt to fulfill the requirement given by Plato in the *Phaedrus* for the ideal rhetorician. Plato insisted that one completely developed in the rhetorical art must analyze the soul (*psuchē*) as the doctor analyzes the body.[63] Aristotle attempts a general analysis of the audience in terms of moral habits, emotions, and what we today call demographics, that is, age, social class, status, and wealth.[64] The purpose of knowing the audience's frame of mind is to draw upon that knowledge in order to reshape the audience's frame.[65] The speaker must identify with the emotional traits of the audience in order to move them to adopt the desired attitude toward the subject. This is the movement toward consubstantiality that Donald Bryant captures in his statement that the "rhetorical function is the *function of adjusting ideas to people and people to ideas.*"[66] This movement of adjustment is a centripetal movement within a communicative ecosystem as "difficult and strange ideas have to be modified without being distorted or invalidated; and audiences have to be prepared through the mitigation of their prejudices, ignorance, and irrelevant sets of mind without being dispossessed of their judgments."[67] The result of rhetors employing this Aristotelian orientation on the audience and adapting to the interests and desires of the audience is an increase in unity among audience members and between speaker and audience.

As we have seen in the appeal to ethos, however, the communicator may choose to exacerbate the differences between generations, classes, and other social groups in order to increase unity within a targeted group. Rhetoric may also take the form of the diatribe in which an outgroup (cynics, atheists, antiwar protestors) reinforces itself by attacking and ridiculing the beliefs of the audience rather than adapting to them.[68] In such cases the principle of audience adaptation continues to operate, but the target audience is the protestors themselves and not the external audience of nonbelievers. The external audience is an object used antithetically to create stronger unity within the outgroup. At the same time, the "normal" majority reassures itself of its correctness by antithesis to the "weirdness" of the outgroup. Again, what is centripetal at one level is centrifugal at another. Intragroup unity is obtained at the cost of intergroup division.

The pistis of logos would seem to be irrelevant to the process of creating consubstantiality. After all, formal logic simply claims to show us what must be the case based on what is the case. From A we logically infer B, whether we like it or not. Formal logic compels assent; it does not adapt to the audience. Indeed, if logos in rhetoric were the equivalent of formal logic then it would not affect the consubstantiality of speaker and audience.[69] Logos in Aristotle's rhetorical theory, however, is not *logic* as we usually think of it. It is instead a logic created jointly by the speaker and the audience in the speech event. Edward Cope recognized the cooperative nature of rhetorical argument in his classic commentary on Aristotle, noting that the rhetor is dependent upon the audience, "for in ordinary cases he can only assume such principles and sentiments in conducting his argument as he knows will be acceptable to them, or which they are prepared to admit."[70]

Lloyd Bitzer explains that perplexing rhetorical syllogism that Aristotle called the enthymeme in terms of its cooperative construction by the rhetor and the audience. Bitzer finds previous explanations of the enthymeme, such as its being a truncated syllogism or one based in probabilities, insufficient to differentiate the enthymeme from both the scientific and dialectical syllogisms. He argues cogently that the enthymeme is a syllogism that the audience helps construct by providing the missing premises.[71] As a result, he notes, "a recorded speech is only partially a speech. The complete speech is the actual speech which occurs when speaker and audience interact, either cooperatively or not."[72]

Here Bitzer has addressed the basic nature of the forcefulness of rhetorical logic. The enthymeme either unites or divides. If the audience and speaker adapt to each other, together they construct the logic of the speech. The result is a common perspective on the problem and agreement on the reasoning involved. If, on the other hand, the audience and speaker do not adapt, they become further estranged by the recognition of their differences. They don't even seem to reason the same way. A similar process is at work in example (*paradeigma*), the second of Aristotle's means of developing logical force. Gerard Hauser's analysis of Aristotle's treatment of example argues that the rhetorical effectiveness of example is found in the perception by the speaker and audience of the same universal form in the example. "If the example and exemplified are identical in form, they are related to each other simultaneously or in a one-step process."[73] Again, the audience's ability to agree with the speaker on the form creates unity and the failure to perceive that form would create disunity. Thus, the logos, the re-presentation of the facts of the situation (pragmata),[74] can act as either centripetal or centrifugal force.

Burke's rhetoric can thus be seen as descended from Aristotelian rhetoric in their common emphasis on the interrelationship between rhetor, audience, and subject. I would simply add that rhetoric invariably affects the actual consubstantiality of the various systems of which rhetor and audience are parts. The systemic forces that are evident in Burke's theory of rhetoric and implicit in Aristotle's can also be found in other contemporary theories of rhetoric. Chaim Perelman points out, for example, that argumentation is built around audience adaptation. "To adapt to an audience is, above all, to choose as premises of argumentation theses the audience already holds."[75] Even "facts" and "truths" are simply what is acceptable to the audience. Common sense by this line of reasoning is *communal sense*. If the agreement about what constitutes fact and truth "is sufficiently widespread, no one can reject them without appearing foolish, unless he gives adequate reasons to justify his skepticism concerning them."[76] The challenging of accepted facts and truths would, of course, be a divisive force; whereas the affirmation of the audience's premises would be a unifying force within that particular system. Perelman adds another aspect to the centripetal function of rhetoric in his discussion of epideictic rhetoric—ceremonial discourse, which Aristotle treats somewhat offhandedly. For Perelman, "the epideictic genre is central to discourse because its role is to intensify adherence to values, adherence without which discourses that aim at provoking action cannot find the lever to move or to inspire their listeners." The speaker "seeks to create a unity around certain values in an epideictic discourse."[77] Perelman gives the example of Antony's funeral oration in *Julius Caesar* as one which unified the audience to the point where they were incited to revolt. In the process, of course, the audience was divided from the partisans of Brutus.

Ernest Bormann's theory of symbolic convergence claims that a dynamic chaining of group fantasies takes place through many different forms of communication. A fantasy is "the creative and imaginative interpretation of events that fulfills a psychological or rhetorical need."[78] As these dramatized fantasies come to be shared within a subsystem, they develop into a "rhetorical vision" that becomes a shared social reality. The participants in the vision form a "rhetorical community."

Interpreting events in terms of human action allows us to assign responsibility, to praise or blame, to arouse and propitiate guilt, to hate, and to love. When we share a fantasy theme we make sense out of what prior to that time may have been a confusing state of affairs and we do so in *common with the others who share the fantasy with us.* Thus, we come to symbolic convergence on the matter and will envision that part of our world in similar ways.[79]

Bormann's theory extends Burke's dramatistic theory and his concept of rhetoric as the means of developing consubstantiality. The vision may be developed by a single speaker's dramatic vision, but it is more likely to arise from a group's sharing of fantasies. The first dramatized message is taken over and elaborated by others. Translated into systems terminology, the rhetoric becomes deviation amplifying through positive feedback from the process of chaining out. The common vision eventually results in a new consciousness within the group, and the group finds it has a need to identify itself as a collectivity: "Dealing with who they are often gets the group to fantasize about who the outsiders are. Thus, a we-they division in the innovative fantasies helps with the setting of boundaries and leads to the group self-awareness which is crucial to the emergence of a new consciousness."[80]

In his theory, Bormann accounts for both centripetal and centrifugal forces at work in the rhetorical creation of communities. He does not address how this rhetorical setting of boundaries and creation of self-awareness has the effect of reducing the cohesion of the larger communicative ecosystem because his level of analysis remains at the group level. One of his examples of a shared rhetorical vision is the Moral Majority. By attacking "secular humanism" the members of the Moral Majority undoubtedly increased their own sense of unity. However, the result has also been an increased polarization between religious and secular elements in American society. Bormann, of course, is not addressing the question of ethical responsibility for the consequences of these types of communicative acts.

The question of the balancing of the centripetal and centrifugal forces of rhetoric, or the creation of homeorhesis, has not been addressed in classical or contemporary rhetorical theories. Nor has the question of rhetorical effects on holon-properties within the hierarchy of systems. But what has been addressed, either explicitly as in contemporary rhetorical theory or implicitly as in classical rhetorical theory, is rhetoric's ability to create a sense of consubstantiality.[81] Since community, in the Deweyan sense we discussed in the last chapter, requires awareness of consubstantiality, rhetoric creates, strengthens, or undermines community. Communication in general has the consequence of creating consubstantiality at different levels of hierarchy within the communicative ecosystem. In this sense, communication that is not intended to be rhetoric in the classical sense of persuasive discourse often turns out to be rhetorical in its effect of unifying and dividing systems. Rhetoric in the classical sense itself may have unintended systemic effects that are at least as important as the intended effects.

By becoming aware of the effects of our communication on the communicative ecosystems involved, we should be better able to estimate consequences realistically. This increased awareness, in turn, should result in better ethical decisions and, eventually, a more satisfactory life narrative. Our communicative actions affect the various social systems in which we fill niches, because a social system must perceive its own consubstantiality in order to be a community in the Deweyan sense. Consubstantiality, of course, like rhetoric or, for that matter, semiotic in general, can be abused. Burke showed this with his analysis of Hitler's rhetoric. We must, therefore, distinguish between pragmatic and fascistic uses of consubstantiality.

Consubstantiality of Blood versus Consubstantiality of Purpose

Kenneth Burke has done the most of any theorist to show the role of communication in creating consubstantiality. His *Rhetoric of Motives* made *identification* the key term of rhetoric:

A is not identical with his colleague, B. But insofar as their interests are joined, A is *identified* with B. Or he may *identify himself* with B even when their interests are not joined, if he assumes that they are, or is persuaded to believe so.

Here are ambiguities of substance. In being identified with B, A is "substantially one" with a person other than himself. Yet at the same time he remains unique, an individual locus of motives. Thus he is both joined and separate, at once a distinct substance and consubstantial with another.[82]

In the *Grammar of Motives*, Burke addressed the ambiguity of substance (literally, that which *stands under*) in a way that makes him seem to be the precursor of Derrida:

[T]he word "substance," used to designate what a thing *is*, derives from a word designating something that a thing *is not*. That is, though used to designate something *within* the thing, *intrinsic* to it, the word etymologically refers to something *outside* the thing, *extrinsic* to it. Or otherwise put: the word in its etymological origins would refer to an attribute of the thing's *context*, since that which supports or underlies a thing would be a part of the thing's context. And a thing's context, being outside or beyond the thing, would be something that the thing is *not*.[83]

Although the term *substance* has lost popularity in metaphysics since Locke criticized it, Burke argued that the concept remains necessary to metaphysics, to any attempt to define what something really is:

To tell what a thing is, you place it in terms of something else. This idea of locating, or placing, is implicit in our very word for definition itself: to *define*, or *determine* a thing, is to mark its boundaries, hence to use terms that possess, implicitly at least, contextual reference. We here take the pun seriously because we believe it to reveal an *inevitable* paradox of definition, an antinomy that must endow the concept of substance with unresolvable ambiguity, and that will be discovered lurking beneath any vocabulary designed to treat of motivation by the deliberate outlawing of the *word* for substance.[84]

Contextual definition reveals itself in the pairing of antithetical terms, like heredity-environment, man-nature, mind-matter, and mechanism-teleology, at high levels of generalization, in which the oppositional term provides the context that gives meaning to its opposite. Apart from Saussurean semiotics, Burke has arrived at a concept of difference underlying ontology so that "the only ground of 'Being' is 'Not-Being.' "[85] Burke also includes the idea of deferral because the pursuit of the "substance" of "man" cannot make the essence of man present to the mind: "Hence, the more thorough one is in carrying out his enterprise, the more surely he opens himself to the charge of failing to discuss man 'in himself.' "[86]

Burke's deconstruction of metaphysical substance does not undermine the pragmatic conception of community as consubstantiality. Pragmatism recognizes the contextual, relational nature of substance. According to the pragmatic maxim, all such concepts refer to differences in practice; so the concept of substance refers to our experience of important continuities of relations in practice. A substance maintains its difference from its context over time, reflecting systemic stability. The pragmatic idea of consubstantiality is captured in Burke's first case, in which two people's *interests* are joined. So a public and a community are formed by the regularity of their relations to consequences over time. Mutual interest means that two people share a desire for the same differences in practice. Most of us, for example, share a desire for peace in our cities, as opposed to the increasing violence that has been our recent experience. That common desire makes us a public; and as we become more aware of our consubstantiality of interest, we will become a community.

Burke's discussion of the paradox of substance, however, alerts us to the possibility of a more metaphysical construction of consubstantiality based on origins:

This is the "tribal" or "familial" sort, the definition of a substance in terms of ancestral cause. Under the head of "tribal" definition would fall any variant of the idea of biological descent, with the substance of the offspring being derived from the substance of the parents or family.

The Christian notion that the most important fact about mankind and the world is their derivation from God is an instance of "ancestral" definition on the grand scale. We find bastardized variants in political doctrines of race supremacy, such as the Nazi "blood" philosophy. The Latin word *natura*, like its Greek equivalent *physis*, has a root signifying to become, to grow, to be born. And the Aristotelian *genus* is originally not a logical, but a biological, concept. We can discern the tribal pattern behind the notion, so characteristic of Greek nationalism, that like causes like or that like recognizes like, as with Democritus' theory of perception. Similarly, there was an *ancestral* notion behind the Platonic theory of forms; in fact, it was this tribal ingredient that recommended it so strongly to the ages of Western feudalism.[87]

From feudalism to fascism, variations on the theme of consubstantiality based on bloodlines have often formed the basis of communities. The origin of the metaphysical belief is understandable. It is based on a primitive, libidinal drive ensuring reproductive fitness and evolutionary survival of genes. "Animals help each other in almost direct proportion to the number of shared genes, thus helping the common genes to survive in later generations."[88] Families are normally closely coupled social systems with shared interests; primitive families are packs of animals ensuring gene survival. Physical family resemblance, standing for genetic communality, can by association be taken as a sign of those shared interests. As a result, physical similarities in general come to stand for community interests. Since blood represents life, begetting life is signified as sharing blood. A bloodline can then metaphysically signify a life essence joining and transcending generations. Blood is now thicker than water, if water stands for pragmatic advantages of association. Blood consubstantiality, based on the primitive libidinal impulse, overrules consubstantiality of common interest in consequences. A "natural" hierarchy of bloodlines is taken to be the a priori determinant of the public interest.

At its most basic, this belief in ancestral consubstantiality shows itself in arguments that the "natural" parents should have priority over the functional parents who have actually nurtured a child. From the pragmatic perspective, a family is a family because it functions as a closely coupled ecosystem supporting its constituent parts. Both the genetic relation and the nurturing relation are real ontological relations, but pragmatically, the relation of nurturing is more important than the relation of begetting. An adoptive family is thus no less authentic a family. From the ancestral perspective, such functional definitions of family neglect the mystical consubstantiality of bloodlines. This same mystical principle operating at a national level can lead to fascism.

Speaking at the famous Nazi book-burning in 1933, Hans Nauman concluded by praising the traditional values of family and *Volk*. The various varieties of fascism emphasized "nationalism, racism, and the longing for a restoration of traditional morality."[89] Mussolini connected his fascism with Julius Caesar and Imperial Rome. The term *fascist* comes from the *fasces*, a bundle of rods with an axe that were carried before the highest magistrates in ancient Rome. The symbol represented supreme power. Mussolini identified himself as the agent of the Italian people, who were the bloodline descendants of the ancient Romans. Given the assumption of mystical identification between the will of those sharing the Roman bloodline and Mussolini, a totalitarian state was the inevitable outcome.[90]

In Germany, Hitler thoroughly worked out the implications of bloodline consubstantiality:

National Socialism [Hitler declared] takes as the starting point of its views and its decisions neither the individual nor humanity. It puts consciously into the central point of its whole thinking the *Volk*. This *Volk* is for it a blood-conditioned entity in which it sees the God-willed building-stone of human society. The individual is transitory, the *Volk* is permanent. If the Liberal *Weltanschauung* in its deification of the single individual must lead to the destruction of the *Volk*, National Socialism, on the other hand, desires to safeguard the *Volk*, if necessary even at the expense of the individual. It is essential that the individual should slowly come to realize that his own ego is unimportant when compared with the existence of the whole people . . . above all he must realize that the freedom of the mind and will of a nation are to be valued more highly than the individual's freedom of mind and will.[91]

In fascism, bloodline consubstantiality is often represented in a bodily metaphor of the community. The leader expresses the will of the organic whole. All of the parts are subordinated to the will of the whole as expressed through the leader. Parts that rebel against the organic state are like cancerous cells in the body. Outside influences may also infect the body. Often the body must sacrifice its own parts to conquer disease. The parts have no meaning of their own other than as functioning elements of the body.

This fascistic, oppressive view of the community is based in a kind of naive realism. Some antecedent substance such as race is considered necessary as a ground for community, thus a metaphysics of originary essence arises. Both Burke and Derrida rightly deconstruct the notion of originary essence, and Lyotard is also right to warn us of the dangers of such totalizing narratives. The fascist version of consubstantiality, however, is not the only alternative to postmodern fragmentation. Instead of looking back to our roots to define our consubstantiality, the pragmatist suggests we look forward to the consequences of our interactions. If we are willing to critically question our own prejudices, we will find a mutuality of interest that goes far beyond bloodlines. Again the role of rationality as critical openness is the key, and it does not require the rejection of a strong sense of truth, merely the recognition that truth is not meaningful if it is not critically tested. The fascists knew their prejudices could not stand such critical testing; fascism allied itself with expressionism, asserting the irrational foundation of human instincts.[92] Contrary to Lyotard's assertion, Auschwitz is not the sign of an excessive faith in rationality; it is the sign of excessive dependence upon libidinal instincts uncontrolled by critical reason.

We began this chapter with an archaeology of sorts. Now we are reminded that all uses of traditions must be critical. The advantage of the pragmatic borrowing from the Aristotelian tradition is that Aristotle's concept of practical wisdom attempts to integrate rationality and libido as does Dewey's theory of valuation. In MacIntyre's discussion of continuing traditions, theoretical rationality becomes subordinated to practical reason arising out of communal life. The validity of our reasoning, both in our communal discourse and in our individual life narratives, depends upon our openness to correction. The good life is not the perfect life but the self-correcting life. The good community is not the perfect community but the self-correcting community. In this chapter we have seen the ontological role of communication in creating community, for better or worse. In the next chapter, we shall consider the communicative virtues that operate ontologically to develop better communities and better life narratives by being epistemologically critical. The quests for truth and justice are unavoidably interrelated.

4

The Cardinal Virtues of the Communicative Ecosystem

In our discussion I have used the term *rhetoric* to mean the aspect of communication that influences audiences in ways that affect the ecosystem. In ancient Greece, rhetoric was the art of oratory, and oratory was the means of managing communal affairs. Although I have broadened the concept of rhetoric, I have kept intact the basic notion of communication affecting community. In later chapters, I will examine this rhetorical aspect operating at different levels of community from interpersonal relationships to mass communication. Before examining those different systemic levels affected by this rhetorical dimension of communication, however, I would like to consider the cardinal virtues of rhetorical practice: practical wisdom (phronēsis)—the controlling virtue—honesty, and openness. These virtues apply at all the various levels of the communicative ecosystem, which in turn have their own particular excellences.

We should note a difference between my definition of rhetoric as practiced and the Greek *tekhnē rhētorikē*. As a tekhnē, rhetoric was planned and deliberate. The rhetorical aspect of communication that I am concerned with, however, may have epistemological or ontological consequences on the community without the communicator's being aware of those effects. Insofar as virtues are habits, deliberation about a particular communicative act may not always be necessary in the ecological ethic as long as the habits of communication are good. On the other hand, if deliberation and reasoning play no part, then Lyotard is right and ethics simply reflect libidinal habits. If an ethic is possible, the chief virtue of the cardinal virtues must be practical wisdom, the deliberative virtue.

Aristotle called this practical wisdom *phronēsis,* and it was the key to his ethical system. Because his virtues were points of balance in practice, practical wisdom was necessary for determining the mean in any particular case. Theoretical wisdom cannot lead to action (praxis). Action is the result of choice (*proairesis*).[1] Choice, in turn, is the interaction of desire (*orexis*) and thought (*dianoia*).[2] Correct choice requires deliberation, and the virtue of deliberating well about practical problems of good and evil is phronēsis.[3] Aristotle also points out that practical wisdom is a virtue for both the individual and the community, belonging to both ethics and politics.[4] Good habits of deliberation are necessary in both aspects of the ecological ethic, the individual pursuit of the good and the ecosystem's function of supporting individuals in their pursuits.

Aristotle's approach thus seems essential to the ecological ethic, or to any practical ethic for that matter. How could one object to the desirability of practical wisdom? Yet McKerrow has, in fact, objected to the use of phronēsis as a criterion of public moral argument.[5] His objection is threefold: in form, content, and gender bias, phronēsis is unsuitable for a critique of freedom.

According to McKerrow, the form of phronesis in our culture has been the form of reasoned argument. The argumentative form "privileging reason precludes access by those whose voice is not expressed in the forms accepted within the dominant culture." In content, phronēsis is "exclusively logos oriented; the practical reason of the community is marked by the exclusion of emotion." Finally, the contemporary conception of phronēsis operating in a Habermasian public sphere is gendered: "The image of males articulating reasoned discourse—shorn of its emotive grounding—in the public sphere is so well inscribed in our culture that we scarcely notice its presence. In contrast, women remain ensconced in the private sphere, ever the emotive beings."[6] Notice that McKerrow is arguing against the *modern* conception of phronēsis. The Aristotelian definition incorporates emotion. We could evade McKerrow's argument by claiming to return to the original meaning of phronēsis as I argued in the preceding chapter about virtue in general. In truth, however, McKerrow's critique applies as well to Aristotle's approach because Aristotle subordinates phronēsis to higher intellectual virtues. Despite his affinity for our purposes, Aristotle was not a thoroughgoing pragmatist. The modern rationalists extended a tendency that was already present in Aristotle. Therefore, if we are going to appropriate phronēsis for an ecological ethic, we must first try to eliminate the elements in phronēsis that make it a system of a priori privilege. Those elements are subtly embedded in Aristotle's philosophy where it seems most pragmatic, in its emphasis on act.

Energeia versus *Kinēsis*

Aristotle did not write in a political vacuum. As the Woods have argued, he was an apologist for a declining aristocracy, in many ways a more subtle apologist than Plato. They call Aristotle the "tactician of conservatism" because of his willingness to compromise with democracy in order to maintain the hegemony of the aristocracy.[7] In his metaphysics and his practical theories, Aristotle upholds aristocratic principles with a more flexible and realistic version of Platonism. The Aristotelian corpus, like the Platonic corpus, serves to maintain the traditional class system against the egalitarian claims of democratic theorists like Protagoras. As an empiricist, however, Aristotle recognizes that he cannot return the evils of democracy to Pandora's box and simply restore the traditional aristocracy. Instead, his work provides methods of cooptation and compromise by which the aristocracy can maintain its hegemony in polities that are likely to include democratic elements. Aristotle's *Politics* wistfully alludes to an ideal monarchy or aristocracy before settling on a compromise polity that mixes some democratic elements with oligarchy. In the same way, the *Rhetoric* wistfully alludes to an aristocratic rhetoric of pure reason before settling on a compromise that incorporates popular appeals based on commonsense reasoning, the passions of the audience, and the image of the rhetor. Rhetoric, in Aristotle's limited sense of discourse in the courts, assemblies, and public ceremonies, becomes one of the means for the aristocracy to regain or maintain control in a democracy or mixed polity.

If we, on the other hand, define rhetoric pragmatically as the aspect of discourse with practical consequences for a public's ability to act as a community, then we must consider even Aristotle's *Metaphysics* to be rhetorical. The rhetorical exigence from the aristocratic perspective is the problem of institutionalizing a temporary system of privilege, ideally to create something like eternal tenure for the upper class. Plato's solution to this exigence is to find the justification for permanence in a world of ideal forms that are not affected by changes in this world of appearances. Whatever its metaphysical appeal, Plato's approach is not rhetorically effective simply because the connection of his fixed essences to the world of practical action is tenuous at best. The consequential discouraging of practical action

supports the aristocracy only when that aristocracy is securely established or when the aristocracy is a priesthood that draws its power
from that metaphysical world. A more effective rhetorical strategy
when democracy has taken hold would be to locate fixed essences
within the world of experience, providing the analogy of permanence within change that would support the tenure of an aristocracy
existing among democratic elements. It is this more subtle rhetorical
metaphysics of Aristotle that we must deconstruct and then reconstruct pragmatically in order to regain the concept of practical wisdom for communicative ethics.

As Kenneth Burke has pointed out, Aristotle's philosophy is a philosophy of the act.[8] With his usual perceptiveness, Burke has also
noted how, in the hands of the scholastics, act and being were identified and that, "sociologically, . . . this identification between act and
being served a feudal society built upon the maintenance of fixed
social status."[9] In fact, Aquinas and the other scholastics have only
made explicit what was implicit in Aristotle's approach. The poten-
tiality-actuality pair, when interpreted teleologically, form the basis
of Aristotle's essentialism, allowing him to bring the world of being
into the world of becoming as its proper ruler. The Greek word for
potential, *dunamis,* means both the possibility to be something and
the power to do something. The word *actuality* is the usual translation for the Greek word *energeia;* however, as Blair points out, *actuality* smothers the sense of activity that is still alive in the Greek. In
the *Metaphysics,* Aristotle relates the word *energeia* to the word *kinēsis,* which is motion.[10] Kinēsis, however, is motion as we experience it as process and change, so Aristotle has had to coin a new term
that he can use to express activity without change. Blair rightly trans-
lates the new term, *energeia,* as *inner activity* rather than *actuality.*
What Blair fails to realize is that the standard term *actuality* is not a
mere oversight in translation but an effect of Aristotle's rhetoric. The
elimination of change from action allows action to have a fixity that
is captured in the term *actuality.* The standard translation attests to
the success of Aristotle's rhetoric in the *Metaphysics* and throughout
his corpus.

Aristotle has, in fact, told us how the rhetoric of his metaphysics
works. In his discussion of style in the third book of the *Rhetoric,* he
points out that an urbane and popular style is achieved when the
rhetor makes the object appear before the eyes (*pro ommatōn*). To
make an object present in this sense, the rhetor must use words that
signify activity (energeia). According to Aristotle, this style accounts
for Homer's popularity. Homer gave the appearance of activity to in-
animate objects, as in the line, "the lance sped eagerly through his
breast." The Homeric style gives motion and life to everything, and

"*energeia* is *kinēsis.*"[11] As with Homeric style, Aristotle's metaphysics allows him to make fixed essences seem more real by giving those fixities the appearance of motion.

We can better understand Aristotle's oxymoron of fixed motion by seeing it carried to perfection in the Prime Mover. The Prime Mover is unmoved. It is pure activity, uncontaminated by matter, because matter would be potential for change. The Prime Mover is thought thinking itself, unchangeably and eternally. As idealized motion, the Prime Mover is the final cause of the less perfect forms of motion found throughout the lower levels of the universe. All the lesser forms of motion strive toward achieving the pure inner activity of the Prime Mover, but they are limited by the conditions of their own existence as composite substances made of matter and form. Matter is the potential of lower beings, and the nature of matter constrains the achievement of pure activity. Heavenly bodies are most like the Prime Mover because their matter is *aither* (ether), which is eternal. The heavenly bodies move only in repetitive cycles that do not change.

Form is not simply shape, as we tend to visualize it, but is rather the organizing principle for the inner activity that results in shape and other properties as well, such as the eternal cycles of heavenly bodies. The form, or pattern of inner activity, depends upon the *telos*, which is the final cause of striving to achieve the highest level of activity possible. Energeia thus depends upon form, which depends on telos, which is maximal energeia, given the constraints of matter, which is the potential, dunamis, both in the sense of to do and to be. Thus, Platonic forms are embodied in composite substances through entelecheia, that is, having the telos inside oneself.[12] Since the telos is the highest level of energeia achievable, *entelecheia* means that the perfected form is internal to composite substances. The acorn contains the form of the full-grown oak.

For Aristotle, essence is a problem of definition. Although he holds that meaning is conventional rather than natural, nevertheless, Aristotle insists that words stand for real objects by means of mental impressions.[13] So definition does not merely clarify words, it signifies the essence of real objects. A good definition is an accounting of the being of the object defined. Witt points out that definitions function epistemologically for Aristotle and therefore have three requirements: (1) "definitions are of things, rather than words"; (2) "definitions are causal or explanatory"; and (3) "definitions are intrinsically common to or shared by a number of individuals; thus, they are of universals."[14] Aristotelian essentialism is different from contemporary essentialism, which treats essences as necessary properties. Because it is explanatory, his essentialism is based in formal and final causes that determine individual substances.[15] Being logically prior to the substance, the formal cause cannot be a property of the substance. Even though essences may be discovered by observing substances in development, the essence is not that process of development but the final form that is the organizing principle of that development.

Notice what Aristotle has accomplished through this metaphysics. He has hierarchically ordered activities based on their purity, that is, on their inability to produce change. Nonproductive activity, thought of thought, is the highest telos because it is the purest energeia. The more a substance is involved in matter and change, the lower it is in the hierarchy. At the same time, Aristotle seems to have provided an account of change in the real world because his essences are activities. His forms do not seem to be removed from the world of becoming as Plato's were; following his own rhetorical guidelines, he has made the fixed forms present to us by using active imagery. His principles thus seem to apply naturally to the social system: the most worthy are those who do not do productive work, who live off the labor of lesser beings; in other words, the most worthy are the traditional landed aristocracy. Within the upper class, the true aristocrats are those who act in accordance with the virtues of an aristocrat. Happiness is energeia of the soul (psuchē) in accordance with such virtues (aretai). The highest form of energeia is speculative thinking (theōretikē) that is done for its own sake and thus produces nothing and is based in leisure (skholē, from which we derive school).[16] In speculative thought, the philosophical aristocrat will transcend his composite substance and partake of the divine.[17] Unfortunately for most people, happiness is only available to those who are blessed with noble birth, good looks, and prosperity.[18] After all, one must have the potential before it can be actualized. The good life is thus connected with living out one's fate.

McKerrow's critique of the disembodied rationality of modernism can be applied to Aristotle. Indeed, the modern tendency to marginalize based on the form of communication applies as well to one of Aristotle's most notable biases, his attitude toward natural slavery. Natural slaves are barbarian (barbarikos), so called because of the strange sound of their speech. The difference in speech is taken to be a mark of essential difference, especially when combined with other differences in physical features. Based on his observation of these barbarians constrained by a language barrier, Aristotle assumes that they are less capable of reasoning and thus have a natural potential to be slaves. Metaphysically, his argument in favor of slavery is based on the analogy of soul ruling body. The soul is the energeia of the body, its form and inner activity, or life. The soul is superior to the body because it is more like the pure activity that is divine; so also is the Greek morally superior to the barbarian because the Greek is more rational.[19] The hierarchy is one of fixed natural categories based on supposedly fixed potentialities.

The difference between men and women is not quite so pronounced. Nevertheless, Aristotle insists that men are superior to women because women have a lesser power to deliberate. Slaves have no power to deliberate, children have an immature form of the power, and women have a somewhat incomplete form of the deliberative power. The rule of man over woman is not the rule of master over slave or father over child, but it is rule of the superior rational power over the inferior rational power in Aristotle's metaphysical hierarchy. Women's virtues are virtues of serving, whereas men's virtues are virtues of ruling. Aristotle quotes with approval Sophocles' dictum that "a modest silence is a woman's crown."[20] Virtue in Aristotle's system is a matter of function, and function depends upon position in the social hierarchy—a position that Aristotle's metaphysics establishes a priori and thus renders permanent rather than a mere a posteriori accident of social practices.

What we would call blue-collar workers are in a similar position to women within Aristotle's hierarchy. This class, which includes day laborers and craftsmen, is a necessary material condition for the existence of any polis, but its members are not truly parts of the polis.[21] The true citizens are the deliberative aspect of the polis related to the laboring classes as the soul is to the body. For Aristotle, a polis is a composite substance, just as the body is, with a ruling and a ruled element according to its natural telos. The best polities are those whose energeia achieves the telos of the polis, which is the good life for its members. The three correct forms of constitution, then, are monarchy, aristocracy, and polity, that is, a mixed oligarchy-democracy. The perverted forms of constitutions are tyranny, oligarchy, and democracy. Each of the perverted forms parallels a correct form but distorts the telos by serving only the interests of the rulers, not the whole polis.[22] Within Aristotle's hierarchy, however, the interests of the members of the polis do not include the happiness of the laboring classes, slaves, or women. Lacking the full form of rationality, these classes of people are incapable of achieving the telos of the happy life; they would not appreciate the goods available through communal practice. Distributive justice is concerned with distributing the goods available according to the function performed within the hierarchy of energeia. Therefore, Aristotle's interpretation of justice will always reward the aristocrats, who because of their good pedigree, free birth, wealth, disposition for justice, and military capability can contribute more to the activity of the city.[23]

The problem with Aristotle's practical philosophy is suggested by Aristotle himself. In his discussion of distributive justice, he points out that previous discussions of justice have erred because the advocates were judging in their own case and most men are poor judges when their own interests are involved.[24] Aristotle has erred in the application of his principle of justice because his own interests were involved. He has written his class and gender interests into a natural hierarchy from which he has then derived his conclusions in practical philosophy. In revising his philosophy pragmatically, we should recognize the natural tendency to reify our own interests as permanent standards. The standards we use should be open to criticism and modification from the margins as well as the center.

Can pragmatism reconstruct the concept of phronēsis? I believe it can. The pragmatists who have addressed the problems of metaphysics have generally arrived at a thoroughgoing principle of *kinēsis* as process. Dewey argued for a reconstruction of moral philosophy to reflect that ontology:

For in what is now taken to be morals the fixed, the immutable, still reign, even though moral theorists and moral institutional dogmatists are at complete odds with one another as to *what* ends, standards and principles are the ones which are immutable, eternal and universally applicable. In science the order of fixities has already passed irretrievably into an order of connections *in process*. One of the most immediate duties of philosophical reconstruction with respect to the development of viable instruments for inquiry into human or moral facts is to deal systematically with *human* processes.[25]

Dewey's reflections on the ethical-political dimensions of process metaphysics directly pertain to our project here. But the most profound thinking on the problem of process is that of C. S. Peirce.

Although an appreciative student of Aristotle, Peirce went far beyond Aristotle in his metaphysics. Peirce developed an ontology that he called synechism (from *sunekhēs, continuous*), based on his triadic conception that includes both change and continuity. This ontology underlies the conception of systemic stability and adaptability in the last chapter. If I make the statement, for example, that I have changed over the years, this statement implies a continuity in the "I" that is doing the changing. To make sense, the statement requires Thirdness, not merely a dyadic model of change; otherwise the statement could mean only that various events occurred with no connection between them. On the other hand, the experience of change is an experience of qualitative difference, the Secondness of difference implying the Firstness of qualities that may differ. Firstness is the realm of pure possibility (tychism, from *tukhē, chance*) that is constrained by continuity somewhat, but not completely. The notion of process, or *kinēsis,* thus requires a concept of a *discontinuous continuum.* Helm explains the concept using the analogy of a rope:

A rope, for example, is continuous but interrupted. A coil of rope fifty feet long has no fifty-foot fibers in it, but is composed of endless overlappings, side-wise interweavings and braidings. The fibers are like the "topical singularities" that interrupt or divide a continuum at a lower level of generality (4.642). A rope can be a suitable image for a discontinuous continuum, discontinuous as regards its partial singularities but continuous as a complex interacting whole.[26]

Individual lives are narrative "ropes" built out of the threads of events. Communities are longer ropes comprising various subsystems that are events of different lengths occurring in time. Time itself epitomizes the discontinuous continuum. Time is real, but Peirce would agree with Derrida that the "present" does not exist. The present contains no time.[27] The present is merely the point where the past meets the future, and a point has no extension on a continuum. Zeno's paradox results from treating points as if they existed separately instead of seeing one event blend into the next. Semiosis is possible because it is a discontinuous continuum. Derrida had it partly right but did not see the triadic alternative. Our signs as Thirdness mediate the past and the future. But the influence of the past on the future is not totally deterministic; chance can enter in. Continuity is probabilistic.

What we conventionally call the present is a combination of the near past and the near future. The immediate past is still influencing the immediate future and so determining it. The distant future, however, is a realm of general possibility that is much less determined, and the distant past is a realm of actuality that has much less effect on the future. Past events are coming to a close, other events are at their peak, and new possibilities are just beginning to grow into events. The continuity between these events serves as a kind of final cause, but it is a vague final cause with room for many possibilities. The future is not fully determined until it is past.[28] Peirce's theory of the discontinuous continuum allows for evolution and real change within the universe. The actions we take now may be the beginning of a thread of new possibilities in the universe. If this statement were not true, we could not be responsible for real change in our ecosystems. Ethics would be meaningless.

To give new meaning to Aristotle's notion of practical wisdom and virtue in general, let us substitute the pragmatic principle of process, kinēsis, for his oxymoron of unchanging motion, energeia. The distinction makes a great deal of difference to Aristotle's classification of people according to their capabilities. Because his concept of energeia includes the concept of entelecheia, he assumes that potential will actualize itself. In his ethics, this assumption leads him to the peculiar belief that knowing what to do will result in doing it and so the morally weak must necessarily lack knowledge. Politically, the assumption leads him to believe that, by studying the evidence of his own culture and the opinions (endoxa) of others in the Greek world, he can uncover the true essences of the various classes. The limit of each class's potential is shown by what its members have achieved. This limit must constitute a difference in kind, not a difference in degree, because Aristotle acknowledges that a difference in degree cannot justify a permanent distinction between ruler and ruled.[29] When we substitute process into the basic principles of this model, however, we end up with a mere difference in degree of actualization of potential.

A process does not necessarily achieve a particular telos. It can be interrupted or diverted in many ways. Ethical knowledge may not lead to ethical action, and the actual state of classes and genders in society may not reflect their potential. As various environmental factors limit development, the difference in underlying potential becomes less determinate. Recent psychological studies, for example, show that the physical development of the brain depends upon the environmental conditions encountered in infancy. "Individuals have different brains because of their early experiences. Of course, later development can also have an effect." Early communicative experiences largely determine later communicative abilities:

During development the mother coos, talks, and makes the sounds of almost every word in the language of the area in which, of course, the child is going to be speaking. At the same time, the child babbles and produces the sounds of almost every known language. Those sounds that relate to the language being spoken (say, English) get wired up in the person; those phonemes and sounds, expressions and gestures that are not used in the language group do not link up.[30]

From the pragmatic perspective, Aristotle's barbarian slaves were potential Attic orators.

Furthermore, if activity without change is no longer privileged, pure theoretical intelligence cannot be the principle of hierarchy. Humans can develop different kinds of intelligence to adapt to different environments. At different times in the life of a community, one form may be of greater value to the community than others. Because communities are themselves processes, the most valuable intelligence cannot be predetermined. Given that we don't know what differences in potential intelligence exist and that we also don't know what types of intelligence the community will need in the indefinite future, the idea of a permanent hierarchy collapses. Community hierarchies are probably necessary as means to particular ends at different times; however, these hierarchies must be adaptive and changeable as circumstances change. No a priori hierarchy can be assumed to represent the best interests of all those involved for all time. Because we do not know ahead of time what specific talents will be most important for the community, we can best serve both the community and the individual by equalizing the opportunities to develop talents in many different areas. Given equal opportunity, people can actualize various potentials while living out their lives according to their own goals, and the community can reward those developed talents that serve its needs in its own process of change. This allows for a principle of distributive justice.

When applied to communication, distributive justice includes access to the forum, which is any site of communal deliberation, any public space. Because new possibility begins with the Firstness of pure quality, it begins as feeling. Therefore, the logocentric model purified of pathos is inappropriate for deliberation. Peirce himself, although emphasizing logical issues in his work, subordinated logic to ethics and ethics to aesthetics. "We cannot know how we are deliberately prepared to aim to behave until we know what we deliberately admire."[31] Logic operates in the realm of thought, ethics in the realm of action, and aesthetics in the realm of feeling. These subjects may be considered both theoretically and practically, but phronēsis clearly requires their interaction. A pragmatic conception of phronēsis should overcome McKerrow's criticism of modern models of deliberation by overcoming the hidden rigidity of energeia.

Narrative Reasoning and Pragmatic Phronēsis

The pragmatic emphasis on process (kinēsis) instead of cyclic action (energeia) seems to fit well with the current emphasis on narrative forms of reasoning. In contemporary theory of argument, Fisher has proposed a "narrative paradigm" as the model of phronēsis. Burke has contrasted the syllogistic style of argument with the narrative by using the analogy of a cycle of terms in syllogism and rectilinear motion in narrative. This focus on narrative does not mean we should dismiss syllogistic forms as useful forms of deliberation. Pragmatism certainly doesn't. Neither, in fact, do Burke or Fisher. The term "narrative paradigm" is misleading.

Burke wished to develop "conceptual instruments for shifting back and forth between 'philosophic' and 'narrative' terminologies of motives, between temporal and logical kinds of sequence, thereby finding it easy to translate discussions of 'principles' or 'beginnings' back and forth into either of these styles, and thereby greatly cutting down the distance there seems to be between poetic and philosophic styles of statement."[32] This ability to shift between modes of discourse is, I shall argue, a necessary condition for any ethical judgment. Ethical reasoning requires the ability to move from personal and communal narratives to general principles and back. Phronēsis, as I conceive it, incorporates both forms of reasoning.

At first glance, Fisher's narrative paradigm seems to eliminate the possibility of ethical reasoning. If narrative is the paradigm of reason-giving, then principles appear to be irrelevant. Narrative can only show sequences of events; comparisons between sequences must be arbitrary. Fisher's idea of narrative incorporates values, however. Furthermore, he would even evaluate these values: "to weigh values, one considers questions of fact, relevance, consequence, consistency, and transcendent issue." This weighing is clearly a kind of ethical reasoning; so "narrative rationality is an attempt to recapture Aristotle's concept of *phronesis.*"[33] But if so, it cannot rely simply on narrative. Narrative cannot evaluate a "transcendent issue." One must move back and forth between narrative and deliberative forms of reasoning to assess the principles incorporated into one's life narrative.

Fisher's terminology is misleading: he does not really offer a narrative paradigm. Insofar as it is limited to narrative, it is not a paradigm because it cannot account for communication in general. Insofar as it is a general paradigm, it cannot be limited to narrative. He admits as much:

To test soundness, one may, *when relevant,* employ standards from formal or informal logic. Thus one must be attentive to facts, particular patterns of inference and implicature, and issues—conceived as traditional questions arising in forensic (fact, definition, justification, and procedure) or deliberative (the nature of a problem and the desirability of proposed solutions) practices. However, use of the narrative paradigm forces recognition that reasons are expressed by elements of human communication that are not always clear-cut inferential or implicative forms. Any individuated form of human communication may constitute a good reason if it is taken as a *warrant for accepting or adhering to the advice fostered* by that communication.[34]

Mythos does not displace logos, but simply takes its place alongside it in ethical reasoning. Contemporary theory has a fascination with the term *narrative*; however, insofar as the term is meaningful as a descriptor of discourse, it is a necessary but insufficient condition of practical wisdom.

This dialectic between narrative and syllogistic forms of reasoning resembles the dispute between Continental schools of hermeneutics, represented by Hans-Georg Gadamer, and ideological criticism, represented by Jürgen Habermas.[35] Gadamer's position is that the moral agent necessarily operates within a tradition. One must participate in a tradition in order to understand it. All human beings find themselves situated in history and are subject to the authority of the traditions within which they exist. Everyone is stuck in a narrative. One cannot distance oneself from all traditions and become independent of one's past in order to criticize that tradition. Habermas counters with a theory that is ahistorical in a utopian direction. He argues that the narrative tradition conceals distortions at the level where work, power, and discourse overlap. The mission of the critical social sciences is the unmasking of these distortions under the direction of an emancipatory interest. But these distortions can be disclosed only in comparison to an ahistorical ideal that must apparently be accepted a priori.

Ricoeur considers the debate between Gadamer and Habermas to reflect complementary elements in the practice of valuation. Gadamer emphasizes understanding through historical tradition; Habermas emphasizes explanation through ahistorical criticism. Understanding requires participation; explanation requires distanciation. In fact, both participation and distanciation are required. Gadamer's "fusion of horizons" in understanding of a text implies a distance between perspectives. The text can be understood only after its structure has been explained. Habermas's detachment of explanation of ideologies from understanding could work only if there were some ahistorical place "from where we could consider from a distance and from on high the theater of illusions, the battle field of ideologies. Then it would be possible to explain without understanding."[36] Ricoeur contends that our ability to perceive and challenge a given ideology depends on our received evaluations. What we can do is "transvaluate" the received values. Transvaluating is done through a constant process of reinterpreting received valuations: "There are no other paths, in effect, for carrying out our interest in emancipation than by incarnating it within cultural acquisitions. Freedom only posits itself by transvaluating what has already been evaluated. The ethical life is a perpetual transaction between the project of freedom and its ethical situation outlined by the given world of institutions."[37]

My ecological approach to practical wisdom agrees with Ricoeur's assessment of the debate between Gadamer and Habermas. To seek the point of equilibrium between individual and ecosystem in a system operating in history requires a *perpetual transaction*. But the disposition to continue to enter into this transaction is what it means to be ethical. Practical wisdom must be informed by a hermeneutical understanding of our own ongoing narrative and the narrative of our community accompanied by a critical comparison of those narratives with the ideal telos of the society as communicative ecosystem. Therefore, practical wisdom requires the practice of both narrative and syllogistic forms of communication. Neither form by itself is an adequate paradigm.

As Fisher's recognition of *transcendent issue* implies, in order to transvalue, the person making an ethical decision must be able to appeal to some concept that transcends the historical situation. Warnick has pointed out that the narrative paradigm is inadequate for judging the values of particular narratives without some rational standard or criterion.[38] The standard offered here is the telos of the communicative ecosystem to nurture each person in the achievement of the individual telos, which is the quest for the good. In the process of seeking the good, all of the individuals should support the ecosystem that supports them. Support of the ecosystem, however, includes attempts to change the ecosystem in order to make it better at supporting all its members over the long term. In a pragmatic approach, the telos does not guarantee its results entelechially. The telos itself is the product of semiosis and can be made concrete only when it is used to guide actions. As we saw in the last chapter, any system can claim to be rational only to the degree that it provides means for challenging its truth claims. This is the most basic requirement for rationality and therefore can be treated as a principle of communicative ethics. It is, in fact, the principle that justifies the critique of traditional reasoning that both McKerrow and Fisher make.

Fisher unfortunately undercuts the value of his critique by devaluing deliberation excessively, opting instead for identification:

The operative principle of narrative rationality is *identification* rather than deliberation. Narrative rationality differs from traditional rationality in another significant way. . . . Traditional rationality is . . . a normative construct. Narrative rationality is, on the other hand, descriptive; it offers an account, an understanding, of any instance of human choice and action, including science. At the same time, narrative rationality (although not necessarily the paradigm itself) provides a basis of critique. Where freedom and democracy are ideals, narrative rationality will imply a praxis constant with an ideal egalitarian society.[39]

The narratives of recent history belie Fisher's optimism. Gadamer and Habermas were arguing with the shadow of Hitler in the background. Hitler's narratives trampled the tender shoots of freedom and democracy in Germany. A sufficient number of Germans identified with his narratives to give him political power. He achieved power not through deliberation but through identification. The transcendent issue was ignored under the charm of myth. Narrative alone offers no principles for evaluation.

Fisher does provide some principles of narrative rationality—coherence and fidelity. Just as Fisher's paradigm is not simply narrative, however, his principles of coherence and fidelity are not merely narrative principles. In fact, within pragmatic realism they are general semiotic principles. These principles refer to the relations between signifiers and interpretants, on the one hand, and signifiers and objects, on the other. Consider Fisher's principles of narrative rationality:

Narrative *coherence* refers to formal features of a story conceived as a discrete sequence of thought and/or action in life or literature (any recorded or written form of discourse); that is, it concerns whether the story coheres or "hangs together," whether or not a story is free of contradictions. Narrative *fidelity* concerns the "truth qualities" of a story, the degree to which it accords with the logic of good reasons: the soundness of its reasoning and the value of its values.[40]

A story hangs together when its elements constitute a reasonable chain of interpretants. In traditional rational argument, an argument is coherent when its premises follow each other reasonably. A story is true when the signifier-interpretant chain stands for a real object just as a rational argument is true when the objects it represents are real. For pragmatic realists, in both cases the objects represented are relationships of events. Fictional stories, if well told, are not untrue; they simply do not index any particular state of the world. Fiction represents a general truth of relations that does not claim to be true in particulars. The equivalent of fiction in rational argument is pure mathematics, which examines the truth of purely hypothetical relations.

Peirce saw that a general logic based on semiotic would require several branches. One branch, equivalent to narrative probability or coherence, Peirce designated "pure rhetoric" with the function of discovering the rules by which "one sign gives birth to another, and especially one thought brings forth another." "Logic proper" (as opposed to the general logic of semiotic) is the study of "the conditions of the truth of representations." These would be the conditions a story or syllogism would have to satisfy in order to have fidelity. So Peirce proposed branches of semiotic to study the principles of coherence and fidelity. In addition, Peirce recognized the need for a third branch of study, "pure grammar." Its function was to study the conditions necessary for a sign (representamen) to "embody any meaning."[41] An interesting finding of Peirce's own exploration of semiotic grammar was the necessity of indeterminacy. This necessary quality of a sign has profound implications for the nature of reasoning, in both narrative and syllogistic forms. Peirce's semiotic leads us further away from Aristotelian categories and points us toward fuzzier realms.

Fuzzy Phronēsis

The transvaluation of a narrative requires that we abstract from our narratives to form ideals. A narrative associates events as causes and effects. Deliberative reasoning abstracts the structure of that narrative and considers its implications. In its simplest form, such abstraction is analogy: when we interpret our present situation by some past narrative, we are making an inferential leap. If we convert the narrative to syllogistic form, we can critically evaluate the analogy. If we do not critically evaluate the narratives we live, we will be determined fully by those narratives. Aristotle was right: choice (proairesis) requires deliberation. When we abstract from the narratives of experience, however, we do not usually achieve the crisp categories of Aristotelian logic. Aristotle was wrong: we cannot reduce kinēsis to energeia. The structure of kinēsis is that of a discontinuous continuum, and our deliberation should reflect that structure. Pragmatically reconstructed, phronēsis should allow for the problems of indeterminacy and vagueness. Phronēsis must incorporate fuzzy logic.

Fuzzy logic has made dramatic inroads into computer decision making. The reason is not that electronic circuitry has some remarkable capability heretofore undiscovered but that human deliberation is being more carefully analyzed and used as a model for expert systems. Deliberation involves working with degrees of vagueness and indeterminacy, not the clear sets of symbolic logic. Fuzzy logic traces its heritage to Peirce, "the first thinker to grapple seriously with vagueness."[42] Most logicians of vagueness, however, have been unable to find his developed theory of vagueness. Their inability is apparently an inability to see the forest for the trees. While some scholars still search through Peirce's papers hoping to find some unpublished manuscript detailing the logic of vagueness, Brock and Nadin claim to have found it right in front of their noses.[43] Peirce's semiotic is his logic of vagueness. For Peirce all symbols are indeterminate, and logic must take this indeterminacy into account. As we saw in chapter 2, Peirce's acceptance of indeterminacy leads not to the cynicism of deconstruction but to the recognition that indeterminate symbols are sufficiently determinate for practical purposes within a given context.

Given Peirce's triadic semiotic, we should not be surprised that there are three aspects affecting indeterminacy. These are breadth, depth, and information. Symbols—that is, terms, propositions, and arguments, both syllogistic and narrative—can be indeterminate in breadth and or depth. Indeterminacy in breadth is indeterminacy about the object to which a symbol applies. Indeterminacy in depth is indeterminacy about the interpretants of that symbol. The statement "Some heterosexuals have AIDS," for example, is indeterminate in both breadth and depth. *Some heterosexuals* does not indicate exactly whom we are talking about; so it is indeterminate in breadth. The terms *heterosexual* and *AIDS* are both indeterminate in depth because we do not know exactly what all of the interpretants of those terms would be. Does heterosexual include bisexual? If someone has tested positive for HIV, does that person have AIDS? These questions reveal an indeterminacy in depth. Narrative coherence is primarily a matter of depth, and narrative fidelity is primarily a matter of breadth. So the question of the appropriateness of an analogy is primarily a question about its breadth: does it apply to this particular situation?

Information plays a key role in Peirce's logic of vagueness. Information is "the sum of synthetical propositions in which the symbol is subject or predicate."[44] "Synthetical" here is used in the Kantian sense. Peirce's equivalent for Kant's analytic is "essential." Thus the essential depth of a term comprises "the really conceivable qualities predicated of it in its definition" even if "the defined term will not perhaps be applicable to any real objects whatever."[45] Peirce's semiotic is a logic for scientific fixation of belief; so information is always the result of experience. A scientific mind is one that learns by experience. Peirce denies any Cartesian ability to know intuitively. Our knowledge, however, may involve both knowledge of definitions and of the real objects involved. The perfect level of information would then have two aspects, substantial information and essential information. Substantial information would be perfect knowledge about all facts, natural laws, and logic. Essential information would be perfect knowledge about the meanings of words and deductive logic. We, of course, possess neither substantial nor essential information. Ordinary information is a partial level of information about both objects and meanings.

Since we are incapable of intuiting substances, substantial information is equivalent to the real—the hoped-for result at the end of inquiry. The concept of essential information serves to remind us that deductive arguments may carry information because our knowledge of terms is not complete. Overall, however, Peirce's logic of vagueness is concerned with essential or informed breadth and depth for a given state of ordinary information. Like essential depth, essential breadth applies to definitions. The essential breadth of a term comprises those objects of which the term *by its very meaning* could be predicated. The term "being," for example, essentially applies to everything. The informed breadth of a term comprises those objects that are actually known to have that term as a predicate in a given imperfect state of information. Suppose we did a computer search of a given library for the term *fuzzy logic* and the result was fifty items found. These fifty items are the informed breadth of the term *fuzzy logic* within that particular universe of discourse.

The depth of a symbol is everything that is implied by the symbol. Essential depth is what is implied in the definition. Depth also includes informed depth, however, which is an implication learned from experience. The informed depth of cigarette smoking, for example, includes the implication of lung cancer even though that is not deducible from the definition. The informed depth might eventually change the essential depth by changing the definition. The definition of cigarette may come to incorporate the predicate *carcinogenic*. Therefore, a term grows in depth. We, ourselves, are symbols growing in depth as we develop the narrative of our lives. What we learn about ourselves from experience becomes part of our definition of ourselves—our momentarily singular essence considered for purposes of transvaluation. The fact that we return to our narratives and continue to grow as symbols indicates that we are not determinate symbols.

A determinate symbol would have no room for growth—specifically, no latitude for interpretation in either breadth or depth. According to Peirce, no sign is absolutely determinate.[46] The ability of deconstructors to exploit that indeterminacy comes as no surprise, but on Peircean terms that exploitation is unfair. According to Peirce's logic, the only form of indeterminacy that gives the interpreter the right of further determination is the indeterminacy in breadth arising from generality. The proposition that "All humans are mortal" invites the interpreter to determine the object to which it applies. The interpreter can choose any human as a test case, so the interpreter has some latitude of interpretation. Other types of indeterminacy do not give the interpreter the right to determine the meaning or application. As Brock points out, of course, we often usurp that right as interpreters and may even come up with a correct interpretation:

In fact a sign which is general in breadth gives the interpreter a license such that it is virtually impossible for him to err in determining breadth. Note, however, that an interpreter may also achieve a *correct though unlicensed* interpretation of a sign which is *indefinite in breadth*, e.g., in the case when the interpreter correctly infers that "a certain man" is designed to refer to him. . . . It is this sort of *unlicensed ability* to come up with a correct interpretation, and not a *right* of further determination, which belongs to the interpreter of a sign which is indeterminate in depth, i.e., a vague or ambiguous sign. The fact that such "freedom of interpretation" is unlicensed will turn up when the interpreter puts a wrong or untoward interpretation on the utterer's words. Then the utterer will assert his *natural right* to reject the interpretation and supply the correct one.[47]

Logic for Peirce is a kind of ethic that imposes responsibilities. Deconstruction achieves its effects by violating that ethic. In some circumstances that violation may be appropriate, but it should not be taken for granted.

The utterer of a sign, of course, has responsibilities as well. Although no sign is absolutely determinate, within a given pragmatic situation, a sign can often be made sufficiently determinate for practical purposes. That was the point of Peirce's example of the Englishmen talking about Charles II, which I discussed in chapter 2. The symbols were sufficiently determinate for their purposes. It is the responsibility of the utterer to reduce the latitude of interpretation that is *relevant* to the purposes of the communication.[48] In terms of the ecological ethic, I would interpret those purposes to be the purposes of the particular system as a whole, not those of the utterer. The utterer's rights to clarify her own meaning do not inhere in the utterer but are a result of her function within the system. Failure to provide enough relevant information is likely to result in misunderstanding.

The demand for irrelevant precision results in the fallacy of overprecision.[49] There is no one standard of precision that applies to all situations. The question of how much precision is needed is itself a question of practical wisdom. Demands for excessive precision can increase the costs of inquiry unnecessarily. *Phronesis* implies wisdom in economical communication. In most situations the interpreter can ask questions if more precision is required. The fallacy occurs when one confuses the refutation of a precise belief with the refutation of a vague belief from which the precise belief was derived.

This fallacy occurs, for example, when the uncertainty principle and indeterminacy of quantum physics are used to generate skepticism about our everyday knowledge of the world. The uncertainty principle does not refute our knowledge of the position and velocity of a tennis ball for practical purposes. "For a flying tennis ball, the uncertainties due to quantum theory are only one part in about ten million billion billion billion (10^{-34})."[50] It is a fallacy to claim that we cannot make true, sufficiently precise statements about the position and velocity of tennis balls just because we cannot make true, sufficiently precise statements about the position and velocity of subatomic particles.

Unnecessary demands for precision can make a true statement appear false. The critical commonsensism of pragmatism recognizes that most observations of common sense are true even though they are vague. Within the purposes of everyday life, the hypotheses of common sense have been well tested over countless generations. Errors arise when the hypotheses of common sense are extended beyond their normal purposes. A classic example is the flat-earth hypothesis of common sense. For most human purposes, the earth is roughly flat. One need not plan a great circle route to plow the back forty. The problem arose when the workable local hypothesis was extended beyond the range of the observations in which it had been tested. That is why commonsensism must be critically evaluated in pragmatic realism. That is also why the narratives of common sense should be respected but not accepted uncritically.

Failure to accept vagueness as a necessary accompaniment of symbol use can increase rather than reduce errors. The problem is worsened by the failure to recognize that the objects being signified are often continua rather than clearly demarcated sets of objects. The recent popularity of fuzzy logic arises from the recognition that many of the decisions of experts deal with continua. Fuzzy logic arose from the need to design computer controllers. Its relevance for phronēsis comes from the fact that ethical decisions are similar to control decisions of expert systems. Despite his own reliance on crisp categories, Aristotle's golden mean in ethics illustrates the kind of balance that is achieved through fuzzy logic. Fuzzy logic is especially appropriate for dealing with the open systems that constitute our ecosystem because they are continua in essence, that is, by definition. Phronēsis, therefore, is the deliberative process of balancing the demands of these various vague systems.

In 1964, Lofti Zadeh, a system theorist in electrical engineering at the University of California at Berkeley, introduced fuzzy-set theory. He was apparently unaware of the work on vagueness done by Peirce; nevertheless, as Nadin asserts, "the semiotic and dialogic nature of thought in Peirce's conception and the model of multivalued logic demonstrated by Zadeh in his definition of fuzzy sets seem to be outright complementary components."[51] The basic insight of Zadeh was graded membership in sets, which complements Peirce's logic of vagueness by relating continua to sets with vague boundaries. Take, for example, the supposed impossibility of altruism. The argument is that if one enjoys doing good for others, one is acting for one's own pleasure; therefore, the act cannot be altruistic. Fuzzy logic denies this dichotomy. Acts may participate in the category of "altruism" by degrees. Suppose, for example, that in a conversation you thought of a witty remark that was clever but hurtful to another. You decide not to say it, in part because of your concern for the other but also because you know it would be unwise to offend the other. Is the act altruistic? In traditional logic your choices are yes or no. In fuzzy logic, you would place this particular act on the continuum of altruistic acts, giving it a partial membership in that set. So in this case the act might have been 75 percent altruistic and 25 percent selfish. On a scale of zero to one, this act has a 0.75 membership in the altruistic set.

This number, 0.75, is admittedly not a purely objective measure and, if misinterpreted, is somewhat misleading. The number is meant not to indicate a false accuracy but merely to make the measure usable in computer programs. For our purposes of deliberation, we could simply say that the act was for the most part altruistic. In any case, by the more careful interpretation of partial membership in the set, we have greatly increased the essential breadth of *altruism*. In Peirce's terminology, we have increased our essential information about *altruism* and about logic in general apart from any information about whether the term actually applies to any existential acts. We have increased the possible cases to which *altruism* could apply. If, in fact, all actual actions are either perfectly altruistic or not at all altruistic, then the informed breadth of the term will not change. In that case, the informed breadth of a traditional "crisp" set and the fuzzy set would be the same even though the essential breadth had changed because of the new logic. Most of us, however, have learned through experience that many actions are altruistic in part. Therefore, the informed breadth of the term has changed significantly and disproves the argument that no actions are altruistic (or that the set of altruistic acts is an empty set).

A fuzzy set incorporates the crisp set's values as limits. In the crisp set, only membership values of one are included; all other values are reduced to zero—a significant loss of information. (Such a loss of information might even lead one to the strange conclusion that all actions are purely selfish.) In the fuzzy set, all values greater than zero are members of the set; one is the high-limit value of membership in the set. The continuum of numbers greater than zero and less than or equal to one stands for the continuum of possible membership values in the set. The value one may be regarded as the *paradigm case* of the set, even though it often is never experienced but exists only in the sense of being the limit of possibility. The normal judgments of our lives operate in the realms of partial memberships, in the range of "somewhat," "sort of," and "largely." Formal logic (*logica docens*) is beginning to catch up with common sense (*logica utens*). As it does so, it confirms the value of much commonsense reasoning and undermines the elitism of "rationality."

Take, for example the problem of multiple-choice questions on an exam. Only one answer will be credited as correct (membership value equals one), but two or three of the choices will be close to the truth. Given the normal vagueness of words, test takers feel justified in the choice they have made. Even when shown what the correct answer is, they can give good reasons for their choice. They feel they should get some credit for their answer, but they receive zero. To them the test seems unfair. Unless the test happens to even out those injustices, they are correct. For most subjects, where the test attempts to measure degree of understanding, the multiple choice grading system is unfair. The grading system does not give examinees credit for the degree of correctness of their answer. Keeping in mind Foucault's discussion of the power involved in examining, we should be concerned about how the logic of crisp categories can lead to an unjust exercise of that power. This injustice is especially discouraging to the disadvantaged. Imagine a young student in college, for example, who comes from an inner-city neighborhood and has just managed to qualify for college. The terms being used are very strange to her, but she struggles to understand them. As she works hard, she comes to feel she is really learning something. She began with very little essential information within this particular universe of discourse, but through hard hermeneutical work her comprehension increases. Then comes the midterm exam. The multiple choice test offers her choices she cannot discriminate between. She knows that one or two answers are definitely wrong, but she can't be sure about the others. So she fails the exam, decides she was just fooling herself when she thought she was learning something, and drops out of school. If the grading system had given her credit for the partial understanding she had achieved, she might have been encouraged to continue. But the grading system increases the apparent difference between those who are familiar with the terms and those who aren't. In multiple choice tests, the rich get richer and the poor get poorer.

The crisp category system supports the Aristotelian and modernist hierarchy in other ways as well. People who lack essential information within a particular universe of discourse are assumed to lack the ability to learn that information. The fact that potential is a continuum is disregarded. Each level of learning has increased the potential for more learning, but that increase goes unrecognized until it crosses a certain threshold. Suddenly the person who lacked potential now has it. Those who are brought up and trained in that universe of discourse, of course, will display more potential than those who haven't. The crisp category system will exaggerate that difference. Differences then can be justified as natural differences in potential, as Aristotle did with his concept of natural slaves. In fact, the difference is economic. The person whose communicative ecosystem has trained her in the essential information of the relevant universe of discourse will be more economical to educate further. Multiple choice tests are also more economical to administer, and they have the additional advantage of clearly identifying those who will be uneconomical students. These considerations of economy tend to support the status quo.

The preference for crisp, analytic reasoning over vague, holistic reasoning has also supported the status quo, not because of its results, but because of the economic requirements of participation. Analytic reasoning in the form of a decision tree requires leisure. One must have time to break the problem down into its many parts and to define each of those parts as a crisp category. It takes time to remove events from time to analyze their structure. One cannot do it under the press of events. People under the press of events, however, continue to make relatively effective decisions (else humanity would not have survived). How do they do it? Well, it depends who is making the decision. If the decision maker is a woman, we are likely to attribute the effectiveness to that mysterious entity *women's intuition*. If it is a man, we are more likely to credit the wisdom of experience, although in sports we often refer to some incredible sixth sense. The successes of fuzzy logic suggest that our effective holistic decision making is a matter of what Peirce called scientific intelligence, which is learning from experience. What we learn is how to deliberate quickly and well using fuzzy logic.

The need to develop expert systems has led to a greater appreciation for the effectiveness of fuzzy logic in practice. A controller using fuzzy logic acts like a deliberative assembly.[52] The controller is given the rules used by experts for various situations in fuzzy categories. In a steam controller, for example, one rule might be, if the pressure is a little high but rising rapidly, reduce the heat a moderate amount. These rules are derived from experience—basic, blue-collar experience. The controller then receives information on the current state of the system and compares that to the conditions for each rule. Because this is a fuzzy system, the current reading will be a member of several different categories to some degree. Every category in which the reading has any membership at all will provide its rule to the controller. Analogically, it is as though every member of the assembly affected by the current condition were able to give its preferred solution. The controller then finds the center of gravity of all the various solutions and uses that as the point of adjustment. The weight each rule has in the deliberation depends upon the degree to which that particular reading is a member of its category. That weighting is involved in the calculation of the center of gravity. Since the response must be relatively precise, the center of gravity provides a precise adjustment for the controller to apply. The success of controllers using this process of fuzzy logic has been amazing.

What is interesting is how this result has been achieved. The controller model is a deliberative model in which common experience is given an input into the deliberation. The role of the logic is to balance these many inputs. It seems to me that fuzzy logic controllers have succeeded in modeling the deliberative process that Aristotle used in his ethic. The center of gravity is a more sophisticated version of the golden mean. It is what the golden mean would be if the deliberation paid attention to every voice weighted by relevance to the actual situation instead of privileging certain voices on a priori grounds. Fuzzy logic is based on the reasoning of the blue-collar worker, the homemaker, and the professional who have learned to quickly balance multiple demands in arriving at a decision. The success of these controllers shows how logical holistic reasoning is when we understand reasoning pragmatically as reasoning governed by purpose.

This is the model of deliberation for an ecological ethic—fuzzy phronēsis. In our individual life narratives we must balance many competing desires and duties. As communities we must balance the competing needs and desires of individuals in pursuit of their goods and of the various levels of the system. This is complicated deliberation, but it is the kind of deliberation we have been doing all of our lives. The purpose of an ecological ethic is to learn how to do this better—to develop better rules for achieving balance and especially to incorporate more voices of experience in our deliberation. As a consequence we must attend to the marginalized voices at all levels of the ecosystem, including the voice of our own emotions. As a postscript to this discussion of phronēsis, we should note that despite its practical successes fuzzy logic has not been well accepted by the theoretical establishment.[53] Perhaps that is simply another sign that we should not confuse theoretical competence with practical wisdom. The practical public sphere is not some Habermasian place of theoretical discourse but is the apparent bedlam of interaction taking place throughout the community. The problem of the public sphere is the failure of our deliberative controllers to listen to all the voices speaking their own expertise.

Our failure of phronēsis is a cause of the increased division and fragmentation in our communities. We cannot solve the problem by returning to some utopian ideal of a purely homogeneous community existing in our mythic past. As McGee has pointed out, we find ourselves in a postmodern culture of fragmentation. Admitting that we are in a postmodern culture, however, does not require excessively valorizing fragmentation at the expense of community as postmodernism does. McGee also noted that we need not give in to the "circle of negativism" found in postmodernism. "It is time to stop whining about the so-called 'postmodern condition' and to develop realistic strategies to cope with it as a fact of human life."[54] Practical wisdom involves dealing with our situation—building community by integrating the voices that are relevant to public exigences, while recognizing the diversity of private exigences. A reconstructed, pragmatic, fuzzy phronēsis that incorporates multiple forms of argument is essential for making ecologically sound decisions. We should not assume that community is there to be found simply and easily, nor should we assume that community is impossible because it is complex and difficult to achieve. Fuzzy phronēsis would warn us not to become victims of this false dichotomy.

Ecological Honesty

The consequences of listening to more voices would obviously include a better community epistemology. We would know more about our communicative environment and about the status of the subsystems within our ecosystem. But these epistemological consequences will also lead to ontological consequences. When marginalized voices find that they are being incorporated into communal knowledge and so influencing decisions, their ties to the community will be strengthened. The result is ontological: the potential community becomes more real. All of this, however, presumes that most basic of communicative virtues, honesty, is the dominant habit in the communicative ecosystem. If we recognize that even truth is a continuum, better represented by a multivalued fuzzy logic than by a simple binary system of true or false,[55] then we can see that truth values do predominate in our communicative ecosystem.

The possibility of lying is a by-product of human use of symbols. Once signs are used to represent a state of affairs that is not present to the senses, those same signs may be used to misrepresent a state of affairs. Umberto Eco goes so far as to define the discipline of semiotics as "the discipline studying everything which can be used in order to lie."[56] Even the success of a lie, however, depends upon a norm of truth-telling. The system of communication that supports the individual pursuit of the good is built upon a presumption that speakers are, for the most part, honest. One cannot even imagine a communicative system operating in which speakers tell the truth only randomly. Such communication would be meaningless jabbering to those hearing it. In order to interpret another's utterance, a listener forms a hypothesis that assumes some predictability about the relationship of the utterance to the shared universe of discourse. Randomness makes such interpretation impossible.

An old puzzle illustrates the problem. In the puzzle a traveler comes upon a fork in the road. The traveler does not know which way leads to her destination. She sees two natives of the land at the fork. One is from a tribe whose members always tell the truth, the other is from a tribe whose members always lie. Between the two of them, they are willing to answer one question from her. What question can she ask that will ensure that she discovers the correct way to her destination? The answer relies on the predictability of their habits of honesty and dishonesty. To solve her dilemma, she should ask either one of them, "If I asked the other man here, would he tell me that the right or the left fork leads to my destination?" The answer will necessarily be the wrong fork: if the truth-teller answers, he will truthfully predict the other's lie; if the liar answers, he will falsely say what the truth-teller would not have said. In either case, the answer will be the wrong fork; so the traveler can simply take the opposite fork and proceed to her destination.

The point of the story is that a predictable liar cannot deceive; the listener knows that the contradictory is the truth. Predictability results in effective honesty because the correlation of signifier-interpretant-object depends on regularity in practice. Tribes of perfect liars and truth-tellers, however, exist only in stories; and only in such a story would the traveler know she was encountering perfect liars and truth-tellers. Actual societies depend upon the presumption of honesty in order to make communication predictable enough to be pragmatically informative. Deception depends upon this presumption so that the victim will form the wrong hypothesis rather than compensating by contradicting the lie. An effective liar is aware that communication depends upon a basic commitment to honesty by the members of a communicative system and so buries an occasional lie among truths.

The judgment of a speaker's ethos by a listener is in part an attempt to adjust the listener's interpretation of the message according to an estimation of the speaker's competence and compliance with the norm of honesty. Ethos is in practice a fuzzy measure of truth value lacking the crisp categories that the traveler's riddle provided. Because listeners continually make fuzzy adjustments based on their estimate of competence and truthfulness in the communicative act, every lie detracts from the overall ability of the system to support effective communication. The lie increases randomness, or entropy, in the system. People tend to generalize, so a loss of trust in predictability spreads through the system and the ethos of every speaker is affected. Cynicism makes concerted action more difficult, and the system may become unable to respond to internal and external changes. Thus honesty is important to the survival of the system.

The requirement to be honest does not, however, entail a standard of Absolute Truth as anything other than an ideal of assertion. Most contemporary theories of meaning point up the epistemological problems involved in determining truth sub specie aeternitatis. Humans deal in signs; the process of signification requires interpretation; and signs can be honestly misinterpreted. What I mean by honesty is not correspondence with the dynamic object but correspondence with lower levels of semiosis and interpretation according to a given universe of discourse, or what Eco calls an encyclopedia of meaning.[57] One hopes, of course, that one's meaning system is to a large degree isomorphic with reality; but if it is not, one is simply mistaken and not dishonest. To be dishonest, one must betray what one believes to be the case. If we took literally the charge to tell the truth, the whole truth, and nothing but the truth, none of us could testify. The "true state of affairs" cannot be the measure of a speaker's honesty because our only means of measurement are different human perspectives conveyed through different human meaning systems. The fact that we may find some areas of agreement between our different meaning systems does not guarantee that this agreement represents the truth that would eventuate at the end of inquiry.[58] Honesty includes a fallibilistic concept of truth. Nevertheless, in asserting a proposition, we assert our belief that it will stand up to the test of inquiry.

Honesty, understood as correspondence between one's utterances and the encyclopedia of meaning, is necessary not only for the proper functioning and the survival of the communicative system but also for the individual pursuit of the good within the system. The epistemological problems involved in seeking the good become compounded by dishonesty. Open systems grow and adapt because they receive information. Dishonesty can distort the growth of a system and cause it to be maladapted to its environment. An individual's cognitive system depends upon accurate feedback to correct the direction of its growth. A married couple, for example, seeks the good within a marital relationship. To the degree that either spouse is dishonest to the other, the relationship cannot adapt to their mutual needs. If the marriage is to grow in its ability to nurture both of them, then the communication between them must be true to both of their underlying experiences. How much they should reveal to each other may be a matter of prudence, but the accuracy of what they reveal is a matter of honesty. Not passing information about how they feel to each other will result in a lack of growth for their dyadic system in that area, but passing the wrong information will result in growth in the wrong direction. One member of the dyad may build his or her expectations on the false communication of the other until eventually the whole system collapses like a house of cards when the dishonesty grows so large that it cannot be sustained. Once dishonesty is discovered, the dyadic system can never again grow normally because trust has been lost. One spouse will not be able to base his or her quest for the good on information provided by the other.

On the other hand, we cannot use truth as a way of avoiding responsibility for our communicative decisions. Since all of us stand in the midst of a flow of messages and observations, we must decide what we will pass on to others. In an ecological ethic this decision would be based on predicted systemic effects. Truth is an important criterion determining whether the consequences of a communicative act will be good or bad. But truth is not always sufficient grounds for a decision to communicate. Truth may be the ultimate legal defense in a libel trial but it is not a sufficient ethical defense for evasion of responsibility. The ethical communicator must consider the consequences of communicating the truth because he or she is responsible for those consequences. Telling the truth about someone's distant past may damage communicative systems built on trust and hurt that person's ability to pursue the good while gaining nothing for the other systems involved and their members' pursuit of the good. Discovery of apparent truth does not necessarily entail the disclosure of truth. Phronēsis requires balancing the needs of the various systems involved regardless of the claimed truth of the message. Truth value alone cannot be used to rationalize an evasion of responsibility for the consequences of a communicative act.

Granted the dangers of dishonesty to communicative systems, there are still times when going so far as telling a lie may be the best ethical choice in a given situation. In making the choice to lie, however, one must accept responsibility for the consequences of the lie. The correctness of lying is most clear in those cases where the communicative-social system has become deranged and lacks even minimal phronēsis. An example is the case of Nazi Germany. If someone living in territory under Nazi control were hiding Jews to protect them from persecution, it would clearly be ethical to lie to the Gestapo to keep them from discovering the hidden Jews. The damage done to the communicative system is an acceptable trade-off for the protection of those endangered lives. The communicative system in this case has, through the lies and distortion of Nazi rhetoric, become maladapted so that it no longer supports the pursuit of the good of its members. Telling the truth in such a maladapted system can cause more evil than lying. Lying is an interim policy until the social system can be reconstructed. Nevertheless, the trust that has been lost because of the pattern of lying throughout the system will make the reconstruction of a healthy system more difficult. This is an inevitable consequence of lying whether such lying is on overall balance ethical or not.

In the example of Nazi Germany, the ethical correctness of lying is justified by the extremity of the situation. But in what would seem to be a much healthier communicative system in nineteenth-century Denmark, Søren Kierkegaard also argued for the ethical use of deception. Kierkegaard's argument is much more problematic. Kierkegaard admitted that "from the point of view of my whole activity as an author, integrally conceived, the aesthetic work is a deception." He considered aesthetic categories to be opposed to true Christianity, yet he presented his works as though they were only about aesthetics. Nevertheless, Kierkegaard defends his action as ethical:

One can deceive a person for the truth's sake, and (to recall old Socrates) one can deceive a person into the truth. Indeed, it is only by this means, i.e. by deceiving him, that it is possible to bring into the truth one who is in an illusion. Whoever rejects this opinion betrays the fact that he is not over-well versed in dialectics, and that is precisely what is especially needed when operating in this field. For there is an immense difference, a dialectical difference, between these two cases: the case of a man who is ignorant and is to have a piece of knowledge imparted to him, so that he is like an empty vessel which is to be filled or a blank sheet of paper upon which something is to be written; and the case of a man who is under an illusion and must first be delivered from that.[59]

If we interpret Kierkegaard's argument from an ecological perspective, we can see similarities with the argument I have presented above; but Kierkegaard is operating at the level of individual semiotic systems rather than social systems. He is arguing that the listener's system of mental constructs has developed in the wrong direction in its dependence on aesthetic categories. One cannot directly proclaim the truth because the other is unable to receive it into this somewhat deranged system of constructs. The tendency of a system to use selective perception and negative feedback to maintain a steady state prevents the "truth" from getting through. Therefore, the interlocutor "begins by accepting the other man's illusion as good money." The purpose is to use the other's constructs to show that the position is untenable. Beginning from the other's position, the interlocutor deconstructs the faulty system of beliefs in order then to reconstruct the system so that the other person's system is more isomorphic with reality. If the other person had not yet developed mental constructs in this area—if the other were "a blank sheet of paper"—the deconstruction-reconstruction would not be necessary. One would simply express the truth to the other.

From an ecological perspective, Kierkegaard's argument is reasonable—setting aside the question of whether he exercised wisdom in its application to the question of aesthetic versus Christian categories. Several caveats, however, need to be added to his general argument. First, one person's illusion is another person's truth. It is a good thing to show others the weaknesses in their system of mental constructs; critical thinking improves the adaptability of individual cognitive systems. To do so from a position of Absolute Truth, however, suggests that one is unwilling to examine the weaknesses in one's own system. Ideally, dialectic should be the occasion for change and growth in the cognitive systems of all involved. Second, by the end of the argument the deception must be corrected. In a Socratic dialogue, Socrates comes eventually to the point where he rejects the position he originally took for the sake of the argument. His intention is that his interlocutor will also reject the position, and they will have reached a new level of agreement. This is not the same type of deception as that practiced by a politician who pretends to adopt a position that he or she does not really support just in order to win votes. The Kierkegaardian deception intends to expose itself in the process of argument. Finally, Kierkegaard's deception was not alien to his underlying beliefs. He in fact found the aesthetic categories very attractive. His adoption of the position reflected what he had once felt and what was necessarily still a part of his understanding even though he had come to reject its conclusions. His deception was intended to lead others on a path he had followed. To understand and appreciate the opposing position while exposing its weaknesses is not the same as setting up a straw man to destroy.

In both the above cases in which I acknowledge that deception may be a prudent choice, a malformation of the systems of information, either external or internal, was involved. In the example of the Nazis, a deranged social system made truth-telling unwise; in Kierkegaard's argument, a deluded cognitive system blocked the direct path for truth. Accordingly, in both cases the deception was a temporary expedient, awaiting a reformation of the troubled system. Yet there exists a class of lies that perpetuates itself in our communicative system without seeking a change in the system. This category is the class of social lies.

Suppose a man and a woman were on their way to an important social event. As they walk out the door, the man turns to the woman and says, "Do you like this suit?" The suit happens to be a style that the woman does not care for; nevertheless, she answers, "Sure do; it looks great on you." At the party, the man develops heartburn and a headache. He has a miserable time. But as he prepares to leave he tells the host that it was a wonderful party and he enjoyed himself very much. In both of these acts of communication, the man and woman have not spoken truthfully. They have told social lies. The question is, are such actions ethical or not?

Consider the particular communicative system in which the couple was operating. In neither case were they attempting to convey misinformation in a system demanding information. When the man asks about the suit, his purpose presumably is not to seek information for a decision about the suit. It is too late for him to decide not to buy the suit or not to wear the suit. He is simply seeking personal reassurance before an important social engagement. The woman addresses his need for reassurance and not a need for information. In speaking to the host later, the man's purpose was not to give information but to thank the host politely. As long as the listeners have the social competence to interpret the speech acts the way they were intended, no deception should occur. Should the listener misinterpret a speaker's intention, the speaker must seek to correct their misapprehensions. If the man suspects that a certain type of food served caused his physical difficulties, for example, he should not allow the host to believe that he enjoyed that food. Otherwise, the host may be led to serve it again when the man is invited. In the same way, at some other time the woman may suggest to the man that he looks better in a different suit. In this way, while not intending to deceive by means of the social lie, the speakers take responsibility for any deception that happens to occur.

Responsibility for the consequences, however unintended, of deception also applies to the myths we teach our children to accept, such as the Easter Bunny and Santa Claus. Obviously, the purpose of such myths is not to deceive the children for our own advantage but to give them pleasure. Such myths also encourage optimism in children by leading them to believe that the natural world is somehow on their side. But not all of the consequences are good. Take the case of the disadvantaged child: if the cultural system encourages belief in

Santa Claus as a benevolent force in the world, how will the child react when it appears as though Santa Claus prefers rich children? Won't these children come to believe that the whole world is against them? Furthermore, all children will eventually come to discover that adults don't really believe in Santa Claus. The children will learn that they have been deceived. This disillusion will affect the ethos of parents and other adults at a time when they will be trying to warn their children about such things as the dangers of drug abuse and irresponsible sexual activity. Furthermore, children may have difficulty distinguishing between the mythology their parents did not themselves believe but taught them anyway and the mythology their parents believe and teach, such as their religious myths. God may be placed in the same category as the Easter Bunny and Santa Claus—a parental deception. These consequences are generally not desired by those who nevertheless maintain the myths.

The point is not that our society must immediately expose our children to the truth about their parent's disbelief in Santa Claus or the Easter Bunny. Rather, the point is that in perpetuating a myth that we ourselves take to be untrue, we must accept responsibility for all the consequences of our apparent dishonesty, both good and bad. We can then take actions that will ameliorate the bad effects. As a community we can try to ensure that if any children are visited by Santa, all children will be visited by Santa. As parents, we can lead our children to an understanding of Santa as a representation of the joy of giving so that they eventually come to understand that myths signify ideas that we hold to be true or wish to be true. In that way, we can communicate the deeper honesty that lies behind our surface dishonesty. Our children will then come to respect mythology as a symbolic representation of some of the most important constructs in our meaning systems. In a sense, these myths are like Kierkegaard's dialectical deception: in deceiving, they seek to reveal deeper truths about our belief systems.

In sum, every exception to the principle of honesty relies on the justification that the act will in the long run promote better consequences for the full communicative system as long as the communicators involved accept responsibility for their actions. Deception is not justified for personal advantage at the expense of the larger communicative system. Deception is justified when the social system has become perverted to the point where it opposes its true telos of nurturing its constitutive systems. It is justified in the short term under careful constraints as a means of adjusting malformed cognitive systems so that they will be more open to growth and adaptation. Apparent deception is justified when the message serves an honest function at another level beyond the transmission of information. Finally mythic deception is justified when it leads to an appreciation of the myth as honestly symbolizing a deeper meaning. But in each exception, the communicator must accept responsibility for the damage caused by the deception and seek to repair it. I am not saying that the end justifies the means. In practice, such rationalization serves to avoid responsibility for all of the consequences of the means used by privileging one consequence and ignoring others. Instead, communicative phronēsis makes decisions by balancing all of the systemic consequences that can reasonably be predicted. With very few exceptions, communication must be anchored in the virtue of honesty. On rare occasions, in exercising practical wisdom communicators may discover that the consequences of deception serve the telos of both the individual and the ecosystem better than the consequences of truth-telling would. The tendency to rationalize lying for personal advantage, however, must be avoided. The virtue of honesty requires its habitual practice. Deception, which increases entropy in the system, must be rare if the system is to respond correctly to its environment.

Others might disagree, of course, with my assessment of each of these particular types of deception. The purpose of the ecological model is not to eliminate disagreement but to provide grounds for argument about disagreements. In other words, I hope to enable proponents of many differing perspectives to present their arguments in a common framework that relates the continuing pursuit of good by the individual to the dynamic balance of the ecosystem. In this way, moral argument itself will be a source of information for the individual and the various levels of social systems. By this process we increase both the essential depth and the informed depth of honesty as a fuzzy concept made determinate in actual practice.

Ecological Openness

Richard Rorty affirms the need for tolerance as a tenet of "postmodernist bourgeois liberalism."[60] He then argues that such tenets can be justified only ethnocentrically. We happen to belong to a society that believes in such tenets, so we believe in them for solidarity's sake. As I have argued earlier, this privileging of communal solidarity has typified fascism more than it has liberal democracy. On the other hand, Rorty is right in the sense that the arguments we make on behalf of tolerance will necessarily reflect our ethnos because that is our universe of discourse, or semiotic encyclopedia. From the perspectives of Peirce and MacIntyre on inquiry that we discussed in the last chapter, however, the assertion that openness is a virtue of communicative ecosystems makes a stronger claim than Rorty allows. I am saying that the virtue of openness is a Thirdness that over the long run is beneficial for any communicative ecosystem, whether or not its members agree. Without openness to challenge, a system cannot be rational. Without openness to the condition of its environment and its parts, a system cannot survive. Ecologically, openness, like honesty, is necessary to the proper functioning of any ecosystem. Attempts to close what must be an open system are doomed to failure.

Honesty was a virtue in most ancient ethical codes. Tolerance, on the other hand, seems to have been less universally accepted as a virtue. As a tenet of bourgeois liberalism, tolerance is indebted to the Enlightenment philosophy of human nature. Enlightenment philosophy presumed that atomistic individuals were born with natural rights, given by a deistic or theistic Creator. Locke described the myth of a natural state of humans, "that is, a state of perfect freedom to order their actions, and dispose of their possessions and persons, as they think fit, within the bounds of the law of nature, without asking leave, or depending upon the will of any other man. A state also of equality, wherein all power and jurisdiction is reciprocal, no one having more than another."[61] In Rousseau's well-known formulation, "Man is born free, and everywhere he is in chains."[62]

The American Declaration of Independence is a classical expression of the Enlightenment philosophy of human rights. The truths that the Declaration takes to be "self-evident" certainly were not evident to most of humanity for most of its history. The claim of self-evidence is simply a begging of the most difficult question by asserting the a priori nature of human rights. The Declaration, for example, appeals to a supernatural source to justify an a priori concept of human equality that contradicts the empirical observation of inequality throughout human society. If all humans are created equal, why are they never found to be equal? The problem is: how does one justify the undoubtedly beneficial practice of treating all individuals *as if* they were equal without begging the question by asserting in the face of opposing evidence that they *are* equal?[63]

From the ecological point of view, equality is the result of not asserting a priori grounds. Having rejected the metaphysical hierarchy of Aristotle, we cannot on a priori grounds justify the claim that any one individual's native abilities or chosen pursuit of the good is worth more than another's. The difference in worth must be observed a posteriori when it becomes apparent that one pursuit better serves the telos of the ecosystem to support all of the individual quests for the good. We cannot claim a priori, for example, that people with a high IQ are worth more than people with a low IQ. IQ is a measurement of one type of intelligence. The fact that there are other types is evident from the constructs "street-smarts" or "horse-sense." Depending on the current state of a system and its environment, IQ may or may not be of greater worth to the system's ability to support its members. All that can be established on a priori grounds is that we cannot predict which shall be of the greater worth. Therefore, on a priori grounds we must treat all individuals as if they were of equal worth. Having taken a process view of potential, we cannot assume that any given state of relative worth is a final state. The question of relative worth must always remain open.

Because we cannot know ahead of time what qualities will enhance the system, openness as a social policy supports a system's ability to adapt to changes. Decreased openness results in a more tightly coupled system. Because divergent views are suppressed, less information is available to the system. As a result, the system is less able to survive changes in the environment or in its constituent parts. If a tightly coupled system were well adapted to its ecosystem and internal systems and there were no change in those systems, however, a tightly coupled system would operate more efficiently than a loosely coupled system. While hypothetically possible, such nearly closed systems are not part of our experience. From an ecological perspective, change is inevitable in a world made up of open systems in constant interaction. Because the full effect of changes cannot be predicted, the social system would do well to allow the largest variety of opinions, no matter how ill adapted some opinions seem in light of present circumstances. A sacrifice in short-term efficiency is the price paid for long-term effectiveness in a loosely coupled system.

The same holds true for the individual. The virtue of openness in a communicative system is the virtue of tolerance in an individual. No individual can predict the direction that his or her pursuit of the good may take. Therefore one does well to tolerate opinions with which one disagrees and to include them in one's deliberation. The information contained in those opinions may at some time turn out to be the solution to a vexing problem. The experience of problem-solving groups shows that apparently absurd opinions often provide the seeds for effective solutions. Furthermore, the suppression of contrary opinions requires the exercise of power. The distribution of power will not necessarily remain the same. If we establish the precedent of suppressing other opinions when we hold power and then lose that power, we are likely to find that our own ability to pursue the good will be hindered by those who have taken power. The history of religious persecution bears witness to the propensity for power relationships and the subsequent cycle of persecution to reverse. An act of persecution retained in the memory of a system festers and diminishes that system's ability to support the pursuit of the good by all of its members—witness the "troubles" in Northern Ireland.

Although we have no a priori warrant to judge any idea or person of greater or lesser value than others, in practice we do so a posteriori in the exercise of prudence. Clearly, the communication of the president of the United States on a question of state has a different weight than that of, say, the average bartender. The issue of *ethos* here is complex and fuzzy. We may, in fact, trust the bartender's honesty more; but because of the presidency's function in our social system, we consider the president's communication to be more important. Because presidential communication has greater effects throughout the ecosystem, the president also has greater ethical responsibility commensurate with those effects. The inequality must be justified by its good effects throughout the system. The divine right of kings and inherited influence make no sense within an ecological ethic. Practical wisdom tests all privilege in communication according to its value to the systemic telos of supporting all the system's members.

Certainly, this ideal of prudential testing of privilege does not reflect the present situation. Actors can parlay the ethos that they have accumulated because of their screen talents into payment for the endorsement of products about which they have no relevant expertise. A prudent audience would reject this transfer of ethos. In a capitalistic society, inherited money allows one to purchase a mass media vehicle and exercise greater influence on public communication. In other societies, criteria such as party membership or high birth are taken as prima facie justification for greater communicative influence. The information needs of the system do not determine which parts are the leading parts; therefore, the system's adaptation is deformed insofar as the feedback mechanism by which it adapts is distorted. The present situation serves the purpose of short-term stability by maintaining received patterns of influence. The distorted information system, however, places the system in danger of long-term failure through malformation.

Privilege is the obverse of toleration. We need only to exercise the virtue of tolerance for those messages and communicators that we hold in low esteem and are tempted to silence. But fuzzy phronēsis insists that we also carefully weigh the manner in which we grant influence to those messages and communicators that we do esteem or on whom our social system bestows special privileges. Both in the area of tolerance and in the area of privilege the prima facie norm should be equality. Just as with the virtue of honesty, exceptions must be prudentially justified by their consequences on the ecosystem and its constituent parts.

Political or Ethical Correctness?

Openness and tolerance do not seem compatible with the concept of "political correctness," at least as it is commonly understood. Part of the problem is that the term is not just vague but is ambiguous. This ambiguity has been very useful to critics from the Right. They lump together everything they disagree with under the label of *political correctness* and then treat it as if it were a conspiracy that had taken over academia. Extremists of the Right and Left love conspiracy theories. They make enjoyable narratives. Some critical thinking would show that these theories lack narrative fidelity, however.

Let us examine the terms. *Correctness* is vague but not ambiguous. The informed depth of meaning implied by the term is indeterminate because we do not know what standards are implied. We do know, however, that it is a measurement against standards. The term *correct* normally implies a binary system of truth values and so may err by eliminating other possible truth values. This is the error recognized by common sense when *correct* is paired with *politically*. In the general American semiotic encyclopedia, *politics* suggests, at best, compromise and, at worst, sophistic deception. The pairing of *politically* and *correct* is, therefore, somewhat oxymoronic in this universe of discourse. Few people, for example, expect the outcome of political deliberation on health care to be *correct* in the binary sense.

The oxymoronic nature of political correctness was recognized by many academicians who used it facetiously. The term originally was used by the Leninist Left to recognize those who precisely followed the party line. Later, it was used ironically by some radicals to caricature other radicals for being too fanatical in their loyalty to the party line. This ironic usage was then adopted by others, who were not necessarily radical, to characterize a general position on race, gender, and class equity.[64] Irony is in-group talk, and it lays a speaker open for misinterpretation when outsiders hear it and interpret it literally. As Peirce noted, the speaker is responsible for making what is said pragmatically determinate. On the other hand, the listener has some responsibility to consider the context and if in doubt ask the speaker what she meant. For example, a student once brought a paper to me on which her professor had circled the word *man* (when both sexes were implied) and written in the margin "not p.c." Because I knew her professor well enough to know that he was not dogmatic, I interpreted it as a facetious reminder that her usage would be offensive to some readers, misinterpreted by others, and so was poor diction. Exactly the same thing could be said, of course, about his usage of the term *p.c.* He had a responsibility to be clearer, and she should have asked him what he meant.

Another sense of *political* in general usage is *partisan*, which in the American two-party system implies favoring either the Democrats or Republicans. The idea that a professor might impose such partisan views on students would naturally raise hackles. Such cases, however, are extremely rare. The more likely case of political influence occurs at higher levels of abstraction—in the political ideology inherent in the theoretical approach being taken. My critique of Aristotle's metaphysics, for example, is *political* in this sense. To ignore the ideological implications in Aristotle's writings would be just as political. An especially subtle form of political correctness involves treating the writings of great thinkers as if they were universal truths that are beyond challenge. Recently, a student complained to me that her professor would not allow discussion of feminist issues in his class. As Scott has argued, however, "while it is surely true that there are within universities—on the Left and the Right—people who would impose their ways of thinking on everyone else, they do not represent the majority and they have never gained control. One of the tricks of publicists has been to conflate serious criticism and intolerant dogmatism under the label of 'political correctness' and thereby discredit *all* critical efforts."[65] Ironically, the political Right is using the topic of political correctness to limit critical thinking in the university. The campaign against political correctness has not been a campaign for tolerance and openness in the academy but a campaign to suppress multiculturalism by association.[66] Overall, the greatest threat to openness and academic freedom is from the Right, not the Left.

On the other hand, real issues of freedom of speech have arisen because of actions by liberals and radicals. Chief among these problems is the question of how to respond to offensive speech. Here the question of *politically correct* becomes confused with the question of *ethically wise.* The term *political* would be proper if it were given its original Aristotelian sense of the art of managing communal problems so as to enable virtue and happiness. The issue is how to use one's authority to restrict offensive speech. The problem reaches beyond the academy to include corporate policies on harassment in the workplace. At some point, the ethical question merges with the legal. In the military, for example, if racist talk is conduct unbecoming an officer, then legal charges could be brought for ethical failures. Sexual harassment legal cases have increased since Anita Hill's testimony. The threat of legal action on issues of race, gender, and class often means that rigid rules are interpreted bureaucratically and then labeled *p.c.* The problem in most of these cases is a lack of phronēsis in applying the rules. The legal turn may make ethical action more difficult. Fear of lawsuits often has this result.

Offensiveness is a difficult question within the ecological ethic, especially considering the semiotic complexity involved. The paradigm case is not difficult. Hate speech is simply unethical because it distorts the system in many ways, affecting not just the target but others. All of us are still suffering from the hate speech against African-Americans that has poisoned our communicative ecosystem. African-Americans are hurt most; but other Americans find that their relations with African-Americans have been damaged because trust has been made more difficult. The difficult cases arise because marginalized groups have been sensitized by past cases of hate speech. The result is that communication not intended to hurt does. In these cases we should first eliminate the term *political correctness* because it confounds the problem. Then we should remember that communication is an interaction. Symbols are interpreted to stand for objects by rules of usage, and these rules of usage vary in different communities. A traditional white southern family might fly the Confederate flag because it stands for the stoic values of the old aristocracy that they wish to preserve. To an African-American the same flag might stand for racism and slavery. The problem is compounded because some southern legislatures adopted the Confederate flag as a sign of resistance to civil rights in the 1960s, and racists regularly wave it at their rallies. In this case, because racism dominates the possible interpretants of the flag, my judgment would be that it should be flown only in contexts that clearly identify it as a historical sign. On the other hand, it is unfair to attribute racist intent to anyone who flies the flag. As in the logic of vagueness, the receiver does not have the right to further determine the meaning of the sender just because the sign sent is ambiguous. Both sides of communicative interactions have ethical responsibilities to be fair to each other.

In some cases, demanding more than tolerance may be unfair. I have heard gay activists demand respect for being gay because it is part of what they are. But we don't respect heterosexuals for being heterosexual. Since some religions teach that homosexuality is sinful, the demand for respect is necessarily a denial of the other person's beliefs. The differences are irreconcilable at that level unless one or the other changes. A loosely coupled relationship for purposes of community, however, is possible if both sides exercise tolerance. We cannot be expected to respect all aspects of anybody, but we can acknowledge everyone's equal right to seek happiness in their own way even if we think that way is wrong. In short, the ecosystem should support both fundamentalists and gays in their individual quests for the good, reciprocating their support for the system. Neither should have the power to silence the other. It is not a contradiction for the ecosystem to support opposed groups as long as the system does not define the good for those groups beyond the good that is a shared communal good. The systemic virtue of openness enables the system to support such diversity.

Conclusion

Openness and honesty could together be considered parts of justice in an ecosystem. They are those aspects of justice that are most directly concerned with communication. Phronēsis is necessary for the application of justice. As we apply these virtues, we make the indeterminate pragmatically determinate. We ourselves act as signs of the ideals we enact. As Peirce wrote, "Through surrendering ourselves to ever loftier ideals, we move toward becoming agents through whom the only truly admirable ideal—the continuous growth of concrete reasonableness—can become more fully actual. Agents *through whom* the ideal is made actual are signs, since such agents perform the essential function of a sign—namely, to render inefficient relations efficient (8.332; 1904)."[67] We are signs to the systems of which we are part because we mediate the virtues to those systems. We are the additional signs by which a vague concept is rendered more determinate. The virtues exist only as ideals until we signify them concretely. The way in which we signify them will be determined within a pragmatic situation by the application of phronēsis. Because we exist in history, we ourselves as signs are determined in large part by our culture. But our possibilities and our responsibilities exceed that determination.

Practical wisdom begins with accepting responsibility for the effects of our actions. In terms of communication, practical wisdom means that we accept the fact that how and what we communicate (verbally and nonverbally) have effects throughout our social system and that we take responsibility for those effects. Responsibility in this sense is not the same as praise or blame. Praise and blame are communicative methods of reward and punishment that are used for conditioning behavior. Praiseworthy and blameworthy actions are those in which we intended or at least could reasonably have predicted the effects of our action. That is why Aristotle emphasizes the importance of showing intention in epideictic speeches of praise or blame.[68] But we are responsible for the effects we did not intend and could not have been expected to predict, even though we should be neither praised nor blamed for them. If my child inadvertently spills a glass of milk, I should not blame her for it; but because she is responsible and insofar as she has the ability to respond, she should clean it up. In the past many factories may have polluted the environment unknowingly. We should not blame these factory owners for lacking knowledge that was not available to them; nevertheless, we can insist that they help correct the damage because they were responsible. In actuality, of course, such responsibility is shared throughout society. We are all responsible for what we have done to the environment, though we are not all equally to blame.

By accepting responsibility for our communicative actions, even in those cases where the damage is irreparable, we will at least become more observant of the results of those actions and better able to predict consequences in the future. Denial of responsibility enables us to continue with actions even after their destructive consequences become apparent. In that case, we become deserving of blame because the damage was caused not by our ignorance but by our failure to accept responsibility. The person of practical wisdom accepts responsibility because that person is aware of the niche that he or she necessarily occupies in a communicative ecosystem. What one ought to do—what one is responsible for—is derived from one's function in the system, not from one's awareness of that function. We comprise the sign system that makes the concrete expression of justice possible; if we do not fulfill our function, we diminish the presence of justice throughout the system. Acceptance of responsibility for consequences is the result of deliberating well about our function as signs within the ecosystem as well as the consequences of an individual act or class of actions.

If we want better communities, we must accept our responsibility to mediate the ideals of justice by our habits of action that are the concrete signs of justice to others. When we enact virtue, we spread virtue throughout our community. We would not understand the virtues if others had not in their actions made the meaning of virtue determinate for us. The ontological status of virtue depends upon our epistemological function of making the meaning of virtue known to others. We must be the signs of virtue in our communities.

5

Ethics in Interpersonal Communication

These next three chapters will deal with specific levels of our communicative ecosystem. We live in various forms of community from our most intimate personal relationships all the way up to international relations. Our communication shapes every level of the ecosystem both epistemologically and ontologically. Accordingly, the possible levels of ethical analysis are myriad; but I will limit my discussion to the levels of interpersonal relations, organizational communication, and political communication. The significance of these levels is shown by the fact that they are traditional areas of research within the field of communication. That history of research has advantages and disadvantages for our own discussion of ethical problems. The chief advantage is that much is known about specific research problems within each area. The chief disadvantage is that most of this knowledge is disconnected from other areas and from ethical concerns. Because each level has been isolated for purposes of analysis, the interconnection and mutual influence between the levels have been neglected. Methodological limitations and differences have made an ecological viewpoint difficult to achieve.

This situation is changing, thanks in part to Foucault's argument that power is distributed throughout society and to the development of new areas of research, such as women's studies, African and diaspora studies, and cultural studies, which have cut across the traditional areas of research. On the other hand, these new approaches have often suffered from postmodernism's cynicism about ethics and have tended to reduce ethical concerns to issues of mere power. Power is, of course, important. But if the ethical ground is surrendered, then the reasons for redistributing power are lost. If, for example, it were true that white males in America held inordinate amounts of power in various levels of the ecosystem and if it were also true that ethics was meaningless, then wouldn't it be foolish for white males to give up their power? Under those conditions white males would be wiser to use their power to gain more power, since power is all that matters. If, however, as I have argued, we are all obliged to improve the ecosystem's ability to support all of its parts, then white males have an ethical obligation to share power. I take that ecological obligation to be real in Peirce's sense; it exists whether or not we are aware of it. The kind of real being that ecological obligation has is the being of a counterfactual possibility—what *would be if* we understood our transcendental relations. My purpose in these remaining chapters is to consider how that real ethical principle can inform our judgment and so be made concrete in the various levels of the communicative ecosystem.

This chapter will look at interpersonal communication from the perspective I have been calling *rhetorical*. By *rhetoric* I mean that aspect of communication that affects the ecosystem by its effect on the participants. From this perspective, I must agree with those feminists who have said the personal is political. Interpersonal communication has effects on many levels of the ecosystem, not just on that particular couple or small group. The personal is not merely political, however. Individuals also seek their individual goods and the good of their relationship through interpersonal communication. Violating the rules of the larger community is one way couples can intensify their own relationship. As long as those violations remain private, they do not damage the stability of the larger community. Privacy is an important means of maintaining diversity within community. Couples, groups, and families should be free to develop diverse models of relationship as long as these models enable all of the members of the relationship to seek the good in their own way. Nevertheless, these models should also take into account the effects of actions at various levels of the ecosystem.

Ecological Considerations of Competence

Many people outside the field of communication assume that the sole function of a department of communication is to teach competence in communication. There is some truth to this assumption in the same sense that history departments teach competence in history, political science departments teach competence in politics, and psychology departments teach competence in mentality. Communication is an important phenomenon of human life; knowing more about that phenomenon should enable one to increase one's competence in living well. In addition to this general competence, however, some areas of communication focus on improving specific performance, such as public speaking. This Aristotelian approach focuses on communication as a *tekhnē*, that is, a productive art governed by rules. One could argue that the function of all the scientific aspects of the study of communication are ultimately subordinate to this *technical* function of improving communicative practice in the long run. In making this argument, however, one should not then presume that scientists must justify every study by its potential for technical application. The practice of science has its own virtues as well. Nevertheless, the field of communication has a strong technical tradition and so has created expectations that it can improve communicative competence.

Behavioral scientists may question the whole concept of competence, preferring to collapse competence into performance. Admittedly, competence can be measured only by performance. The concept of competence, however, is necessary to connect the scientific study of communication with its practical outcomes. A behavioral scientist may discover, for example, that a moderately firm handshake is more effective in creating a first impression in an interview than a weak handshake or an overly strong handshake. This general rule will most likely be included in textbooks on interviewing so that students can improve their interviewing techniques. A student who learns this general rule has knowledge that she may not have had before. Such knowledge increases her potential to behave effectively in an interview. In the future, she will know what response is called for in this situation. This knowledge alone, however, will not suffice. She must also develop the ability to give a firm, but not too firm, handshake, which may require practice. After practicing, she has increased her competence in interviewing even if she has not yet performed an actual interview. Her increased competence will have practical consequences apart from the specific performance of shaking hands: for example, it may make her less reticent at interviewing because she feels more confident. The construct of competence allows us to distinguish different aspects of the habit patterns necessary if the behavior is to be both effective and regular, not random luck. A particular performance considered as action-reaction is Secondness, but competence is Thirdness. By converting observations of behavior to rules of Thirdness, the scientist—even the behavioral scientist—influences future behavior by changing people's competence.

If competence were merely a nominalistic construct, then communicative skills could not be taught, and the only purpose of communication research would be the self-satisfaction of the researchers. The happiness of researchers is certainly a good; but we would then have to conceptualize the research establishment as an exceptionally expensive welfare system for behavioral scientists. On the other hand, if we conceptualize the research establishment as a public investment, then we should believe that communicative competence is a reality worth investing in because of its effect on communicative behavior. As Cooley and Roach argued, "A theory that separates competence and performance and states the relationship between the two supplies a way to explain human behavior."[1] Insofar as this explanation is true, it provides a way to change human behavior, to teach an art of communication.

Aristotle recognized that an art (tekhnē) of rhetoric must reduce the manifold of common experience to a unity of rules for practice. Such is the function of theory within art.[2] Without theory, art is mere knack arising from experience (empeiria) because it is unable to explain its own workings.[3] Furthermore, for Aristotle the art comprises the theory, not the performance. His stipulative definition of the art of rhetoric is that it is the faculty of observing the possible means of persuasion in any particular case.[4] What I have translated as *faculty* (in the neo-Aristotelian tradition) is the word *dunamis*, which, as we saw, was Aristotle's key concept of potential in the potential-actuality pair. In this case, the potential is a learned potential that allows one to observe (*theōrēsai*) possibilities that one would not see otherwise. The act of observation is seeing with the mind's eye; so the product of the art of rhetoric is the mental act of grasping a particular case with the appropriate general principles. Aristotle's metaphysical hierarchy shows again in his privileging of the mental action over the actual physical performance. He gives short shrift to delivery (literally, the hypocritical art) in his discussion of style, which in general is required only because of the corruption of the audience.[5] To be sufficiently general, the theory must encompass these distasteful problems of dealing with corrupt audiences, as seen from the aristocratic point of view. In the ideal community run by true aristocrats or a superior monarch, one would not have to put these principles into practice; however, in the real world of mixed democracy, the aristocrats are responsible for using rhetoric to ensure that truth and justice prevail.[6] Even so, Aristotle does not go as far as to recommend practicing rhetoric. As in his ethics, he assumes that this rhetorical dunamis will necessarily actualize itself in the situation. Competence in this approach amounts to theoretical grasp of the general principles of rhetoric and takes for granted a correlative grasp of the general principles of ethics and politics to which it is closely related.[7]

A contrasting, more pragmatic tradition developed out of the school of Isocrates. Isocrates argued that natural ability (dunamis in the sense of personality traits) is the most important factor in communicative competence and practical experience (empeiria) is second. Theoretical knowledge is a distant third but important because it is the only factor that can be gained through education (paideia).[8] Although his notion of natural ability is simplistic in treating dunamis as fixed rather than developmental, his hierarchy is reasonable for a particular moment in that development. A student who has not developed her ability through prior practice cannot suddenly become competent in communication by taking a college course. She can, however, improve if she uses the knowledge she gains to develop her abilities further through practice. Isocrates also taught that rhetoric should be a force for good in the community, not merely a means of private gain.[9] Both Isocrates and Aristotle recognized that communication was the ontological foundation of community and its virtues.[10] One would expect rhetorical competence to include a consideration of the good of the community and the virtues of communication if it were true to either Aristotle or Isocrates.

Unfortunately, under the influence of the nominalistic individualism of the Enlightenment, the neo-Aristotelian tradition left behind the community framework inherent in the Greek tradition to focus on the rhetor's ability to work his will. This rhetor-centered approach led to such oxymorons as considering a community destroyer like Hitler to be a good rhetor. Whatever accomplished the rhetor's purpose was taken to be good rhetoric, regardless of its consequences for the ecosystem as a whole. At best, the neo-Aristotelian approach subsumed the values issue under the character of the rhetor, choosing as models the "great men" like Lincoln who could be treated as true aristocrats with noble purposes. At worst, this rhetor-centered approach blinded itself to the value implications of reducing the criteria of rhetorical practice to mere effectiveness in achieving the rhetor's purpose. If pedagogy follows this idea of competence, then the neo-Aristotelian teaches that whatever works is good rhetoric.

The area of interpersonal communication developed within this atmosphere of rhetor-centered studies in communication even though the methodology of interpersonal communication was often opposed to the methodology of rhetorical analyses. Spitzberg and Cupach's influential work on interpersonal competence acknowledges that "the study of effective interpersonal behavior has its roots in the discipline of rhetoric."[11] The classical emphasis on persuasion that had lost its communal context was transformed into an interpersonal concept of control. This subject-centered approach to interpersonal competence is well illustrated by Parks's conception of communicative competence: "Communicative competence represents the degree to which individuals perceive they have satisfied their goals in a given social situation without jeopardizing their ability or opportunity to pursue their other subjectively more important goals."[12] Consequences to others and to the ecosystem are reduced to their impression on the individual. This model of competence is solipsistic; it ought to be called a model of *intra*personal competence. All that matters is that one feel satisfied with one's performance. What this statement means is that one has at least temporarily resolved conflicts within oneself as a system. This sense of satisfaction says nothing about what has occurred in the interpersonal system.

Parks actually uses a systemic analysis of the lower levels of system. He considers how various levels of control are necessary from basic muscular control up to idealized self-concepts.[13] His systemic analysis, however, goes no further. Even though interpersonal communication by definition involves a system of more than one person, Parks does not extend his level of analysis to the relationship level, much less to higher social levels. Perhaps it is a problem of method; he has constructed a concept of competence that allows him to rely on self-reports. Examining control operating at higher levels of system is not easily done with traditional forms of empiricism. The method seems bound to the form of Enlightenment nominalism that treats only individuals as real.

Parks admits that individual judgments of the behavior of others are "riddled with shortcomings":

Among the biases we routinely bring to the attribution process are tendencies to give more weight to information that is vivid, concrete, or readily available; to treat a very small amount of information as if it were highly representative; to search only for information that confirms our preconceptions; to distort or ignore information that violates our expectations; and to overestimate the consistency and constancy of others' behavior. Our efforts to understand behavior are also biased by tendencies to rely on a priori ideas of what types of causes ought to go with certain types of effects, to prefer simple explanations over complex ones, to prefer explanations that easily present themselves, to underestimate situational influences on others' behavior and to prefer instead internal or dispositional causes for their behavior, to undervalue information about how a person's behavior compares to others' behavior in the same situation, and to treat genuinely irrelevant information as if it were relevant.[14]

Despite these shortcomings in judging the behavior of others, Parks assumes we are well qualified to judge our own competence in communication. This could only be true if the behavior of others were irrelevant to our relational satisfaction and if we had some special method, perhaps Cartesian introspection, that keeps us from making the same errors in judging own behavior.

It seems as though an abusive relationship could demonstrate competence under Parks's conceptualization. Suppose a man had been trained in the cultural a priori that women were inferior at reasoning. He would tend to interpret her behavior according to that prejudgment. Let us also suppose that whenever she dared to question his decisions he verbally abused her, destroying her self-esteem until she no longer argued with him but was docile and obedient. This behavior on her part fit his expectations of a well-trained wife. If you asked him whether he was competent in this relationship, the man might very well respond that he was. He is not suffering any internal dissonance over his communication; so, according to Parks, he is competent. Even if, as an observer, you suspected that she was building up resentment toward him that was going to explode someday, you would still rate him as competent. She, apparently, is the only one who is incompetent because she is suffering the dissonance. Under Parks's concept of competence, for a given state of communication, the more perceptive one is, the more incompetent one is likely to be. Ignorance of the long-term consequences is not just bliss but competence because it does not interfere with one's satisfaction.

Parks would like foresight to be an aspect of competence, but that inclusion undoes his whole system because foresight is not internal and subjective. Foresight is prediction of reality. It can be evaluated by subsequent occurrences; or, possibly, it can be compared at the time to the known probability of those occurrences by an expert observer. In either case, the evaluation is based on public information, not introspection. In the hypothetical case of the abusive husband, the observer knows that the husband's lack of foresight renders him incompetent, but Parks's conceptualization of competence does not allow the observer to make that judgment. He objects to the use of social appropriateness as an additional criterion that limits control because it relies on observers' judgments of competence. Parks would subsume social appropriateness under self-interest as a means and product of personal control.[15] Something like the invisible hand of the marketplace must be the source of fairness in interpersonal transactions as individuals pursue their own self-interest through methods of control. "Antisocial behavior probably results more often from the inability of individuals to satisfy personal goals than from overzealous and unprincipled control attempts."[16] Apparently we ought to label the hypothetical case of the abusive husband the case of the incompetent wife. Parks's theory is simply the atomistic individualism of the Enlightenment with a touch of social Darwinism applied to interpersonal competence. From an ecological perspective, this type of theory carries the worst aspects of the neo-Aristotelian rhetorical tradition into interpersonal communication. Pedagogy based on it would be totally rhetor-centered, lacking the communal concerns found in the classical theories of Aristotle and Isocrates.

Spitzberg and Cupach attempt to synthesize approaches from rhetoric, psychiatry, marital relations, and interpersonal communication into a concept of "relational competence." Their approach also integrates the Isocratean factors of ability (traits, such as cognitive complexity) and practice (behavioral social skills) into the theoretical model. Pedagogically, these personal factors translate into knowledge, motivation, and skill training, in each case coupled with situational analysis. Contrary to Parks, Spitzberg and Cupach emphasize the interdependence of communicative interaction. "This inherent interdependence leads to the premise that a person can be interpersonally competent *only* in the context of a relationship." It follows that "competent communication is considered a coordinated process in which individuals achieve goals in a prosocial fashion."[17] Spitzberg and Cupach's model of relational competence thus includes both appropriateness and effectiveness.

The problem with Spitzberg and Cupach's approach is that they also ultimately bog down in dyadic nominalism. They assume that appropriateness and effectiveness are merely "perceptual phenomena" that are "susceptible to change over time."[18] This claim refers to the fact not that our habits in a relationship may change and become better or worse but that the appropriateness or effectiveness of a past act changes with our changing interpretation of it. In other words, if your romantic partner were to send you a Valentine gift, say a box of candy, that you interpreted as appropriate, your partner's behavior was appropriate. If later you find out that a friend received a better gift from a lover, you might change your mind about the gift you received. Now you interpret your partner's gift as inappropriate. Therefore, your partner's behavior was inappropriate. According to Spitzberg and Cupach, the quality of your partner's behavior actually changed when your judgment of it changed. Competence, then, is not a reality determining actions that affect relationships: "it is an impression that a person has of self or other. This impression is based on the behavioral minutae [sic] of a given episode and the history of the relationship that contextualizes the behavioral choreography enacted within it. Competence is not enduring; it is ever-changing."[19]

This is dyadic nominalism because it collapses the object signified into its interpretant. Spitzberg and Cupach's nominalism is illustrated by their confusion of "the locus of measurement issue" with competence itself.[20] Competence is an ability, which is a poten-

tial. Considered semiotically, this potential determines performance, which is interpreted to stand for that potential. A misinterpretation of performance does not change the potential that determined
the performance. Recently, for example, I called for assistance to
jump-start my car because I thought the battery was dead. I had tried
to start the car and failed. Taking that performance as a sign of the
potential in the battery, I interpreted the battery as having very low
voltage. When the mechanic arrived, he proved me wrong. The battery measured twelve volts on a voltmeter. The negative ground was
loose, and the potential could not be actualized to the starter. Once
the connection was tightened, the battery started the car with no
problem.

Notice the difference in my triadic explanation of the battery's potential. I acknowledged that I was *wrong*. I had misinterpreted the
battery's potential by limiting myself to one obvious measure and
not the many other interpretants implied in the concept. My misinterpretation resulted in a semiotic object—low voltage—that was not
the same as the physical object (Peirce's dynamic object)—sufficient
voltage. The potential in the battery did not change because of my
interpretation. Once I acknowledged that I was wrong, I was motivated to correct the actual problem. If we reconsider the hypothetical
case of the Valentine gift triadically, we can see the same sort of error.
Your changing interpretations of your partner's performance do not
affect the physical object, your partner's competence. If you recognize that fact, you are more likely to see that the problem could lie in
your interpretation, and you are thus more likely to be motivated to
correct your own habits of interpretation. The failure of my car to
start resulted from my incompetence in interpretation, but I learned
from the experience and became more competent. A triadic interpretation allows us to recognize errors and improve our competence and
subsequently our performance.

I am not saying that interpretation depends only upon the competence of the interpreter. If your lover had sent you a drain auger for a
Valentine's gift, you could reasonably interpret it as a sign of incompetence in most circumstances. Interpersonal competence requires
some empathy. Those of us who appreciate tools as gifts have to learn
that others expect gifts to symbolize the relationship more directly.
As we learn, our habits change, and our competence improves. Although personality traits may be involved, competence is not fixed.
Not only do we learn new habits, but the relationship and its environment changes. What is appropriate and effective at one stage of a
relationship may not be at other stages. Different kinds of relationships function differently both in nurturing individuals and in the
niches they fill in the larger ecosystem. The same relationship in dif-

ferent stages also functions differently. Although the question of appropriate behavior is necessary for an ecological conception of competence, no particular kind or stage of relationship is appropriate per se. Therefore, no fixed sets of ethical rules will suffice other than as general guidelines to be applied with fuzzy logic.

Although Spitzberg and Cupach's approach is clearly preferable to Parks's rugged individualism because it raises the question of competence to the level of the relationship, it falls short of ecological competence because of its ultimate dependence on nominalistic individualism. It falls into the category of approaches that, as Deetz points out, "lead to an unnecessary tension between effectiveness and ethics where effectiveness is the positive force of influence and personal expression and ethics is the negative bridle keeping the individual within socially appropriate bounds."[21] Deetz takes a more ecological perspective on the relation of competence and ethics by raising the issue to the level of the ecosystem, noting that "individual behaviors take on meaning from their system function rather than from the speaker's intent or external social conventions." Individuals in a relationship may act reasonably and still participate in an unethical system. "From such a view, it is not the actions, decisions, or even reasons for decisions that can be ethical, but the system of interaction in which they have a place. Such a view does not eliminate personal responsibility but focuses it on the development and maintenance of relational systems rather than individual actions or attitudes."[22] Deetz has swung the pendulum to the other side, understandably so, considering the individualistic orientation of the discipline. Nevertheless, an ecological ethic must also consider the individual's life narrative and not discard the importance of the individual. The individual is the site where much ethical deliberation and action occurs. It is those "individual actions or attitudes" that make possible "the development and maintenance of relational systems." Some tension between the desires of the individual and the needs of the relationship is inevitable. In learning to be ethical, we will have to make some sacrifices, at least in the short run. In the long run, however, as we perceive ecological virtues as excellences of our own practice, they will enrich the quality of our own life narratives. Part of their value will be their cost.

Despite some differences with the ecological ethic, Deetz's model is a significant advance on prior theories. First, it recognizes that competence cannot be separated from ethics. All theories of competence have ethical implications. Effectiveness simply means that something has a desired effect. What desires should be included in our model of effectiveness is a value decision. Some theories avoid the issue, belittling the ethical component of competence. Others view the ethical component as a constraint. Deetz points out, however, that if we move our focus from the individual to the interaction, we will see that the interaction produces values for its participants. Through interaction, individual interests are transformed by their coordination with others' interests. Deetz presents a true systemic view in which the whole is not simply the sum of its parts but is the product of the interaction of its parts. This approach stands in stark contrast to those that take a transmission theory of meaning in interaction. Powers and Lowry's Basic Communication Fidelity (BCF) model of competence, for example, reduces competence to the successful transmission of a cognition from one person to another so that the received cognition is congruent with the original cognition even if that was erroneous.[23] While there are situations in which fidelity is important, they are not the norm for relational interaction; instead, they are normally relationships of inequality in which fidelity for the subaltern requires performing correctly the desires of the superior. While some individuals may presume that a relationship of inequality exists, the very presumption has ethical implications. Deetz's model, on the other hand, is more compatible with the model of fuzzy phronēsis discussed in the last chapter.

The controller in fuzzy logic makes a decision based on a center of gravity derived from inputs from all parts of the system. Notice that the control takes place at the level of the system, not at the level of individuals within the system. The effectiveness of control depends upon how well the controller integrates the various inputs. Relational interactions occur similarly. A new resolution is achieved through interaction. That resolution is a decision made by the relational system, not by any individual. Compare Deetz's discussion of the "ethical force" of argument:

The making of an argument can function to give voice to a position being left out, can reveal aspects of the subject matter being hidden or overlooked, can force an opinion over others, or can lead the group to respond to an image rather than that which the image is of. In the former two cases it has an ethical force and in the later two an unethical one. The systemic function rather than what was wished to be accomplished is the key issue. The ethical "knowledge" proposed is a kind of critical insight or *phronesis* in Aristotle's sense of practical wisdom born of experience and cultivated in relation with others. . . . This contrasts with a kind of knowledge which can be possessed by an individual or taught as a list of standards.[24]

Just as Peirce's model of inquiry occurs at the level of community, Deetz's model of understanding occurs at the level of the relational system. Just as Peirce warned us not to block the way of inquiry, Deetz warns us not to block genuine conversation.

Blocking genuine conversation has the same effect at the interpersonal level as ideology does at the level of society. Ideology blocks the way of inquiry by not allowing certain beliefs and values to be included. "Unethical interpersonal communication systems perpetuate interpersonal ideologies and limit the ability to engage in genuine conversation."[25] The language we use, for example, has its ideological biases that infect our conversations with unexamined sexist and racist assumptions. We may also "freeze" our images of each other instead of recognizing, as Peirce did, that we are living symbols, developing and changing. This frozen stereotyping is a product of the interaction when "the response of each participant is interpreted within the context of the image which is not (can not) be discussed." In addition to linguistic and imagistic blockage, Deetz lists five practices that are often unethical and hence incompetent in conversation: disqualification, naturalization, neutralization, topical avoidance, subjectification of experience, and meaning denial.

Disqualification is the opposing vice to the ecological virtue of openness. "Statements such as, 'You're saying that because you are a woman [manager, lover, angry . . .],' function within certain systems to exclude the expressed view from the discussion. Such an activity skews the development of mutual understanding." On the other hand, we often overvalue claims of expertise instead of recognizing that ethos is part of the rhetorical process and open to argument. Naturalization, as Deetz uses the term, seems to be the process of essentializing, in which "one view of the subject matter is frozen as the way the thing is" so that "the object created stops discussion on the ethical dimensions of its creation."[26] In terms of Peirce's logic of vagueness, naturalization is the failure to recognize the indeterminacy of symbols. In Peirce's logic, the essential depth and breadth of a term may always be changed by new information. Actual determinacy is pragmatic and produced in a particular interaction. Although the speaker has the right to interpret further what she means, the communal, public meaning is determined in the interactive semiotic process. The "true" definition of a term, that is, its essential information, could be known only at the end of inquiry. Naturalization aborts that inquiry.

Neutralization is the act of suppressing the value implications of positions taken. "Presumed 'objective' claims hide both the activities that produced the claim and the values carried with them." In a conversation on household management, for example, a husband might assert as a fact that he contributes more economically because he brings home the larger paycheck. This supposed fact neglects the economic value of women's work inside and outside the home. It assumes that the method of monetary compensation accurately reflects the economic contribution of labor. By asserting his claim as a neutral fact, the husband closes inquiry into the values underlying it. Neutralization subtly blocks inquiry; topical avoidance is more obvious. Every communicative system has its taboos. In fact, the criterion of social appropriateness in traditional theories of competence is in part a measure of compliance with taboos. In contrast, considered ecologically, compliance with taboos may at times reflect incompetence at the relational level. Many couples are unable to resolve problems of sexual intimacy because of communicative taboos. Deetz argues that social prohibitions "often preclude a discussion of the values which define propriety and order and the benefits to certain groups from those values."[27] Topical avoidance, combined with the other practices mentioned, can be a way of muting marginalized groups. Even dominant groups, however, may be muted by taboos. Men are muted in their ability to express feelings and other aspects of their "feminine" side. On behalf of propriety and often to avoid conflict, topical avoidance distorts communication by limiting what can be discussed. True interpersonal competence would find ways of incorporating all relevant issues and would deal with conflict instead of hiding it. Appropriateness of time and place is a factor in competence, but blind adherence to taboos is not.

Subjectification of experience is a relativist tactic of closure. "Private decisionalism and relativism appear open to others but usually function to preclude questioning of normal routines and assure closure of experience." When we say, "Well, that's just a matter of opinion," we are signaling a close to the discussion. De gustibus non est disputandum. As Deetz points out, however, "[T]he difference between opinions represents the opportunity to escape from self-blinders and indicates that more is to be learned about the issue. In fact, it represents a major reason to seriously talk at all." From the semiotic perspective of pragmatic realism, signs represent something. Opinions are fallible, but they are attempts to organize real semiotic experiences; therefore, they are necessary inputs into that fuzzy phronēsis operating at the level of the interpersonal system. We cannot operate ecologically without knowledge about our ecosystem. From his own perspective, Deetz warns, "When meaning is personalized, difference of opinion can only be resolved in power politics."[28]

Meaning denial is a traditional political tactic that we regularly criticize in our politicians but then employ ourselves in our relationships. It is the exploitation of vagueness or ambiguity to maintain deniability. An example would be my saying to my partner, "Do what you want; don't worry about me," in a tone of voice that implied she ought to worry about me. The meaning is ambiguous and leaves her in a double bind because the ambiguities are contradictory. An example Deetz offers is inappropriate sexual innuendo in the workplace, which exploits vagueness for the sake of deniability. In both cases, "the effect is to shift meaning production to the listener, thus enabling the speaker control without responsibility and precluding the critical examination of what was said (because it was not said)."[29] In discussing Peirce's logic of vagueness in the preceding chapter, I pointed out the speaker's responsibility to reduce the latitude of interpretation sufficiently within a given situation. I also argued that deconstruction usurps the speaker's responsibility. In the case where the speaker may be exploiting indeterminacy, however, deconstruction is an ethical response by the listener. In this case, deconstruction serves to return the level of control to the interpersonal system when the speaker has sought to make the control individualistic and thus tyrannical.

To correct these ecological vices of interpersonal communication, Deetz suggests that we develop competency in three areas: metacommunication, rhetoric, and strategy. Metacommunication in Deetz's use is actually analysis of argument. He calls it "a type of social therapeutic deconstruction," but it is not Derrida's type of deconstruction. He recommends discourse about the cause of blockage and analysis of the warrants used and, if necessary, of the backing for those warrants. This approach would require some sophistication in argumentation. In associating skill in argumentation with interpersonal competence, Deetz is tangentially supported by the empirical studies of Infante on argumentativeness and verbal aggression. In Infante's conceptualization, argumentativeness is a subset of assertiveness, whereas verbal aggression is a subset of hostility. Argument attacks issues or positions, but verbal aggression attacks the self-concept of the other. Significantly, those who are highly argumentative are not as easily provoked into using verbal aggression. In fact, verbal aggression can be the result of an argumentative skill deficiency.[30] Infante's findings support the principle of argumentative skill as an element of interpersonal competence. We should note, however, that the connotation of "attack" found in Infante's concept of argument is the result of the underlying ideology of atomistic individualism in his approach. As Deetz pointed out, argument functions both cooperatively and uncooperatively at the level of the interpersonal system. Both approaches, however, imply that training in argument could improve interpersonal communication.

In the real world, understanding of argument is lacking, so Deetz suggests that rhetoric may be necessary. His definition of rhetoric is related to what I have given here, but he emphasizes the subversive aspect of rhetoric. I agree with him that "the rhetorical dimension of interaction, private or public, is the politics of the interaction" if by *politics* he means the influence on various levels of system within the ecosystem. Rhetoric shapes community at all levels. In my definition, however, rhetoric can support stability as well as change; it is not necessarily subversive in its overall effect.[31] Nevertheless, Deetz's point is well made that rhetoric provides the potential to open up closure. He calls for a reinterpretation of Hart and Burks's concept of rhetorical sensitivity to incorporate "the interpenetration of self and other."[32] I would treat rhetorical sensitivity more broadly as an acceptance of responsibility for the systemic consequences of communication. Rhetorical sensitivity is thus ecological sensitivity, which can and should be manifest at the level of interpersonal communication as well as at other levels.

But what shall we do if reason and rhetoric fail? Deetz suggests that under those circumstances, "strategy may be necessary to develop systems of interaction in which genuine conversation is possible." Deetz admits that his concept of *strategy* is vague and needs further work, but it seems to connote its origins in war. Subversion has been stepped up to outright conflict in various forms of disruption. Deetz is right. Under extreme circumstances, even a revolution may be the correct ethical choice, but "ethically, strategy cannot be supported in the advocacy of one's own position whether that position is about some issue or the very nature of the relationship desired with the other person."[33] If by this statement Deetz means that we should not resort to radical actions merely because we did not get our way, he is correct. But if he means that we must tolerate systems that do not allow us to develop our own life narrative in an ecologically ethical manner, he is wrong. We can take strategic action in our own interest. Breaking up a relationship that unfairly constrains us and does not yield to reason or rhetoric is an eminently ethical act under most circumstances. An ecological approach concerns itself with the intrapersonal system as well as the interpersonal system.

Hearing Women's Voices

Deetz's approach is certainly more ecological than the traditional approaches to interpersonal competence, but is this talk of reason, rhetoric, and strategy truly ecological? Or is it simply a masculine version of an ecological ethic that is not truly holistic? Admittedly, any discussion of the ecosystem is going to be partial; the holism can arise only through the interaction of many voices. Since more than half of the communicators in our ecosystem are women, however, we certainly need to incorporate women's voices in our analysis. Unfortunately, I can only write about a woman's perspective from my own perspective as a man. Still, if we are to develop ethical communities, we must begin the hermeneutic process of attempting to understand each other's perspective, even while admitting we can never fully understand the other. Certainly, our failure to understand should not be used to justify devaluing the other's perspective.

Kramarae has found evidence supporting muted group theory, which claims that male-dominated societies render women inarticulate in some ways: "The language of a particular culture does not serve all its speakers equally, for not all speakers contribute in an equal fashion to its formulation. Women (and members of other subordinate groups) are not as free or as able as men are to say what they wish, when and where they wish, because the words and the norms for their use have been formulated by the dominant group, men."[34] Despite what may be superior verbal ability, women report that they have difficulty expressing their experiences. Because of physical sexual differences and enculturated gender differences, women have different experiences from men, but the linguistic forms predominantly reflect male experience.

Muted group theory is readily understandable from the perspective of Peircean semiotic. Feelings and percepts are semiotic experiences of reality that may or may not be accurately reflected in language. Dyadic semiology, however, has great difficulty explaining how women could have experiences apart from language because in dyadic theory language alone determines experience. Having dropped the object from the semiotic process, dyadic semiology lacks the theoretical resources to explain distortion. On the other hand, in a triadic semiotic, the possibility of symbols as conventional signs inaccurately representing their objects is an ever-present source of fallibility. Peirce's discussion of the methods of fixing belief by tenacity, authority, and a priori argument illustrated those dangers. If men have had the authority to determine "proper" language, then deductive argument derived from that language will only reflect the partial worldview of men. The tenacity of language will reinforce that ideology. That is why critical practice requires opening the language to correction by other levels of semiosis. Although Spender treats *science, reality,* and *objectivity* as further means of male domination, she is really critiquing the authoritative method in which science becomes the new dogma.[35] This sense of science is not Peirce's notion of the communal process of learning from experience. Insofar as muted group theory is true, it serves as a scientific critique of pseudoscience that has refused to open itself to critique by experience.

All of the supposedly scientific findings based on observing males and generalizing to the whole population are scientifically flawed. Sampling is a kind of synecdoche; when the part does not adequately represent the whole, synecdochic error occurs. Synecdochic error also occurs when we use pseudogeneric terms like *man* or *he* when the object being represented could be male or female. The interpretants of these symbols are predominantly male, and so these terms continue Aristotle's synecdochic error of taking the male to represent the principle of humanity. MacKay found that both men and women interpreted *he* in generic contexts to mean *male* much more often than *either male or female*. No one interpreted *he* as *female*.[36] The continued use of pseudogeneric terms supports the contention that our language primarily represents a male perspective. Ideology is itself a kind of synecdochic error in which the interests or perspective of one group are mistaken for those of the whole. Our language and our social science have been ideological because of their accumulation of synecdochic errors. A large body of research is available as evidence.[37] A truly scientific mind would accept the critique of our commonsense sexism.

Kramarae points out that muted group theory cannot adequately explain male problems of expression. "Men are writing increasingly about their inexpressiveness and the problems they encounter when they try to find modes of speaking that can serve them in both their private life with family and friends, and their public life in which they are often encouraged by others to be competitive and relatively unconcerned with people's feelings."[38] Sattel argues, however, that male inexpressiveness is a way of maintaining power:

My argument is that one reason little boys become inexpressive is not simply because our culture expects boys to be that way—but because our culture expects little boys to grow up to hold positions of power and prestige. What better way is there to exercise power than *to make it appear* that *all* one's behavior seems to be the result of unemotional rationality. Being impersonal and inexpressive lends to one's decisions and position an apparent autonomy and "rightness."[39]

This modernist "rationality" contrasts with the concept of *phronēsis* given in the last chapter, which incorporates emotions into decisions. Men's silence about their emotions can prevent genuine conversation at the interpersonal level, substituting power for true deliberation. Sattel claims that increased expressiveness by men will not affect sexism in society because power relations must be changed. But this claim seems to neglect an insight offered by Foucault, that power is distributed throughout the discursive structures of society. The personal is political. If interpersonal communication between men and women becomes more genuine conversation, the power relations will change. Overcoming this learned incapacity will be difficult for men, however, even if they are willing to equalize power.

A major synecdochic error exists in the traditional conceptualization of ethics, as Gilligan has illustrated. Psychological studies of morality and moral development have taken a masculine perspective. According to Gilligan this perspective emphasizes the ethic of justice and neglects the ethic of care that is more common to women. "A justice perspective draws attention to problems of inequality and oppression and holds up an ideal of reciprocity and equal respect. A care perspective draws attention to problems of detachment or abandonment and holds up an ideal of attention and response to need."[40] Justice emphasizes the autonomous self dealing fairly with other autonomous selves in the Kantian tradition. The care perspective correlates with a definition of self through its connections in relationships.[41] The care perspective and its correlative definition of self were discovered by listening to women's moral voices. Studies of men and women show that the care orientation occurs much more often in women than in men.[42] Men also take the care orientation into account but they are not likely to make care the focus of their moral decision. If women had not been listened to, the care focus would not have been observed but would have been subsumed into the justice focus. By studying the care orientation, men can also learn more about the complexity of their own ethical decisions.

A truly ecological ethic of interpersonal communication must draw upon both orientations. As we saw in the discussion of transcendental relations in chapter 2, the self cannot be understood apart from its relations. On the other hand, the self is conceptualized as a singularity because the individual life narrative, while relational, is also singular. So the living symbol that is the self must be understood as both bounded and open. Our communicative ecosystems serve a nurturing function because we give and receive care. Without a care orientation in its members, the ecosystem's nurturing function will fail. On the other hand, justice is necessary in the distribution of power and goods within the system and between various levels of the ecosystem. So, for example, the principle of justice prevents us from deceiving others as a means of supporting our family. The principle of justice also requires us to share power in our interpersonal relationships and correct the problems muted group theory has revealed. Although justice and care may conflict at times, phronēsis requires us to take both into account in our decisions.

Following Gilligan, Bloom calls for a transcendent ethic that integrates both the ethic of justice and the ethic of care. She claims that such an ethic is the final stage of development of universalizing faith, illustrated by such figures as Ghandi, Mother Theresa, Martin Luther King, and Dietrich Bonhoeffer. "The result of integrating the two moral perspectives is to value the individual while, at the same time, create community and reduce divisions."[43] Bloom acknowledges that in an imperfect world a transcendent ethic will result in conflict out of which universalizing faith arises. From my ecological perspective, such faith is simply a belief in the reality of the ecosystem and our responsibilities to it. The ecological ethic provides the possibility of integration. Developing a truly ecological perspective will be difficult, however, because we have been trained to take one or the other perspective through our gender enculturation.

Gilligan and Wiggins attribute the development of both moralities to the experiences of inequality and attachment in childhood. Children learn to love those who care for them and to appeal to the love of others. Children are also aware of their own powerlessness and the need to appeal to principles of justice for their own protection. They learn moral feelings:

> Shame and guilt, love and sorrow can be traced to experiences of inequality and attachment in that shame and guilt imply falling below a standard while love and sorrow imply connection. In the individual person, however, these feelings, like the experiences themselves, intermingle. Guilt may be engendered by the inability to reciprocate love; shame as well as sorrow may be provoked by a loss of attachment or by inattention; and sorrow as well as shame and guilt can accompany the experience of oppression or injustice. These feelings define moral experience and clarify moral violation; yet the power of moral feelings coexists with the recognition that such feelings can be interpreted differently in different contexts.[44]

Ideally, the individual would find the intrapersonal center of gravity of these emotions through *phronēsis*. Because of gender differences in interpersonal interaction in childhood, however, our decisions may be distorted.

In our society, women are given most of the responsibility for nurturing children, especially infants. Therefore, the primary relationship of children of both sexes is with the mother. As Wood points out, however, the nature of the relationship is very different:

> Because mothers and daughters have a sameness that mothers and sons do not, boys and girls form distinct relationships with their mothers. Mothers tend to identify with daughters more closely than with sons, they seem to experience daughters more as part of themselves, and they encourage daughters to feel connected to them. . . . With sons, mothers are inclined to emphasize the difference between them and to encourage sons to differenti-

ate from them. Through a variety of verbal and nonverbal communications, mothers fortify identification with daughters and curb it with sons.[45]

So boys develop their gender identity by separating themselves from the relationship with their mothers. Girls find their gender identity within that relationship. Boys are thus encouraged to develop a sense of self that is autonomous and separate, while girls develop a sense of self that is connected and relational. As a result, most of us are less likely to develop a truly ecological ethic. Male gender identity is more rigid than female gender identity, so it would follow that a man is more likely to be limited in his ethical perspective.

If these theories of gender and ethical development are true, they have serious implications for the ethics of interpersonal communication, especially within families. In those families that include a father, the father must involve himself more in the nurturing of children to help those children develop an ecological perspective that includes both justice and care perspectives on ethics. This approach would encourage girls to develop a greater sense of autonomy and boys to develop a greater sense of connectedness. Again, this change will not be easy for men who lack competence in nurturing communication because of their own upbringing. Another implication is that our intrapersonal deliberation is more likely to be imbalanced than our interpersonal deliberation with members of the opposite sex. If we listen to each other with understanding, we should in general be able to achieve a better ecological balance in our decisions. Paradoxically, as women obtain more justice at all levels of our communicative ecosystem, the ethic of justice is more likely to be balanced by the ethic of care in our deliberations.

Finally, these theories should help us understand the motivation for "telling it slant" and its ethical dangers. Spender explains the phenomenon in terms of muted group theory:

> That there is a block between the generation of meaning and the expression of meaning for women is a premise which is shared by many feminists. It is the block which arises when it is necessary to 'tell it slant' so that it is expressed in the form of the patriarchal order. . . . Subversive meanings can also incur penalties. Even Copernicus, Galileo and Darwin discovered that there is not always encouragement and acceptance for those who try to introduce meanings for which there is no conceptual space in the social order, and it would be surprising if women—particularly as individuals—were to find their new meanings fostered and their efforts in generating them praised.[46]

If telling it slant is an act of deception, then it violates the ethic of justice. In the sense that male domination has made language unsuitable for women's expression, the injustice occurs at that level. On the other hand, when women use indirection to avoid penalties, they may be neglecting justice in favor of care for the relationship. If fear of detachment leads to distortion of meaning, the relationship will not adapt to the needs of both. Ironically, the ethic of care may lead to the eventual failure of the relationship because the relationship as a level of ecosystem needs accurate information to adapt and achieve long-term stability (homeorhesis).

On the other hand, indirectness is not necessarily related to powerlessness. Both Japanese men and women use indirection in saying no to avoid threatening face. The Malagasy men on Madagascar are more indirect than the women; they find the directness of women to be artless. Greek men use indirection in displaying power.[47] This technique is also common in the military where a superior officer, instead of giving a command, will express a preference. The officer is powerful enough that the preference will have the weight of a command. Natanson has explored the role played by indirection in mundane life, in rhetoric, in philosophy, and in pedagogy. All of his examples are men.[48] Telling it slant is not a purely feminine quality. As Tannen has demonstrated, "Indirectness . . . is not in itself a strategy of subordination. Rather, it can be used by either the powerful or the powerless. The interpretation of a given utterance and the likely response to it depend on the setting, on individuals' status and their relationship to each other, and also on the linguistic conventions that are ritualized in the cultural context."[49]

Although the problem is worse for subaltern groups because of their limited power, our language does not adequately represent all men's experience either. As Peirce argued, our symbols are necessarily indeterminate and must grow to represent our experiences. Indirection can be a result of the poor fit between our total experience and our linguistic resources. In that case, indirection is more honest and authentic than direct discourse. Indirection may also be a means of polite recognition of the relational aspect of the message. Depending on context, for example, the statement "You left the door open" could either mean "Close the door!" as a command from a superior or "Would you please close the door?" as a request between equals. The nonverbal aspects of the communicative act would help determine which relational interpretant is correct. In either case, the use of indirection shows an awareness of the relational aspect of the act. The problem with this indirection is that it may be used unethically to deny meaning as Deetz warned. If one used the tone of command with an equal, one could then deny it by saying, "All I said was you left the door open." In that way, the power distribution within the relationship is denied as a topic for discussion. In the same way, the use of indirection by the person with less power avoids confronting the issue of power in the relationship. As a result, the relationship will not become more just. Under an ecological ethic, the ethic of care includes care for the self and so draws upon topics of justice to maintain the overall health of the communicative ecosystem.

The ethical issues that may arise in interpersonal communication are innumerable.[50] Time, space, and my own personal limitations prevent my discussing more of them. What I have attempted to do in this chapter is show how the ecological ethic may provide an overall approach that is able to integrate the ethics of care and justice. I have also emphasized the importance of the ethical component of interpersonal competence. We cannot teach competence in communication at any level without incorporating training in ethics. Avoiding the issue of ethics simply teaches a bad ethic by implying that ethics are irrelevant to effective performance. Doing so is the equivalent of saying that a factory is effective if it produces widgets while destroying the environment. As Dewey's theory of valuation showed, we are not being more scientific by ignoring unwanted consequences of actions. Blinding ourselves to certain *effects* of communication is not the proper way to determine the meaning of *effective*. In the same way, not listening well to over half the population is not the way to improve our communicative ecosystem.

To listen well is to treat women speakers as subjects. By *subject* I mean the pragmatic, a posteriori subject that is a result of semiosis. Postmodernism has difficulty accepting a subject as anything other than a space in discourse. As Spivak points out, the antihumanists have a strategic problem in dealing with problems of subaltern consciousness because the radical intellectual must grant to the subaltern class "either that very expressive subjectivity which s/he criticizes or, instead, a total unrepresentability. . . . [I]f the Subaltern Studies group saw their own work of subject restoration as crucially strategic, they would not miss this symptomatic blank in contemporary Western anti-humanism."[51] She argues that much of subalternist analysis is grounded on an essentialist proposition "that the *nature* of woman is physical, nurturing and affective." The pragmatic position I am arguing, however, claims that the essence of the concept *caring* is related not to its breadth of extension in existing women but rather to its depth of meaning as a desirable possibility. Insofar as women in practice happen to have greater understanding of the concrete experience of caring, their explanations of caring deserve special attention. In attending to women on this and other topics, we treat them as equal subjects of discourse and undermine the discursive structures that reduce them to objects of a Foucauldian gaze.

Men and women can achieve community while respecting difference if we are willing to work at it. Spivak attacks the notion that "only the subaltern can know the subaltern, only women can know women and so on . . . for it predicates the possibility of knowledge on identity."[52] As a follower of Derrida, Spivak can base knowledge not on identity but on différance. As a follower of Peirce, I would add that interpreters are capable of perceiving a similarity of differences. So subaltern publics are better able to understand each other's experiences because they are different in similar ways from the dominant public. All of us have had subaltern experiences of some sort, however. Rhetorical invention can connect those experiences through rhetorical figures and arguments. This invention should be a product of both speaker and listener in order to strengthen the bonds of community on which our relationships depend. A neo-Isocratean approach would recognize the current state of our abilities and try to improve these rhetorical skills through education in theory and through practice. In this chapter, I have discussed the theory and its possible application. As Isocrates realized, the practice is much more important than the theory. Better practice gives greater depth to our theoretical understanding, which in turn leads to additional improvements in practice, constituting an improvement in the communicative ecosystem.

6

Organizational Ecology

Like chapter 5, with its limited study of interpersonal communication, this chapter makes no pretense of covering all the ethical issues that could arise in the context of organizational communication. Many different organizations (for example, religious, social, and therapeutic) influence both our happiness as individuals and the welfare of the larger ecosystem that supports them and us. In this chapter, however, I will focus on communication in business organizations because these are so important in contemporary life. Consider how much of a lifetime is spent earning a living. Business organizations have evolved in our society in such a way as to make them major factors in the construction of our own life narratives. In addition, some of the communicative issues involved can be extrapolated to other organizations. I cannot, of course, even cover all the ethical issues of communication in business organizations. My purpose is to stimulate thought about the ecological implications of our organizational communication by using business as a paradigm case. A great deal of research on business organizations has previously been accomplished using systemic theories. My contribution is a shift in perspective to the ethical demands of an ecological approach.

In the ecological approach, the business organization is another level of community within the overall ecosystem. We saw in the previous chapter that even a dyadic relationship between two people forms an ecological community of sorts that results in mutual obligations. The ecological obligation is to support these various levels of communal systems as they, in turn, support us in our narrative pursuit of the good. Supporting may in some cases mean transforming the system so that it is better able to nurture all of its members in their pursuit of the good. For the typical business organization, the ecological approach requires, at the very least, a radical change of perspective on the meaning and responsibilities of a business.

Traditional organizational theory has been neo-Aristotelian in the sense of being rhetor-centered. In Aristotle's theory the rhetor was aristocratic; in organizational theory the rhetor is managerial. What is called "classical" organizational theory is less than 100 years old, but it is true to the older classical tradition in its fixed hierarchical disposition. Weber's bureaucratic theory and Taylor's scientific management take for granted that the purposes of an organization are determined at the top and enacted at the bottom of a hierarchy.[1] The organization is, in this neo-Aristotelian view, a composite substance with its higher part (mind) and its lower part (body). The contrast is exaggerated further by Cartesian rationality, which substitutes theoretical wisdom for practical wisdom by completely separating mind and body. The result is a conception of an organization as a reactive machine whose function is to carry out the will of its mind, which exists at the top of the hierarchy. This conception then becomes intertwined with capitalist ideas of ownership to create a very distorted view of the business organization. From an ecological perspective, the idea that an investor can "own" an organization is absurd, since the organization is itself a complex open system comprising many parts and dependent upon a larger ecosystem. Admittedly, investors might lay claim to owning the machinery in a plant, but the machinery is not the organization. Cartesian dualism, however, treats bodies as machines to be measured quantitatively. This can lead to the assumption that investors own the machines and the labor that has been hired. The fact that workers are persons with purposes and life narratives is suppressed by the mechanistic view.

Communication in the classical system was primarily a matter of issuing clear commands, the means whereby the mind controlled the machine. The labor struggles of the early twentieth century and the Great Depression encouraged skepticism toward traditional organizational theory. In the late 1930s, Barnard argued that business organizations were systems of people, not machines. Executives depend upon communication to gain acceptance for their authority. Therefore, "Communication techniques shape the form and the internal economy of the organization."[2] At about the same time, Mayo was directing the Hawthorne studies that led to the human relations school of management. Those studies purported to show that paying attention to people as human beings can lead to greater productivity.

The Hawthorne studies also emphasized the importance of communication within a group for morale and performance.[3] The changed attitude toward the role of communication in business organizations led by Barnard and Mayo resulted in a more rhetorical approach to organizational communication but only in the Aristotelian meaning, not in the full ecological sense. Just as Aristotle recognized the practical need for the aristocracy to learn the art of rhetoric in order for the aristocracy to get its way in a mixed democracy, so the human relations theorists saw communication techniques as the means by which the owners could get their way. Like Aristotle, the new theories had to consider ethos, logos, and pathos from the audience's perspective; but the purpose, the telos, was always determined by the aristocrat. In Aristotle's case, at least the aristocrat was supposed to aim at the good of the community. In the case of the capitalist oligarchs, the end was merely to increase profits by increasing productivity.

Certainly, in our current environment, profits are very important for the organization as a system. From an ecological perspective, however, profits cannot be the telos of an organization, even a business organization. Considered as a level of the ecosystem, the business organization has the telos of nurturing all of its members and of supporting the larger ecosystem of which it is a part. In the last chapter we saw how the research into interpersonal competence begged the question of telos: competent at what? In organizational communication, systems theory has been very thoroughly developed, but it has suffered from a similar problem: for what (or whose) purpose does the system exist? As a result, ethical concerns seem to be patchwork additions to theories of organizational communication. From an ecological perspective, ethical concerns are the primary reason that organizational communication deserves study. An oligarchical approach emphasizing input-output has distorted much of the systems analysis of organizations, justifying Lyotard's critique of systems theory as mechanistic. On the other hand, alternative approaches have tended either toward Marxist (or even fascist) totalizing or toward postmodern cynicism. I intend to draw insights from all these theories while shifting the perspective to the ecological aspect of organizational communication.

Oligarchic Open Systems

Whereas general systems theory, discussed in chapter 3, emphasized similarities between physical and social systems, Katz and Kahn point out an important difference: human social systems lack apparent structure.[4] We can observe the structure of most physical bodies to see how various subsystems interact. Our social systems lack that physical structure, however. A business may have a physical plant, but this capital investment does not constitute the system. People come and go. Swing shift replaces day shift, and night shift replaces swing shift. New employees are hired, others are fired or retire. Where is the structure? Katz and Kahn argue that the structure exists in the relations between events. From the Peircean perspective, this makes eminent sense. The structure of a system is the pattern of relations between events, the habit of interaction that is thirdness. As I argued earlier, our own bodies comprise relatively stable relations between events of various duration. Social systems are as real as our own bodies. Our ability to observe those relations, however, is more limited when those relations exceed the scope of normal perception. The fallibility of our interpretation of those relations does not make those relations less real. On the other hand, as we act on the basis of our interpretations, we may change the patterns of interaction and so change the nature of the real system. Our epistemological limitations may have ontological consequences.

All real systems, with the possible exception of the universe itself, are open systems. Human organizations are precarious open systems depending for their stability on a continuous flow (homeorhesis) of input and output. As Katz and Kahn note, "the organization lives only so long as people are induced to be members and to perform as such."[5] Traditionally, systems theory has focused on production input and output and has neglected what Katz and Kahn call maintenance inputs that are necessary to sustain the system. This neglect is due in part to the mechanistic metaphors that have dominated systems theory. Of course, the term *maintenance input* is not necessarily less mechanistic. I prefer the old Aristotelian distinction between praxis and poēsis, practice done for intrinsic reasons versus production done for the sake of the work produced. This change in terminology should change the vector of interpretation away from the machine (presumably owned by the investor) toward the living of life in community.

My point is that a truly sustainable system is an ecological community from which all members benefit by their membership. Production is a function performed for the purpose of sustaining the community so that it can continue to nurture its members. Production is thus an end in view that serves as a means to the further end of the practice of community building. Production is important because of entropy; the system needs a continual renewal of resources to maintain itself. In our social environment, both inputs and outputs are converted semiotically into money. The organization must make a profit as a source of negentropy. Some of that profit is returned to investors to ensure a regular input of investment capital. Some of the profit goes to maintain the physical plant. Some of the profit goes to improve the life of the various members of the organization, both in the form of wages and in the form of improved working conditions. Here the improvement in working conditions is not for the sake of improved productivity (although that is a desirable consequence), but the improved productivity is for the sake of improved working conditions.

At this point, my ecological perspective may seem utopian. I actually expect a business to operate on behalf of its employees. But the ecological perspective is not utopian; it is counterfactual in the sense that it considers the possibilities that could arise if we changed our perspective. These counterfactual possibilities arise when we no longer look at the organization only from the perspective of the oligarchy of investors, owners, or founders. If, as Katz and Kahn claim, systems are cycles of events, no particular individual, group, or subsystem owns the system. Granted, some individuals, groups, and subsystems are leading parts that could destroy the system. The ability to destroy, however, is not ownership. All that anyone owns are parts of the system. Regardless of one's ownership rights, one also has obligations to the whole system that gives those parts value.

Loyalty, then, is a virtue of communal practice. If the system as a whole works for the good of all its members, then these members should act to sustain the system. Communication plays a large role in the development of loyalty in an organization. Interpersonal communication is an important aspect of making work enjoyable. Some resources must be expended to maintain the capability of interpersonal communication on the job, even when the practice seems to interfere with production. Sexual harassment, racial insults, and the like undermine loyalty by making the work environment unpleasant for many—not just for those involved but for others observing. The organization as a whole must expend some resources to ensure that ethical standards of interpersonal communication are maintained.

When an organization does devote resources toward praxis, it should also devote resources toward internal rhetoric to build loyalty and cohesiveness. The members need to become knowledgeable about their organization so that they can reciprocate with loyalty when it is earned. Internal newsletters, when written honestly from the perspective of the whole community, can increase consubstantiality deservedly. Newsletters can also be a source of information about problems that need to be resolved in the organization. If workers at various levels report problems and then see those problems addressed, their loyalty and thus the stability of the system will be enhanced. On the other hand, internal rhetoric that serves only as a mouthpiece for the oligarchy is unethical. Cheney has shown how the "assumed we" is a prevalent feature of policy statements by top executives in corporate house organs.[6] The assumed *we* avoids real issues of community by taking it for granted. The executives presume their own opinions represent the community. The oligarchy, however, has no inherent right to dominate the channels of communication within the organization. In light of the concept of fuzzy phronē-sis, such domination actually reduces rationality in an organization.

The difficulty in making the counterfactual ecological ideal into a concrete, factual reality for business organizations arises from the current state of the larger ecosystem in which businesses participate. Systems theorists have recognized that organizations "are embedded in an environment of other organizations as well as in a complex of norms, values, and collectivities of the society at large."[7] Boulding even labeled this environment an *ecosystem* more than forty years ago.[8] The problem is in the stance we take toward it. Evan, for example, reduces the ecosystem to *organization sets*, which constitute the network of organizations with which a given organization interacts. His analysis of these organization sets focuses on input and output, using the traditional oligarchical perspective. Even his example of an external *normative reference organization* that influences values within an organization is concerned with production goals. He cites the case in which the Department of Defense's desire for a certain type of airplane causes an organization to try to produce that airplane, adopting the goal of the department as its own goal.[9] In general, Evan is concerned with the ways in which the organization set constrains the autonomy of any given organization. The discussion of autonomy, however, is limited to the oligarchical purposes of production, not the communal praxis in which the ability to nurture employees is constrained by external competition. In general, of course, it is the oligarchy that hires consultants and finances studies of organizations; so the oligarchical perspective is not surprising.

From a Marxist perspective, an organization is constrained at high levels of the ecosystem by the mode of production of a given historical period. That mode of production determines relations of production that are the relations between classes—in our historical period, the relations between capitalist and worker. In his Marxist analysis, Burawoy perceives the possibility of praxis at the level of production where relations between workers exist. "It is in this practical activity [of labor] that the human species exhibits its potential for creativity, while the relational aspect expresses the potential for an ethical community of freely associated producers."[10] Apparently, for Burawoy only the workers have the potential to develop an ethical community.

In Marxist theory, however, this ethical potential cannot be actualized within the environment determined by the current mode of production. In sustaining itself, the capitalist ecosystem distorts our "experience." The market system, as the systemic analysis of organization sets illustrates, is a system of relations between organizations. The exchange value of any product is the result of this complex relationship in which the value added to a product by the labor embedded in it is related to the value added to other products by labor. The result is a price that seems to be the value of the object as determined by impersonal forces of supply and demand. Thus the system of social relations is obscured by commodification. This arrangement is what Marx called the fetishism of commodities, and Burawoy argues that it is inescapable: "Lived experience presents what is socially produced as 'natural' and beyond human control. It is unaffected by knowledge and the consciousness individuals carry. It makes no difference whether the occupant of a place of production be Karl Marx, John Rockefeller, or Joe Hill, the fetishism of commodities will be equally real to all."[11] From this very traditional Marxist perspective, "it is lived experience that produces ideology and not the other way round."[12] The ancient appearance-reality dichotomy is thus transformed into the failure to see the reality of social relations because we perceive only the appearances of commodities. Under these conditions, even honest communication will be ideologically distorted, and the ethical community is impossible.

Burawoy illustrates his argument with his own experience as a machine shop operator in Illinois. Pay for machine shop operators was based on a piecework incentive. On top of a basic hourly rate, the operators would be paid a bonus for achieving rates above a base rate of 100 percent. If the operators consistently achieved too high a rate, however, the industrial engineers would raise the base rate. So the workers developed a game of "making out" at the piecework rate. A shop culture developed around the game, with expert players achieving higher status. Burawoy himself, despite his Marxist theory, became absorbed in the game: "I found myself spontaneously cooperating with management in the production of greater surplus value."[13] The work game, which satisfied a need generated by the ecosystem's treatment of labor, sustained that ecosystem by reproducing "not only 'voluntary servitude' (consent) but also greater material wealth."[14] The workers were not motivated simply by the monetary reward of piecework; they turned the process of production into a praxis with its own pleasures. In doing so, however, they further obscured the relationship between the value of commodities and the labor in production. From the Marxist perspective, profit is the value of unpaid labor. The game, the shop culture, the communication of both union and management, all obscured the exploitation of labor necessarily involved in making a profit. The problem was not honesty but the inability to see beyond the appearances of commodities. Even the Marxist was taken in.

Perhaps this is why Deetz has argued that "ethical communication cannot take place within conditions of domination."[15] The problem with this statement is that it treats *ethical* as a crisp category instead of the fuzzy category it is. In Deetz's binary logic, an act is either perfectly ethical or it is unethical. In fuzzy logic an act has a greater or lesser membership in the category of ethical. Deetz's argument that we should "keep the conversation going," that "communicative action and communicative research should have as a normative aim an attempt to establish the conditions for further less restrained communication,"[16] makes more sense using fuzzy logic than binary categories. We cannot declare an ethical moratorium until we live in an ecosystem that no longer exploits anyone. Unless we act ethically in the fuzzy ecological sense, we will never reduce domination. To act ethically, of course, we must be able to think and talk critically about our current ecosystem. Burawoy's argument seems to lead to the conclusion that ethical deliberation is impossible within the current ecosystem.

At this point, Burawoy's argument directly contradicts the pragmatic realism of Peirce. Peirce held the doctrine of "critical commonsensism."[17] This doctrine included the proposition that some of our beliefs are indubitable. It does not follow that those beliefs are infallible, however. Peirce simply means that we are unable to doubt certain beliefs. These are the beliefs on which we stand when we doubt other beliefs. These beliefs are vague, and the objects signified may or may not be real. Peirce opined that these indubitable beliefs change very little from generation to generation; but they do change, especially as we increase our means of perception. Burawoy seems to be saying that the fetishism of commodities is an indubitable belief of the historical period of capitalism. If it is, then we cannot think critically about it until we evolve different beliefs. That is why absolute truth is associated with the end of inquiry. Burawoy's own writings contradict the claim that fetishism is an indubitable belief, however. He criticizes the belief as he reflects critically on his own experience. In the process he leads the reader also to reflect critically on capitalist presumptions. He has raised genuine doubt; therefore, the fetishism of commodities is not an indubitable belief but one subject to criticism. Burawoy's habits of action in playing the game were not interpretants of a changed belief in commodities but an attempt to relieve drudgery in practice. That such practices might lead to belief in commodification does not place such beliefs beyond criticism. The existence of Marxism as a critique of capitalism gives evidence that capitalism's beliefs are not beyond criticism. By using the methods of tenacity and authority, of course, individuals and groups may resist critique of their beliefs; but these methods suggest that the beliefs are, in fact, dubitable. Fetishisms are more like Foucauldian "positivities" that are the product of a historical discursive regime than they are like Peirce's indubitable beliefs. Indubitable beliefs are so basic and primitive that they do not depend upon methods of defense. We have no need of Descartes to prove Augustine's *cogito, ergo sum*, since it is impossible really to doubt it. We also cannot doubt the percepts of zoosemiosis. Capitalism's beliefs are not of the same nature even if they do resist change.

In short, Burawoy confuses the resistance of current beliefs with indubitability. Certainly, all of our beliefs are fallible; so, like any other decision, our ethical decisions may turn out wrong. Our ethical obligation cannot exceed our capabilities; we can only try to do our best. What the Marxist critique shows us is how the ecosystem limits the ability of a business organization to form an ethical community by distorting our communication. That limitation does not remove the obligation to try to improve the situation through critical deliberation, both internally and externally. The Marxist tendency to totalize leads to disdain for incremental improvements. Ethically, we are obligated to choose among likely alternatives based on all of their foreseeable consequences. Marxism provides a useful dialectical critique of the current ecosystem, but it has not yet demonstrated a realistic alternative with better overall consequences. Until it does, we must focus on improving the ecosystem we have. The ecological perspective allows us to move away from the oligarchical perspective on business organizations while recognizing the need to deal with the oligarchy as well as the workers in forming a more ethical community. The ecological perspective also recognizes the constraints on community at the organizational level that result from the nature of the larger ecosystem. The ecological ethic may require "political" action to improve the larger ecosystem. From my perspective, of course, the internal communication shaping the organization is also *political*.

Theory Z: Homogenized Ecology

Given my emphasis on community, one might think that the Theory Z approach to business organization would be close to ideal. Based on the Japanese model, Theory Z treats the organization as a community, developing intimacy through close social relations.[18]

Through community, the organization develops a common culture that allows for subtlety in communication: "Because the underlying premises or theoretical position from which each person proceeds is held in common with the others, each can assume certain responses or agreements without actually taking the time to negotiate them."[19] In rhetorical terms, the increase in consubstantiality allows for greater use of enthymemes, which, in turn, reinforce consubstantiality, as we saw in chapter 4. Greater consubstantiality leads to greater consensus in decision making and an increased sense of responsibility for the decisions made. One of the problems in bureaucratic organizations is the diffusion of responsibility that occurs as each person is responsible for only a small part of the overall process. What seem to be small ethical errors can accumulate into a major ethical problem. Exaggeration in reporting the success of battles in Vietnam, for example, was compounded at the various levels of bureaucracy, resulting in grossly inaccurate figures contributing to tactical and strategic errors. Acceptance of responsibility for the overall product can help organizations avoid lying to themselves and others.

The Japanese also have found fuzzy logic compatible with their appreciation of subtlety, and their method of making decisions seems to approximate the fuzzy phronēsis I have called for. "When an important decision needs to be made in a Japanese organization, everyone who will feel its impact is involved in making it."[20] If everyone's opinion enters into the final decision, then the method of control appears to be that of a fuzzy controller seeking a center of gravity that balances conflicting opinions. Theory Z, however, actually relies on the fact that there will seldom be real differences of opinion. The theory requires a totalized, homogenized corporate culture. Opposing opinions are filtered out long before they reach the level of control.

Ouchi acknowledges the problem. He writes, "Type Z companies have a tendency to be sexist and racist." "At Company Z the cast of top managers is so homogeneous that one member of my research team characterized the dominant culture as 'Boy Scout Macho.' That is, the top management is wholesome, disciplined, hardworking, and honest, but unremittingly white, male, and middle class."[21] Theory Z is based on Japanese business organizations, and "probably no form of organization is more sexist or racist than the Japanese corporation."[22] The desired characteristics of intimacy, subtlety, and trust require "cultural homogenization" of the whole ecosystem. Ouchi recognizes that for the United States such consensus on beliefs is "yet some distance away," so we cannot achieve the organizational solidarity of the Japanese.[23] Presumably, when the melting pot finishes its work of reducing our differences, we will no longer have to concern ourselves with balancing individual and communal needs. Ouchi is not a fascist, but his theory suffers from the same vulnerability to fascist exploitation as Rorty's neopragmatism. The emphasis on solidarity and consensus for its own sake offers no defense against fascism. Such consensus cannot achieve rationality because rationality requires real criticism.

Let us consider how a business organization can become fascist in fact, albeit unintentionally. First, "a concentrated form of ownership or control may be a necessary condition for the development of Type Z organizations."[24] This concentration allows for a homogeneous beginning to the organization as a system. The organization is an open system, of course, so it is susceptible to heterogeneous influences from the environment. As Katz and Kahn point out, "the open organization is subject to transformation by its members and may have difficulty in the single-minded pursuit of given objectives." The degree of openness, however, is determined by the permeability of the system's boundaries:

An organization which seeks to avoid such influence must make itself less permeable to self-nominating new members. It must screen potential members more carefully and define more broadly the individual characteristics which are relevant in the screening. By so doing the organization will perhaps sharpen its sense of mission and minimize the possibilities of internal disruption. It may pay the price, however, of tending to replicate its current membership characteristics and thus coming to resemble itself more and more closely as time passes.[25]

The interview process is a way of assessing the homogeneity of prospective new members, especially when combined with a probation period. Selective promotion further ensures that the oligarchy reproduces itself, as in the "white boy scouts" whom Ouchi researched.

In Japan, the educational system is a means of reducing permeability for business organizations. The top businesses and government agencies hire primarily from the imperial universities. The placement officers at those universities have the duty of selecting students for particular organizations by matching characteristics to ensure homogeneity. But this selection is only the final phase of a national filtering process. Because the imperial universities are the entry point into the most sought after jobs, competition for admission into the imperial universities is intense. Admission is determined by a national examination. All high school students take the same courses and use the same textbooks, but certain high schools have the reputation of better preparing students for the examination. Admission, then, to get into those high schools is also keen; so the primary schools become important and competitive as well. Ouchi describes a Japanese friend who was worried about his four-year-old son's entrance examination for one of the top kindergartens that would improve chances at a better elementary school.[26] Although the examination system seems to be a meritocratic method, it also reinforces homogeneity throughout the system. Examinations test only limited forms of intelligence and reinforce the cultural biases inherent in language. The Japanese system thus reduces permeability at every level of the educational system and then matches the homogeneously intelligent survivors with proper organizations. Comparatively, the American system of entrance exams, reputable colleges, and interviews seems much less efficient at enforcing homogeneity.

Furthermore, since the higher level of ecosystem in America is more heterogeneous, reduced permeability to new members by itself is insufficient to develop fascistic homogeneity. Open systems are open to messages that contain heterogeneous information. So the fascistic system must have ways of excluding information. Katz and Kahn indicate that organizations do have means of restricting informative inputs:

These criteria may specify that only information relevant to the questions posed by organizational leaders will be accepted, or that only members of a certain status or functional position will be heard on certain questions. More generally, the practice is to have specialized structures for the reception of information so that any message will have to traverse and survive the "proper channels" in order to get a hearing.[27]

Coincidentally, Katz and Kahn wrote this passage the same year that Foucault published *Les mots et les choses* in France. They certainly seem to be describing a Foucauldian *discursive regime* viewed at the level of an organization. At that level, the possibility of a discursive regime enforcing homogeneity seems greater than in the larger ecosystem of Foucault's analysis. In fact, Foucault's argument is strongest when he discusses specific practices in specific organizations such as prisons. Foucault has deemphasized hierarchy, but a self-reproducing oligarchy is best able to develop a consistent discursive regime that eliminates disruptive information.

Again the Japanese illustrate the homogenizing method of a discursive regime in its purer form. We have already seen how the Japanese system of examinations preserves homogeneity. Foucault noted that the "examination combines the techniques of an observing hierarchy and those of a normalizing judgment."[28] But the Japanese system goes even further in developing discipline through observation. The hyperbolic model that Foucault uses to illustrate the principle is the *panopticon.* The panopticon was Bentham's design for a prison that arranged space to allow total surveillance of both prisoners and staff, controlling them by means of "a permanent gaze."[29] Now consider Ouchi's description of the physical layout of a typical Japanese company. The employees work in one large room with no internal partitions. Each department has a long table.

The section chief sits at the head of each table, and the division general manager has a desk at the head of the room, much like a school teacher. Around each table the staff and their secretaries sit side by side, with telephones and order books piled in the center of each table. With a constant hubbub of talk, both serious and playful, everyone notices just what each person is up to. . . .
This very public way of life can be intolerable to anyone whose values and goals do not conform, and it can be oppressive even to the Japanese.[30]

Within the Japanese system, the panopticon is not merely a hyperbolic metaphor; it is instantiated in the business organization.

Now, the possibilities for fascistic development of a Z company should be clear. Beginning with concentrated control, the oligarchy reproduces itself through selective recruitment and promotion. Contradicting information is eliminated through the discursive regime. Values are enforced through the panopticon, and members who are "different" are driven out by the stress. Homogeneous employees are rewarded with job security. In this way the purity of the organization is assured; it descends from the founder as though through a bloodline. Consensus will easily be achieved; those who won't consent are eliminated by the system. A false appearance of phronēsis results. The falsity may not be revealed until the ecosystem in which the organization operates finally imposes its reality on that organization.

The values of community that Ouchi desires are not wrong, but his organizational theory does not escape the one-sidedness of the Japanese system. Ecologically, diversity is a value. Ouchi recognizes the importance of deviants for the survival of a population. He argues that type Z organizations are such deviants. He fails to compensate for the fact that type Z organizations are also ecosystems that tend to eliminate deviants from their own population. Research indicates that in the United States white males are likely to equate loyalty with homogeneity, while minorities and women do not.[31] This shortsighted sense of loyalty is likely to damage the system in the long run. As Buhler has argued, a diverse workforce brings more information to the creative process of solving problems.[32] Lester points out, for example, that women bring qualities to the organization that are in short supply in male-dominated organizations.[33] Among these qualities is a sense of relatedness that makes women at least potentially more ecologically sensitive. Whether these qualities in women are the result of culture or nature, they certainly contribute to ethical reasoning in the organization. The tendency toward homogeneity in Theory Z organizations reduces the fuzzy phronēsis of those organizations by creating a partially blinded consensus.

Some aspects of Theory Z, such as quality control circles and walk-around management, can contribute to an ethical theory of organizational communication. A type Z organization might be able to develop an ethical communicative climate overall here in the United States; but it would be ethical because the larger ecosystem forced it to be more heterogeneous than its native tendency would have led it to be. Ouchi's own research, however, does not show much heterogeneity in American type Z organizations. From an ethical perspective, the danger is that type Z organizations will tend to be totalizing on behalf of the oligarchy.

Postmodern Organizing

Directly opposing the homogeneous consensus of Theory Z, post-modernism emphasizes the fragmentation and irrationality of organizations. Perhaps the most striking example is the "garbage can" metaphor of organizational decision making. Cohen, March, and Olsen argued that organizations were garbage cans into which people, problems, situations requiring decisions, and solutions are dumped.[34] They claimed that decisions were made more to avoid problems than to address problems; so organizations rarely solve problems. The garbage can metaphor of course directly contradicts the systems approach, because a garbage can is a heap, not a system. As Alvesson and others have pointed out, however, the garbage can metaphor, while catchy, is misleading. "The degree of overlap between the type of decision-making addressed and the garbage can is too small."[35] The clustering that causes decisions is not random but shows some degree of regularity. Their theory actually seems based on the fact that we tend to avoid difficult decisions when we can. Rather than providing a root metaphor, their approach merely confirms the fact that organizations tend to diffuse responsibility. Perhaps it would help to remember that compost piles normally develop into complex biological communities of interaction.

Weick's theory of organizing offers more useful insights into the problems of organizations from a postmodern perspective. Lundberg called Weick the "white rabbit" of organizational theorizing who can lead each of us Alices to new domains of thought.[36] Weick attacks the mechanistic metaphor that has limited organizational systems theory, and he offers a more meaning-oriented system. From my perspective of pragmatic realism, I view Weick as nominalistic and psychologistic—more like Rorty than Peirce. As a result, even his own insights are presented as mere vocabulary changes, "ways to talk about organizations."[37] That these new ways to talk might better signify real relations in organizations is an interpretation beyond his postmodern neopragmatism. Many of his insights, however, are compatible with, and, I believe, can be enriched by, a more realistic, Peircean semiotic.

Weick's most important insight is that organizations are processes so that the object of study is organiz*ing* not organiz*ation*. The difference is similar to the distinction I made between pragmatic kinēsis and Aristotelian energeia in chapter 4. Weick reduces the concept of an organization acting to double interacts between individuals because he is still captured by the atomistic individualism of modernism. In fact, double interacts between individuals are not more real but simply more easily observed because of their scope. The same individuals are complex processes just as the organization is; both are real patterns of interaction. Although Weick claims that "any assertion that organizations act can be decomposed into some set of interacts among individuals," he also concedes that "the fact that forms transcend specific individuals means that it is reasonable to say that an organization acts, because it is the persisting form that coordinates actions of transient personnel and that produces the outcomes." From a Peircean perspective, double interacts are signs of the organizing process and hence are useful for analysis; however, when the form of an organization is decomposed into those interacts, thirdness and secondness become confused, and the real form of the organization is obscured. This point becomes important in the ecological ethic when we consider the responsibility of the organization for its consequences on the larger ecosystem. Just as analysts tend to "decompose" organizations into double interacts because they are more easily observed, so members of organizations tend to diffuse responsibility to atomistic levels for ease of observation. The result of such ease of observation may be blindness at the higher scale of systemic consequences.

This danger is compounded by a narrow view of rationality. Rejecting the totalizing, modernist view of rationality, Weick argues for a more limited concept. Rationality requires some agreement on ends and means. Because it is unlikely that a large organization can attain agreement, "it is likely that rationality will characterize mostly small groups of actors and that, at any moment in time, organizations will have several different and contradictory rationalities."[38] In the postmodern mode, Weick emphasizes the fragmentation of sensus communis. His argument contains considerable truth and is certainly preferable to the fascistic achievement of consensus through homogeneity. It also underestimates the possibility of rationality understood pragmatically, however. The consensus that establishes truth and defines reality ultimately is the consensus that *would* occur at the end of inquiry. Rationality is the opening up of current consensual beliefs to criticism in the hope of more closely approximating that final consensus. A current consensus does not define rationality, although it does (and should) limit our ability to doubt without cause. Every organization has some consensus of indubitable beliefs.

In addition to the pragmatic conception of truth, the idea of practical wisdom as fuzzy phronēsis also weakens Weick's argument. The fuzzy controller incorporates contradicting opinions in seeking a center of gravity. Therefore the contradictory rationalities observed by Weick are part of the overall deliberation of the organization. Most of us as individuals are divided in our purposes, at least at the libidinal level. Indeed, the lack of division is more a symptom of obsessive-compulsive behavior than it is of rationality. The more open we are to our conflicting desires, the better we will deliberate, as long as we accept responsibility for all the consequences of our actions. In this model of rationality, sensus communis is something we achieve through deliberation, not some a priori we bring to the table. Weick senses this truth. "How can I know what I think until I see what I say?" is the basic theme of his book.[39] As individuals we achieve consensus by talking to ourselves. Organizations also must have communicative openness to know what they think. Weick encourages this openness but fails to acknowledge that this process, if it occurred throughout the organization, could constitute practical rationality.

If sensus communis follows deliberation, then we can also account for common values in an organization that can lead to the development of community. As Weick points out, individuals often have diverse goals. I concur. As I have repeatedly argued, the ecosystem supports the individual in the pursuit of his or her own unique life narrative. I have also borrowed from Dewey's theory of valuation (consistent with Peircean synechism) the concept of ends and means as a continuum, as described in chapter 2. A means to an end is itself an end in view and so is valued. Weick points out that in the process of organizing, people with divergent ends come together on a common means of achieving those ends. That pursuit of common means takes on a structure of interlocked behaviors whose preservation then becomes a common end. "By positing that common means precede common ends, and by restricting the concept of common ends mostly to events that preserve a collective structure in which diverse ends can be pursued, then it is possible to look more closely at group behaviors and make sense of them in their own right."[40] In Deweyan terms, Weick is describing the ends-means continuum as it leads to the development of a public that, when it becomes aware of its interdependence, forms a community. Because a community is a system existing within other levels of ecosystem, diverse behaviors are necessary to support it. Therefore, individual members use diverse means in support of the common end of sustaining the community. Those diverse means also are ends in view; so an organization must be a complex of community and diversity in ongoing interaction. If diversity obscures community, the system is too loosely coupled and centrifugal force destroys it; if community obscures diversity, the system is too tightly coupled and centripetal force destroys it.

From a pragmatic perspective, the interaction that sustains a community is semiotic. Weick's approach also appears to be semiotic, but the terminology may be misleading. Weick uses the terms *enactment, selection,* and *retention* to mark different aspects of what I interpret as semiotic processes. He agrees that we exist in an environment that undergoes change. "Ecological changes provide the *enactable environment,* the raw materials for sense-making."[41] Ecological change would be Peircean secondness, the sense of resistance that is event, fact, or thing. Enactment is semiotic experience, thirdness. One form occurs when we bracket off some aspect of our experience to examine it. Another form occurs when we act on our environment, causing ecological change, which then constrains our subsequent enactments, producing more changes, and so on in what Peirce saw as potentially infinite semiosis. Enactment seems to be simply different types of semiosis based on objects and events encountered at the system boundaries. Both Peirce and Weick agree that these signs are indeterminate in some sense. Weick emphasizes that enactment is "equivocal," that is, comprising multiple meanings. The difference between indeterminacy and equivocality is the difference between an essay question and a multiple choice question on an exam. Both require further interpretation, but one offers determinate choices. Weick's point is that in enacting our environment, we have already reduced it to multiple choices through some filtering process. From a Peircean perspective, such equivocality could be a mistake or could be the result of the indeterminacy of the original sign.

Selection, then, is the reduction of equivocality by the use of some internal structure, often taking the form of correlations based on past experience. In answering a multiple choice question, for example, if I don't know the answer, I may fall back on using a schema (such as: the correct answer is not usually the first choice) to reduce equivocality. The point is that we have these general patterns that we use across situations to reduce equivocality, often in the form of maps of causal relations. Those causal maps that work well at reducing equivocality will tend to be selected. A successful interpretation of a situation will also be retained as a possible analogy for future situations. Retention, then, is simply storing of "enacted environments" that are the result of our trying to make sense out of equivocal displays. Retention, in turn, results in beliefs that affect further stages of enactment and selection. Weick's conclusion is nominalist: "people create the environments which then impose on them."[42]

In the postmodern custom of dyadic semiology, Weick has dropped out the real ecological change from his model, focusing only on the internal stages of interpretation. What he neglects is the fact that the real ecological change already existed as a sign, or it could not have been perceived. The change was not just secondness but thirdness; it had continuity to it, the ability to re-present itself. People may misinterpret the signs of the environment, but they do not create their environments ex nihilo like the God of medieval theology. Granted, we use psychological schemata to interpret signs based on previous experience, and we tend toward the method of tenacity in making new signs fit the old schema. I agree that an organization can become more closed to its current environment by imposing the past on it. But if the ecological change is enduring, it will re-present itself for continued interpretation. The original indeterminacy, if attended to, will reduce itself. Still, the simplification of that indeterminacy by the various coding mechanisms that reduce indeterminacy to equivocality and then reduce equivocality may lead to loss of retention of the original indeterminacy. This statement is especially true when alternative perspectives are kept out of the deliberation so that early closure can be achieved.

Weick's dropping out of the real object from his analysis makes his recommendations seem anarchistic. He calls for "frequent discrediting" of enacted environments.[43] Such discrediting must be random and haphazard because he fails to recognize the reality of the signs of environmental change. His form of discrediting is like Cartesian doubt, which cannot justify itself. Real pragmatic doubt is a belief that something is wrong with another belief. Pragmatic doubt occurs because the pragmatic realist believes that environmental change can represent itself. Weick also points out that compromise is often an ineffective way to make decisions. Compromise as averaging destroys the original positions of all sides. Compromise must be ambivalent, that is, incorporate multiple opinions.[44] Weick's theory, however, doesn't offer any reason to hope that multiple opinions will help the organization. On the other hand, pragmatic realism values multiple opinions as a means of better interpreting the real environment. Hence the importance of a fuzzy approach wherein conflicting opinions are preserved as inputs, not absorbed or hidden in the overall balance. An effective fuzzy controller requires retention of minority reports and various contingency plans. Speaking one's disagreement should be seen as contributing to the ability of the organization to deal with its external environment or its internal membership.

In Foucauldian style, Weick argues that power occurs wherever interaction takes place in an organization. Especially in loosely coupled organizations, the real power is not in the oligarchy, but in the multiple cycles of double interacts that take place throughout the organization. One might argue that double interacts involving the oligarchy are more important than others; nevertheless his basic point is sound. The oligarchy is not the system and does not hold the bulk of positive power in the system; instead it is "the pattern of alliances, causal loops, and norms that exist *between* people that accomplish or defeat efforts at control."[45] If so, then all levels should accept their ethical responsibility for the communicative climate of the organization. At the same time, our traditional systemic perspective leads us to focus power and responsibility primarily at the level of the oligarchy. Our ethical theories of organizational communication are often still pre-Nuremberg, encouraging loss of ethical accountability throughout the organization. If we incorporate Weick's insights, we can begin teaching ethical responsibility throughout the organization.

Weick also provides an important warning about loyalty. He points out that "anything that heightens commitment" makes discrediting more difficult.[46] This statement may, in fact, be true about most organizations today. It does not follow, however, that loyalty necessarily contradicts rationality in an organization. If we understood the necessity for expressing real doubt to ensure rationality, we could couple loyalty and critical reasoning. We might also preclude those extreme cases in which an employee must choose between loyalty to the organization and loyalty to family, friends, and the larger ecosystem. When an organization does not encourage open internal criticism and when it does not incorporate all criticism in its deliberation, an employee may be forced to "blow the whistle" on the company to outsiders.

Jensen has explored what he calls ethical tension points in whistleblowing. His approach has some similarity to fuzzy phronēsis in his recognition that ethics is a continuum, not an either-or judgment. Jensen points out that, in making judgments, we must set priorities among the competing factors, but he offers no general ethical principle to assist us. Some of his tension points presume an oligarchical understanding of communication in an organization. He notes that "in most organizational structures, superiors, not subordinates, have the designated role of making judgments." So he asks, "is the whistleblower thus attempting to play God?"[47] Subordinates are continually making ethical judgments, however. Avoiding ethical responsibility is itself an ethical judgment. Jensen neglects the fact that responsibility is also a continuum. Those with more power have more responsibility; but as Weick and Foucault argue, we all have some power. In the game of life, there is no sharp distinction between players and referees. If exercising ethical responsibility is playing God, then we all must play God or Satan.

On the other hand, Jensen helps clarify the conflict in loyalties. He points out that loyalty involves confidentiality. Most organizations do not want to wash their dirty laundry in public because they exist in a competitive and unforgiving ecosystem. It is unfair and unnecessary to publicize internal problems that the organization is working on unless those problems require informed action by others outside the system. The question, of course, is whether the organization is washing dirty laundry or hiding it. Whistleblowing is an ethical response only in the case of a cover-up of events that seriously threaten other elements of the ecosystem, such as the larger environment or the members and their families. If the company is covering up the fact that it is poisoning a river, for example, whistleblowing is an appropriate response. Or if the oligarchy is secretly raiding the pension fund or saving money by firing workers before they qualify for pensions, that threat to the members of the organization also justifies whistleblowing. Whistleblowers must then balance the likely damage to their own careers when their "disloyalty" is discovered. They and their families are likely to suffer financially and may even be ostracized by their colleagues. These facts should prevent unnecessary or premature whistleblowing. Still, the decision whether or not to blow the whistle in a serious situation will affect the quality of one's life narrative. A former medical technician recently told me that he was still bothered by his own silence about a case of medical malpractice he had observed more than fifteen years earlier. A woman had died as a result, but all of the medical technicians and nurses were told to keep quiet about the doctor's carelessness. They did. Even though he was the lowest-ranking person present, the medical technician knows that he should have blown the whistle. To this day, he cannot forgive himself; his life narrative has suffered permanent damage. So loyalty to the self and family is not simply a matter of job security.

The fact that whistleblowing must even be considered as an ethical alternative is a sign of communicative problems within the organization. Either the opinions of the members of the organization are not attended to within the control processes, or the fact that the organization does hear and react to those opinions has not been publicized to the members. The problems may be technical problems of poor listening and speaking. On the other hand, these technical problems may exist because the organization as a whole doesn't care, doesn't accept responsibility for its communicative climate. Although an unhealthy communicative climate may make the oligarchy feel more powerful, in the process the system will be weakening the larger ecosystem that supports it and the members that comprise it. Eventually, the system will be unable to sustain itself.

Deetz and the critical theorists are right to a degree when they emphasize the importance of the larger system in determining ethical behavior. In an ethical system, individual ethical decisions would be much easier than the severe choice of whistleblowing. It is unfair to put anyone into that ethical situation. We cannot set aside our ethical responsibility awaiting a utopia, however. As Peirce points out, we have the function of transforming the ideal into concrete reasonableness. Cast into unfair situations, we must attempt to make fair decisions. On the other hand, we may be able to avoid those decisions if we accept our ethical responsibilities in our day-to-day communication so that we use the power of our double-interact cycles to make the organization as a whole more ethical. The ecological ethic calls not just for maintaining the systems that we partake in but for improving them when we can. In that way we will better the system and our own life narratives. The organization of course is itself a system within a larger ecosystem, which we also must sustain and improve. Although all levels of communication are political, or rhetorical, in an ecological sense, the larger ecosystem is the realm of political communication in more traditional usage. That realm of political communication is what we shall consider next.

7

The Politics of Representation

The promising season ends next Tuesday [Election Day], and at about 8 o'clock that same night, the alibi season opens, and lasts for the next four years.

—Will Rogers

With his incisive wit, Will Rogers regularly addressed ethical problems of political communication.[1] As we've seen, however, from an ecological perspective the scope of political communication is much larger than the scope of communication by "politicians." I have equated polis with community, and communities may exist at all levels of the communicative ecosystem. Using the Deweyan notion of a public as comprising all those affected by the consequences of a transaction (see chapter 2), we would have to envision the public sphere as virtually the entire sphere of discourse considered in terms of its consequences on others. Not all discourse has important public consequences, but all levels of discourse potentially have public consequences at some level of community. We do not have to shift levels of discourse in order to enter into a public sphere. In this sense, the ethical and political are intertwined in an ecological ethic.

On the other hand, popular usage does indicate a vague sphere of discourse called political because it is done by politicians. This is the discourse of the promising season and alibi season to which Will Rogers refers and to which this chapter is devoted. Politicians play important roles at various levels of our ecosystem, so the ethical problems of this political communication are important to us. This type of political discourse is unique because it involves the politics of *representation,* the means by which we supposedly govern ourselves. I have argued through the course of this book that the dyadic semiotic of postmodernism makes ethics meaningless. In this chapter I will argue that the ethics of political representation is better interpreted by a triadic semiotic. Politicians perform a semiotic function within the ecosystem; the ecological ethic requires them to perform that function well as they advance their own objectives. In other words, ethics requires them to support the system that supports them.

Because politicians operate in a communicative system, they are not the only ones responsible for the ethics of political communication. News media are also part of the semiotic process of political representation, and they have ethical responsibilities ensuing from their function. Furthermore, academics, especially those who specialize in analyzing political communication, also serve a systemic function and are obliged to support the system that supports them. Rhetorical criticism, for example, should serve the needs of the public, not merely the rhetor. Effective criticism, regardless of the method of research, should aim at improving the system of political communication and its ability to represent the public interest. This chapter will examine the issues involved in that semiotic process involving politicians, news media, and academics.

A Semiotic of Representation

Many critics claim that our system of political communication has declined, reaching its nadir (we hope) in 1988. Jamieson uses the 1988 campaign to illustrate the failure of politicians and press to engage the argument on real issues.[2] Bennett refers to 1988 as an example of the "postmodern election," that is, "politics in the age of unreason."[3] Both Bennett and Jamieson presume that reasoning about facts and reality is possible in an election. Jamieson states, "Postmodernism aside, at some level, political discourse presupposes the existence of brute, verifiable facts."[4] The problem is, we cannot simply set postmodernism to the side; we must engage its argument as well. Bennett claims that "the difference between 'reality' as constructed within healthy political rituals and 'realism' as constructed within commercialized empty rituals is all the difference that once mattered politically."[5] But if reality is merely constructed by ritual symbols, on what grounds should we prefer it to realism? If one accepts the dyadic semiotic of postmodernism, one can hardly quibble with postmodern elections that simply play with symbols. If symbols cannot stand for anything but can merely construct "reality," the only grounds for complaint is libidinal, not rational. If the resulting reality goes against one's feelings, the only option seems to be to obtain the power to define reality in accordance with those feelings. Any appeal to a more rational approach requires one to engage with postmodernism at its semiotic core.

Cooper attempts to develop an ethic for political communication by synthesizing the ethical approaches of Foucault and Habermas. She couples Habermas's concern for the rationality of full, open discussion, epitomized in the ideal speech situation, with Foucault's ethic of resistance, emphasizing the individual's construction of self, often in opposition to a discursive regime's definition of rationality.[6] In forcing this synthesis between modernism and postmodernism, however, she must distort one or the other. She argues that "postmodern perspectives recognize that truth may be elusive and information partial, and therefore place more value on access to the means of communication"; but this is hardly a postmodern discovery. Postmodernism is much more radical on the question of truth and information, so much so that it brings into question the relevance of process. If truth and information are impossible, what difference does process make? Cooper also argues that "from a postmodern perspective, the guiding principle for motives of political advocates is the preservation of others as autonomous subjects."[7] This guiding principle is simply a restatement of Kant's categorical imperative. Postmodernism, however, denies the autonomous subject, treating it as merely a positivity created within a particular discursive regime (see chapter 1). So Cooper's postmodern ethic is, in fact, ethical only insofar as it is *not* postmodern. She is admirably concerned with the need to balance the public and the private; however, postmodernism does not provide the resources for such a balance. Postmodernism, at best, expresses ethical desires that it cannot justify. An ecological ethic, on the other hand, addresses Cooper's concern for both the individual and the larger social system but does so on the basis of pragmatic realism.

Pragmatic realism is semiotic at bottom and so can provide a basis for an ethics of political representation. Political power is derived from the claim to represent a public. Smith has observed that political leadership is relational: "leaders and followers are interconnected systemically, and neither role exists without the other."[8] He also recognizes that "representation is a relational role";[9] but he fails to connect the two. From the perspective of a pragmatic semiotic, legitimacy of leadership is a function of true representation. To whatever degree a leader accurately stands for the object that is the will of the people, to that degree the leader is legitimate. Legitimacy is, therefore, a logical interpretant of the representative's relation to the object in a triadic semiotic. I have pointed out that Peirce's semiotic logic is an ethics of inquiry, indicating that the purpose of science should be to refine its ability to represent real objects by means of discourse and experimentation. Science is the practice of a self-critical art of representation; that is why blocking the path of inquiry is unethical. In the same way, politics is an art of representation that is ethical only insofar as it is logical in this Peircean sense. By means of discourse and learning from experience, the political community must aim more and more accurately to reflect its object, the will of its members, which itself changes in the process. How this representation can best be achieved is the problem at the heart of political communication.

A review of the Peircean categories of signs will help us better understand what is involved in political representation. Based on his phenomenological categories, Peirce divided signs into three trichotomies:

first, according as the sign in itself is a mere quality, is an actual existent, or is a general law; secondly, according as the relation of the sign to its object consists in the sign's having some character in itself, or in some existential relation to that object, or in its relation to an interpretant; thirdly, according as its Interpretant represents it as a sign of possibility or as a sign of fact or a sign of reason.[10]

According to the first trichotomy, a political representative is a sign having the nature of a general law, established by convention. The significance of political representation comes from being a type, which must be instantiated in replicas or tokens. When Mr. Smith went to Washington, he was not a representative because he was Mr. Smith, but because he was a token of a constitutionally determined type. Peirce calls these signs *legisigns,* and they are of a general nature. The tokens are thus replaceable. The large turnover in the 1994 congressional elections, for example, did not change the nature of the representative as a sign. All that happened was a change of tokens. Both the Republicans and the Democrats they replaced were able to function as signs because of a general law, not because of who they were as individuals or their particular qualities.

According to the second trichotomy, a political representative would be an icon, an index, or a symbol, depending on how it was related to its object. An icon does not have an existential relation to its object; it can function as a sign only when some similarity is observed between a quality of the sign and a quality of the object, "whether any such Object actually exists or not."[11] An icon can function as a sign of an object because it possesses a quality in itself that may re-present a similar quality in the object. Because the icon possesses the quality whether or not the object does, icons can be very deceptive. A typical example is a campaign photo of a candidate with his or her family as an icon of a good family relationship. Regardless of smiles and hugs, the icon actually may offer no information about the real nature of that relationship.

An index, on the other hand, can offer real information because it is in an existential relation with the object signified. This relation means that as the object changes, the sign changes. A good example is a weathervane, which is really acted upon by the wind that is its object. The action of the wind upon the weathervane does not make it a genuine sign until it is interpreted, but the real relation between object and sign makes the weathervane a different kind of sign from an icon. Indexes must include iconic elements, however, that is, qualities that are associated with qualities of the object. A weathervane, for example, normally uses an arrow as an iconic element indicating wind direction. A politician who simply reacted to opinion polls would be the political equivalent of a weathervane. Proposals for direct democracy also treat government as pure index of the will of the people. Because indexes are based in real existential relations, however, their objects must be "individuals, single units, single collections of units, or single continua."[12] Therefore, the will of the people would have to be a preexisting consensus. Although politicians readily claim the existence of such a mandate, the actual will of the people seems much fuzzier. Preliminary information on the 1994 election indicated that fewer than 40 percent of registered voters participated; so 20 percent of the people could account for the Republican "mandate." In addition, although these people seemed unhappy with the way things were going, they gave little indication of having a clear idea of what should be done. Because the object is not singular, political representation cannot be simply indexical. Nevertheless, the people's representatives must somehow remain connected with the vague and general will of the people.

The kind of sign that is related to a general object is the symbol. A symbol "refers to the object that it denotes by virtue of a law, usually an association of general ideas, which operates to cause the Symbol to be interpreted as referring to that Object."[13] In other words, a symbol is related to its object through its interpretant because of a convention or correlating rule. By *law* Peirce means a "regularity of the indefinite future."[14] The relation of a symbol to its object depends upon this continuing regularity. Words, propositions, and arguments are typical symbols. So long as and so far as the conventions associating sign and interpretant are real, the relation of sign and object is real. In English, the word *star* stands in a real relation to the general kind of heavenly body it denotes simply because it will be so interpreted by convention. The so-called arbitrariness of language is simply a recognition that, in themselves, symbols need not be iconic or indexical; nevertheless, they are governed by law and so are not truly arbitrary. "You can write down the word 'star,' but that does not make you the creator of the word, nor if you erase it have you destroyed the word. The word lives in the minds of those who use it."[15]

The reality of the law, however, does not guarantee the physical reality of the object. The law really exists because people habitually associate *star* with the idea of a heavenly body, whether you or I or anyone else thinks about that law of association or not. The reality of the law parallels the reality of a dream. Suppose I had a dream last night. The dream was a real event, whether I or anyone else thinks it so. Of course, the events in the dream were not real if they existed only in the dream. In the same way, the ontological relation between the symbol and its semiotic object is real because the law of interpretation is real, but the semiotic object may not have real existence as a dynamic or physical object. As Peirce notes:

[T]hat which is general has its being in the instances which it will determine. There must, therefore, be existent instances of what the Symbol denotes, although we must here understand by "existent," existent in the possibly imaginary universe to which the Symbol refers. The Symbol will indirectly, through the association or other law, be affected by those instances; and thus the Symbol will involve a sort of Index, although an Index of a peculiar kind.[16]

Peirce's approach requires us to draw careful distinctions between concepts like *social reality* and reality itself.

Furthermore, symbols change, drawing upon icons and other symbols in this process, which Peirce sees as evolutionary:

Symbols grow. They come into being by development out of other signs, particularly from icons, or from mixed signs partaking of the nature of icons and symbols. We think only in signs. These mental signs are of mixed nature; the symbol-parts of them are called concepts. If a man makes a new symbol, it is by thoughts involving concepts. So it is only out of symbols that a new symbol can grow. *Omne symbolum de symbolo.* A symbol, once in being, spreads among the peoples. In use and in experience, its meaning grows. Such words as *force, law, wealth, marriage,* bear for us very different meanings from those they bore to our barbarous ancestors.[17]

Symbols are the primary form of deliberation and argument. Symbols, like icons, are susceptible of error and falsehood, however. Since political representatives are symbols, they could stand for a supposed will of the people that does not really exist. Whereas the postmodern approach is to deconstruct the symbols by showing that the interpretant is indeterminate and so the object cannot be known, the pragmatic approach is to make the symbol more determinate in ways that bring it more into line with reality. This need to make symbols more determinate brings us once more to the pragmatic maxim: "[C]onsider what effects, which might conceivably have practical bearings, we conceive the object of our conception to have. Then, our conception of these effects is the whole of our conception of the object."[18] From the discussion of types of signs, we should now see this maxim as a rule to connect symbols with indexicality. Let us recall from our earlier discussion in chapter 2 of the ways of fixing belief that Peirce's idea of the scientific method was simply that method "by which our beliefs may be caused by nothing human, but by . . . something upon which our thinking has no effect."[19] Therefore, the logical meaning of a symbol must be all of the possible practical effects implied by that symbol. In that way, our conceptions can be tested against experience. Experience, in turn, is our interaction with the indexical signs of that "something" that is reality. Therefore, when I claim that *legitimacy* is the logical interpretant of the relation between politician and will of the people, I am saying that legitimacy is the general term for a set of antecedent-consequent propositions that could conceivably be experienced. *Legitimacy* has cognitive meaning only if the will of the people can somehow show itself in actual experience. If so, then the political representative can grow like any symbol and determine a semiotic object that is more like the real object because the symbol is, in turn, determined indexically by that real object. Because the symbol is general, however, neither it nor its object can be as fully determined as a pure indexical sign. It must instead be of the nature of a general rule incorporating many indexicals, projecting them into the future as that "regularity of the indefinite future" that constitutes Thirdness. Based on past indexicals—brute facts—the symbol can be refined to better represent the future. As the postmodernists have shown, indeterminacy is a problem that can never be completely resolved. Using pragmatic realism, however, we can make the indeterminate more determinate. The likelihood that legitimacy will always be a matter of degree does not negate its meaning.

Representation as Argument

In his later years, Peirce restated the pragmatic maxim in a form particularly appropriate for our discussion of political representation as symbol: "The entire intellectual purport of any symbol consists in the total of all general modes of rational conduct, which, conditionally upon all the possible different circumstances and desires, would ensue upon the acceptance of the symbol."[20] Here he makes the generality of the symbol more obvious. He also points out the indeterminacy inherent in that generality because it must apply to "all the possible different circumstances and desires" as antecedents of the "modes of rational conduct" that "would ensue upon acceptance of the symbol." Rational conduct captures the sense of both logical (cognitive) and energetic (behavioral) interpretants. Emotive interpretants may enter in indirectly by underlying desires as conditions for hypotheses. The emphasis in both science and ethics, however, is on deliberate conduct, "and deliberate conduct is self-controlled conduct."[21] Peirce does not deny the importance of what Lyotard would call the libidinal; Peirce acknowledges "an occult nature of which and of its contents we can only judge by the conduct that it determines, and by phenomena of that conduct."[22] By the pragmatic maxim, we can, therefore, deliberate only about the conduct that arises from our occult nature.

Self-control, whether ethical or logical, imposes order on the libidinal chaos, even when the ultimate purpose is to satisfy the libido. Lyotard's attempt to develop a libidinal economy failed because *economy* as a concept implies thirdness that is rationally discerned. Rational consciousness is not the same as immediate consciousness, which is "simple Feeling viewed from another side."[23] For Peirce, rational consciousness is a form of self-control:

The machinery of logical self-control works on the same plan as does moral self-control, in multiform detail. The greatest difference, perhaps, is that the latter serves to inhibit mad puttings forth of energy, while the former most characteristically insures us against the quandary of Buridan's ass. The formation of habits under imaginary action . . . is one of the most essential ingredients of both; but in the logical process the imagination takes far wider flights, proportioned to the generality of the field of inquiry, being bounded in pure mathematics solely by the limits of its own powers, while in the moral process we consider only situations that may be apprehended or anticipated.[24]

Both the logic of science and the practical wisdom of ethics depend upon a kind of mental experimentation aimed at determining possible consequences. The difference is a matter of the scope of this mental experimentation; but both aim at conclusions that are better habits of thought and action.

The pragmatic understanding of reasoning as self-controlled mental experimentation leads us to consider the political representative's relation to the third trichotomy of signs—classification according to how the sign's interpretant represents it. The three types of signs according to this classification are the rheme, the dicisign, and the argument. A rheme "is understood to represent its object in its characters merely"; a dicisign "is understood to represent its object in respect to actual existence"; and an argument is understood to represent its object "as being an ulterior sign through a law, namely, the law that the passage from all such premisses to such conclusions tends to the truth."[25] A typical rheme (the Greek *rhēma* means *word*) is a word like *red* that by itself is understood to stand for a possible quality; but *red* by itself does not imply the actual existence of that quality. In a political advertisement, a flag may be understood as standing for a possible quality of patriotism. Considered in itself, the flag is a rheme. The producers of the ad, of course, did not place the flag there to be considered in itself. The flag is supposed to be associated with the candidate. In that case, the sign relating the flag and the candidate is a dicisign. A typical form of a dicisign is a proposition, such as "This pen is red" or "George Bush is patriotic." In interpreting these dicisigns, we understand them to signify the actual existence of these qualities in the designated subjects. The visual dicisign of George Bush's image in front of the flag is a vaguer form of the proposition "George Bush is patriotic."

Rhemes and dicisigns are clearly involved in political representation; however, the political representative as legitimate sign (that is, as logical and ethical sign) of the will of the people must be interpreted as an argument. No possible quality, no single proposition suffices to represent the complex will of the people. To stand legitimately for the admittedly vague will of the people, political representation must be interpreted as a valid process of joining together rhemes and dicisigns so that the conclusions will be habits of action agreeing with that will.

Inference is the process of joining together rhemes and dicisigns to reach conclusions. The method we use to make inferences is not random but regular, following what Peirce calls "leading principles," which are habits of thought.[26] Any given inference may be good or bad either because its premises are true or false or because our habit of making inferences of that type will or will not generally lead to the truth. An argument is a sign that is interpreted as the sign of an inference. Interpreting a sign as an argument makes it possible logically to criticize the leading principle employed as well as the truth of the premises. Recognizing that political representation is argument therefore enables us to criticize the premises used and the leading principles that should presumably be general methods of achieving legitimate representation.

Peirce divides inference into two major types, explicative and ampliative. Explicative inference is deductive; the conclusion makes explicit what was implicit in the sign system being used. The general leading principle of explicative inference is "that in a system of signs in which no sign is taken in two different senses, two signs which differ only in their manner of representing their object, but which are equivalent in meaning, can always be substituted for one another."[27] Explicative inference is concerned with the essential depth of a sign, as described in chapter 4. As we experiment with transformations, we increase the essential depth of a given sign. This deductive inference can produce real insights. Deductive inference, for example, allows us to solve mathematical problems by substituting equivalent values, formulas, and diagrams.

In Peirce's approach, abstraction is a form of deductive transformation that can be very important in explication. Hypostatical abstraction is the transformation of a concrete predicate to an abstract substantive. A transformational grammar, for example, allows us to convert "These stoves are black" to "Blackness is a common quality of these stoves." Blackness is a hypostatic abstraction that can be useful to us because it allows us to focus on the quality black while maintaining equivalence of meaning. In political representation, however, such abstractions often suffer from equivocation. To increase the likelihood that our representatives will represent our communal interests, for example, we would prefer them to be motivated by a real care for the community. By hypostatic abstraction, this care could be labeled *patriotism*, as in "George Bush's service in World War II is a sign of his patriotism." This statement, however, also reflects a popular interpretant of patriotism as "willingness to go to war." Given a true caring for the community, under some circumstances willingness to go to war would not be rational conduct ensuing from that sense of patriotism as caring. Thus the argument contrasting the patriotism of George Bush and Bill Clinton because of their war records relies on an equivocation. The argument is not a valid argument because it does not follow the leading principle of deduction that only equivalent meanings may be substituted. Willingness to go to war is not equivalent to caring for the community.

Foucault's analysis of the positivities of a discursive regime also points to the equivocation of hypostatic abstractions like *madness*. Foucault's argument shows that *madness* has had different implications in different regimes. These implications both depend on and form power relations in that regime. In some cases, simple opposition to the dominant power of a regime is taken as a conclusive sign of madness. Through such equivocation, political enemies can be silenced. We should recall here that hypostatic abstractions are made, in practice, from a given perspective in a given context, that is, according to a given interest. Hypostatic abstraction directs our attention to the quality abstracted by converting it from a predicate to a potential subject, which may then be considered in terms of its own implications. Zeman compares this focusing of attention to the process of gestalt formation that occurs in problematic situations.[28] Abstraction as a means of organizing our environment is real insofar as the elements it unifies are real, but the scope of the reality is limited by the interest involved in the process of abstraction. The deductive problem arises because the same symbol, for example, *madness*, is used to stand for different objects that were the result of different processes of abstraction. The unity of the abstraction is then illusory. To guard against ambiguous uses of such abstractions, political argument should follow the pragmatic maxim and indicate the general modes of rational conduct that the term implies, in short, the policy implications. What kinds of behavior, for example, would justify institutionalization under a particular understanding of *madness?*

Deductive inference that makes the implicit explicit can be especially useful in exploring the "promising season" of political representation. A deductive argument presumes the truth of the general premise and works out its implications. So when a candidate states "No new taxes" or promises a middle-class tax break, deductive logic can be used to explore the implications of that claim. The deductive processes of mathematics can be used to show what the results on the budget will be. The argument is often complex, because other assumptions must usually be made in a multistep deductive argument. Each step's assumption must be evaluated for the strength of its claim to truth. While the validity of a deductive argument depends on its adherence to the leading principle, its strength comes from the credibility of its major premise, or rule, that is applied to the particular case, leading to a result.

The fact that we must use assumptions to work out the implications suggests that we are often uncertain about the rule that applies. Developing an accurate general rule then becomes the objective of the inference. This is a case of ampliative inference, in which our knowledge of the world, rather than just our codes, is increased. The problem is that observed facts are simply observed facts related to a particular set of circumstances. No observed fact can, in itself, tell us what would be appropriate conduct in the future. For this reason narrative as the simple relating of events is not inference. When the narrative leads to a belief in general patterns that would hold true in the future, however, the narrative is an inference. An ampliative inference adds to and enlarges knowledge (*amplus* means *large*) by providing new rules to guide future action or by modifying the rules we already believe. The two types of ampliative inference are abductive and inductive.

Abduction is the invention of a hypothesis to explain some surprising fact. Under invention I include discovering, selecting, and what Peirce calls "entertaining" a hypothesis for interrogation.[29] The point is that abduction only holds a hypothesis for interrogation; nevertheless, it is a logical inference taking the following form:

The surprising fact, C, is observed;
But if A were true, C would be a matter of course,
Hence, there is reason to suspect that A is true.[30]

The leading principle here is that the hypothesis must account for the fact or facts that it claims to explain. The antecedent-consequent relation must be true. The abductive inference then leads from consequent to antecedent. The result of the inference, however, is merely a plausible explanation. Furthermore, a large number of hypotheses $(A_1 \ldots A_n)$ might just as well explain the fact C. For this reason Peirce suggests that "the whole question of what one out of a number of possible hypotheses ought to be entertained becomes purely a question of economy."[31] If the concept of economy includes all of the costs to the ecosystem involved, then Peirce's notion of scientific hypothesis applies as well to political argument.

Consider, as an example of abductive reasoning in political deliberation, Lincoln's repeated use of a conspiracy hypothesis in the Lincoln-Douglas debates. Lincoln claimed that the surprising fact that slavery could no longer be prohibited in the territories could be explained as the result of a conspiracy between Senator Douglas, Presidents Pierce and Buchanan, and Chief Justice Taney. Even though a conspiracy would account for the fact, the hypothesis is not justified economically because of the cost to the system of political discourse that arises from entertaining it. Such conspiracy theories vilify the opposition and create hatred among an already divided community. Furthermore, although the conspiracy theory was repeatedly denied by Douglas, it could not be easily disproved. A hypothesis that is not easily tested is also a poor economic choice. Conspiracy theories may make aesthetically pleasing narratives, but they are generally ethically undesirable as abductive reasoning in political discourse.

Although ampliative because it adds a hypothesis to the facts, abductive reasoning accepts the hypothesis only as an interrogation. Our knowledge does not grow until we have reason to place some confidence in the hypothesis. The form of inference that gives us reason for confidence is induction. Induction is the testing of the hypothesis against experience to allow reality to influence our belief in the hypothesis indexically. Given a hypothesis, we must determine what other implications it has in practice under some condition and then test to see whether, in fact, when the condition occurs, the implication holds true. The hypothesis that the United States has the finest medical system in the world, for example, has been treated as an assumption in deductive argument about government medical programs. It would be better treated, however, as a hypothesis to be tested. If the United States has the best medical system, then we could reasonably expect to have lower infant mortality rates than other countries among comparable population groups. If this is not true, then the hypothesis should be modified. In this case, we could employ fuzzy logic to modify the hypothesis so that the claim becomes that the United States has some degree of excellence in some regards and less in others. This continual testing and modification of our hypotheses result in the approximation of our inductions to truth in the long run. The reason is simply that inductions are reasoning from part to whole, and "a sufficiently long succession of inferences from parts to whole will lead men to a knowledge of it, so that in that case they cannot be fated on the whole to be thoroughly unlucky in their inductions."[32]

Effective inductive inference requires openness and honesty, which is especially difficult to achieve in partisan political discourse. Once we recognize political representation as argument and we also recognize that confidence in our major premises depends upon inductive testing, then we must conclude that effective criticism of our political discourse must incorporate criticism of the openness and honesty of that discourse. Here the openness of the process of arguing becomes a factor in the validity of the argument because representation cannot stand for the will of the whole community if parts of that community are excluded from participation in the process. Legitimacy thus demands open, honest argument.

Ampliative inference is especially important to the politics of representation because of the vague nature of the semiotic object. As a community, we know our own will only vaguely. Our system of political representation is how we determine our own will. The ongoing arguments constitute the mind of the community. This statement is so whether we recognize it or not, just as our own personal processes of semiotic inference constitute our minds whether we recognize them or not. Recognition of the nature and role of semiosis, however, makes logical criticism of that process possible. This logical criticism of the community's semiotic processes is the basis of ethical criticism of political discourse.

Politicians are, of course, more than symbols. They are mothers, fathers, lawyers, bankers—people with lives apart from their role as symbols. This statement is true of all signs, however: they have a material nature that may be considered apart from their nature as signs in a particular semiotic process. The ethical problem for politicians is that they must balance their needs as individuals with their responsibilities to serve as symbols for the mind of the community. Yet this is simply another example of the ecological ethic. The whole community is the ecosystem that enables a politician to accomplish his or her goals. This politician is, therefore, obliged to fulfill his or her function within the ecosystem as effectively as possible. A politician's function as a symbol is to improve the quality of argument in the community.

Although it was first expressed more than 200 years ago, Edmund Burke's explanation of his responsibilities as a representative of the electors of Bristol reflects a partial recognition of the necessary role of the representative in deliberation:

> Certainly, gentlemen, it ought to be the happiness and glory of a representative to live in the strictest union, the closest correspondence, and the most unreserved communication with his constituents. Their wishes ought to have great weight with him; their opinion high respect; their business unremitted attention. It is his duty to sacrifice his repose, his pleasures, his satisfactions, to theirs; and above all, ever, and in all cases, to prefer their interest to his own. But his unbiassed opinion, his mature judgment, his enlightened conscience, he ought not to sacrifice to you; to any man, or to any set of men living. These he does not derive from your pleasure; no, nor from the law and the constitution. They are a trust from Providence, for the abuse of which he is deeply answerable. Your representative owes you, not his industry only, but his judgment; and he betrays, instead of serving you, if he sacrifices it to your opinion.
>
> My worthy colleague says, his will ought to be subservient to yours. If that be all, the thing is innocent. If government were a matter of will upon any side, yours, without question, ought to be superior. But government and legislation are matters of reason and judgment, and not of inclination; and what sort of reason is that, in which the determination precedes the discussion; in which one set of men deliberate and another decide; and where those who form the conclusion are perhaps three hundred miles distant from those who hear the arguments?[33]

For the most part, I agree with Burke. The process of adequate representation and the determination of the "general good," however, are not as simple as he indicates. We cannot simply turn over our deliberation to our representatives as though they were ideal Aristotelian aristocrats. If we do, they will lose touch with the indexical signs of our own self-representation that are the source of their legitimacy. The process of representation as argumentation must build out of a complex of signs that eventually connect with indexicals.

The general public also shares in the responsibility. We the people are the source of the indexical signs that should improve the hypotheses in the ongoing argument. Despite my emphasis on logic, I do not believe we can logically neglect feelings; feelings are important elements in the argument. The screams of pain from the inner city are indexical signs that our hypotheses need correction. Ignoring these feelings is both illogical and unethical. Nevertheless, the feelings in themselves do not provide guides for modes of rational conduct that will address those feelings in the future. We must, as a community, reason about those feelings. This statement implies that we all should express our feelings to our representatives and that we should suggest hypotheses for policies, but we should also recognize that those hypotheses are to be interrogated and corrected inductively by information from the whole community. Each of us should realize that our individual desires must be balanced against the needs of the whole community if rational conduct is going to be possible at the communal level. Not just our politicians, but we ourselves must accept our ecological responsibility.

An effective community is possible only to the degree that public and politicians accept responsibility for their role in shaping public discourse. An effective community is an ecosystem that works at supporting all of its members; all of its members are then obligated to support the community. In practice this will involve confrontation as well as cooperation. Arguments don't arise unless there are differences of opinion. The communal spirit does not avoid conflict but channels it into reasonable argument in the belief that the good of all will be served in the long run. This belief is itself an inductive inference that must be continually supported by the symbolic actions of politicians and public. If the belief is not supported, the indeterminate will of the people cannot be made more determinate. The communal mind will be the schizophrenic mind of postmodern fragmentation. Modes of action will not be rational but will be chaotic reactions to feelings whose effect on the community will be determined by equally chaotic distributions of power in the community. The ecological model suggests that something better is possible, but achieving a good community requires ethical action on the part of politicians and public.

Some members of the public play a larger role than others because of the nature of our communicative system. Our levels of community far exceed the bounds of an Aristotelian polis. As a result, the system of political communication is multiply mediated. This mediation has profound effects on the nature of our political argumentation. Members of the media, because of the role they play in the communicative ecosystem, have a special ethical responsibility regarding political communication. Politicians, in turn, have an ethical responsibility to use media wisely, that is, ecologically.

The Ecosystem of Mediated Politics

Considering the semiotic function politicians play in our communal deliberation, the current ecosystem of political discourse shows symptoms of ecological disaster. As Bennett has shown, our postmodern system of representation is dominated by three factors: money, marketing, and media control.[34] These factors are all related to the problem of media. Advertising and marketing costs have risen, creating an ever-increasing need for money. News media are themselves expected to be profit centers. While the reach of our media makes deliberation on a national scale possible, the expense of such coverage makes effective deliberation less likely.

We have always had media involved in politics, of course. A medium is merely something that comes in between the sign and its interpreter. Media require the translation of signs into other signs, which are interpretants of the original sign. As I write this, I am translating my ideas by means of the keyboard into electronic signals that will then be printed so that eventually you will read them in the medium of a book. As Derrida argues, even my conversation with myself cannot be truly immediate because the original sign must always undergo some translation through a system of signs. This lack of immediacy is not a problem, however, as long as the mediate interpretants are equivalent to the original sign or are more developed versions of that sign. In either case, the original sign can be carried forward into the ongoing argument by means of effective interpretants.

In our political discourse, the original signs that should be carried forward into the argument are the experiences and desires of all the members of the community. As the argument progresses, these original signs will be synthesized into more advanced signs, resulting in hypotheses that must then be tested against the experiences and desires of the community. In a local organization, for example, the members' experiences and desires give rise to an awareness of a problem through discussion. In the organization, this problem may then be referred to a committee for further discussion and development of hypotheses. The committee seeks out further information in developing and initially testing its hypotheses. The hypotheses are then brought forth as committee proposals at a general meeting. In the deliberation at the general meeting, the proposals may be further modified on the basis of the members' experience and desires. The modified proposal is then tested by being put to a vote. If the proposal is approved, it becomes organizational policy. Policy should remain open, however, to inductive testing and continued modification based on experience. Any attempt to block this continuing process of inquiry by manipulating parliamentary procedure, for example, is unethical and illogical. The purpose of parliamentary procedure is to bring together these various elements in the inquiry as a kind of fuzzy logic controller to ensure that all inputs are accounted for. If the fuzzy logic controller works well, everyone should achieve some satisfaction out of the result. If some members use their status or parliamentary knowledge to advance their own interests unfairly, however, the logic fails.

Naturally, the problem of synthesizing and testing becomes more difficult as the numbers of people and the levels of mediation increase. Any political representative should be a locus of argument that incorporates the needs and experiences of all constituents. The representative serves as mediating sign in the same way that a committee does in the local organization. At these larger scales, however, the input to the representative is normally previously synthesized by other mediating signs, which include the news media and special interests. Since there is no voice speaking for the general interest, the news media assume that role by default. If this ecosystem is to function at all effectively, the news media must effectively synthesize all of the relevant opinions of the general public as well as report on the activities of that public's representatives. In that way, the community deliberates through the mediation of news media and political representatives in forming hypotheses and also in testing those hypotheses before and after they become policy. I have oversimplified the issue of mediation, of course, because entertainment media can also affect our deliberation about public policy and the line between news and entertainment has become more and more blurred. Many forms of media constitute our system of public deliberation.

The common complaint that government is out of touch with its constituents indicates either that our system of political discourse does not carry the original signs of all community members into the further steps of argument or that the proposed and actual policies resulting from the argument are not effectively communicated back to those members. A third possibility is that those complaining have failed to take into account the needs of the community as a whole in assessing the effectiveness of government. All of these possibilities involve ethical failures by different elements of our political ecosystem.

The failure of the system of argument to represent all of its constituent voices involves both news media and political representatives. Political representatives have become more and more dependent upon special interest money. Bennett notes that contributions to Congress by political action committees (PACs) rose from $55.3 million in 1980 to $150 million in 1990.[35] PAC money may not buy votes, but it does buy the PAC a hearing for its case. The more representatives depend on special interest money, the more those interests are able to dominate the argument. The time to hear all points of view is limited, and the lobbyists are buying greater proportions of it. The abductive process of developing ideas for policies is thus distorted because the input is distorted. Sometimes the distortion is simply the result of special interests' dominating the time available for argument; at other times the threat of withdrawing the money is used to directly influence policy. Philip Morris executives reportedly asked New York city arts groups that had received millions in grant money from the company to contact city lawmakers during deliberation about regulations on smoking. The arts groups were requested to remind the lawmakers about the importance of the grants.[36] In this case, the implied threat appears to be an attempt to subvert the argumentative process. If the attempt was made as reported, it is unethical on the corporation's part. On the other hand, to the degree that representatives allow lobbyists to dominate an argument unfairly, the representatives are also acting unethically because their arguments no longer represent the general public interest.

These representatives, however, must have alternative sources available to improve the argument. Some of the responsibility for listening to a broader range of interests belongs with the representatives. They can improve communicative access with their constituents. Relying only on advanced technology like FAX machines and e-mail will also distort the input. Representatives must earnestly seek out their constituents' opinions. Since the well educated and the well-to-do are more likely to be heard, a representative must learn to listen to the poor and less educated whose voices are most often ignored. Even so, all representatives will still depend on news media for more information about their constituents. The news media also have responsibility to help keep the public and its officials informed about the state of their whole community.

Unfortunately, the news media are also limited by financial constraints. Many of the same corporations that are effective lobbyists are also major advertisers. Media organizations depend upon the advertising. Sometimes this dependence upon advertising constrains the content of the news. Many local newspapers depend heavily upon automobile dealers' advertising. The coverage of new models in those newspapers' automobile sections is generally much more complimentary than the coverage in a consumer magazine that does not depend on advertising support. The need for advertising money is at least a constant temptation to distort coverage, but most journalists recognize the temptation as an ethical problem. Less obvious is how the need to draw an audience can also have ethical implications. To some degree, news must entertain as well as inform. In this regard, news is no different from any other form of rhetoric; Cicero recognized that effective rhetoric must delight the audience as well as inform them. As the entertainment function comes to dominate, however, the informative function is weakened. Much of the information we as a public need is about problems in the community. We need to know who is suffering and why. In short, we need to know the bad news. Audiences grow tired of bad news, however. In order to hold an audience, news media must limit the bad news and incorporate more entertaining good news and celebrity gossip. As the competition moves toward a tabloid style that emphasizes entertainment and gossip over information, our system of political discourse suffers. This decline is intensified by our increased dependence on television as an information source. Because of time limits, television simply cannot convey as much information relevant to public argument as print media. The more time that television news must devote to entertainment, the less relevant information the public and its representatives obtain. The balance between hard news and entertainment is itself an ethical decision.

The well-known emphasis by the news media on the "horse race" aspects of politics is an example of their being driven by the need to entertain. The drama of the race is more entertaining than a detailed analysis of the issues involved. The confrontation on issues, however, offers the public an opportunity to examine the current state of the political argument and offer course corrections. Experience shows that politicians must be pressured into revealing their true positions on the issues. Some vagueness about future plans is necessary because of unseen conditions that may arise, but politicians tend to use vagueness to avoid offending any elements of the audience. This type of vagueness blocks the path of inquiry by running from the confrontation that is necessary to advance the argument. Members of the news media have the opportunity to ask questions that can lead to confrontation with the real issues of public concern. Many news reporters seem to relish their adversarial role in relation to politicians. The ecological function of their adversarial role, however, is to advance the argument on issues of public interest. The adversarial questions must be relevant to the public interest, which is not to be confused with the curiosity of a potential audience. Arousing and satisfying curiosity is an entertainment function if it is not related to questions of public interest.

As a public we need to deliberate about the consequences of our general policies; that is the public interest that news media can serve. Individual cases are important as indexical tests of the correspondence between our general beliefs and reality. Journalists, however, tend to focus on the indexical itself and ignore the general issue that is related to the public interest. By losing track of the general issue, they often focus on irrelevant indexicals. Asking a candidate how he would respond if his wife were raped does not gain information about the general issues involved in prison furlough programs. It confuses the candidate as a person with the candidate as a public representative. Currently, as I write this, we are inundated with coverage of the O. J. Simpson trial. Most of this coverage is celebrity gossip and soap opera stories. This entertainment function of satisfying the audience's curiosity does great damage to the people involved; yet it is justified on the basis of the "public interest." The public interest lies in observing how our system of justice works. The forensic issue of this particular case will be determined by the judges and juries directly involved. The rest of us are concerned with how well the justice system handles problems such as racism or celebrity privilege. Stories that provide information on how well the system operates are stories in the public interest. Other curiosity we may have about the lurid details of the case is not *public* in the Deweyan or Peircean sense. A public is not simply a collection of curious individuals but a group with a shared general purpose of controlling future consequences as a group. The public interest is a thirdness, a generality of the indefinite future. Our beliefs about the current state of our justice system are hypotheses that require testing by specific cases. But the public relevance of those cases is simply the relation to those hypotheses, not the satisfaction of our personal curiosity.

In the same way, many of the tabloid stories about President Clinton's alleged affairs were examples of celebrity gossip with little or no public relevance. The president functions as a symbol of broad generality in the nation, representing the whole country as his or her constituency. A presidential campaign provides an opportunity to integrate ongoing arguments with new information at this higher level of community and test the results with the public. The character of the president is certainly relevant but only insofar as it relates to public function. Clinton's marital successes and failures are important only if they affect his ability to function as a public representative in developing and executing policy. Extramarital affairs that involved abuse of public power, for example, such as using the state police to assist in those affairs, would be relevant if substantiated. Allegations of purely private relationships are irrelevant, however, and allegations of abuse of power should focus on that abuse more than on the lurid details of the supposed affair. The claim that Clinton's failure to maintain marital vows is a public matter because it is a sign that he would not uphold his official oath seems to be based on a flimsy analogy. Research into his public career would offer much more relevant information about his adherence to official oaths. The claim that a president with a history of extramarital affairs cannot be a good role model does address a symbolic role of representation; however, if the news media have introduced the stories of irrelevant affairs, their actions are primarily responsible for the destruction of the role model. Without the lurid gossip, the simple fact that the Clinton marriage has survived difficult problems would serve as an effective symbol of the importance of family relationships. In fact, most of the major media coverage of the supposed affairs has been framed by the horse race approach to coverage, addressing the question of how this might hurt his election or reelection chances. For the most part, the entertainment aspects of the horse race and of celebrity gossip have overwhelmed the small amount of public information involved in these stories.

Commentators have complained that today there is no end to campaigning. The difference between the promising season and the alibi season observed by Will Rogers has now disappeared. The complaints are misdirected. Insofar as campaigning involves effective two-way communication with constituents, this would be a desirable change. Effective two-way communication would eliminate the problem of community voices being heard in the formation of policy and also the problem of communicating the current state of the argument back to the community. As we have seen, these problems are likely sources of the common belief that government is out of touch with the people. So the complaint should be directed not against the continuity of campaigning but against the nature of political campaigning today. Bennett warns against "the conversion of the national political scene into an endless election in which the goal is to dodge the problems and the issues of the day, keep one's image strong, and make it to the next election with a full campaign chest and no mistakes to live down."[37] The endless election is not the problem; the use of marketing techniques to avoid real argument is the ethical and political problem confronting contemporary democracy. Since the function of political representatives is to serve as argumentative symbols in the communal process of deliberation, marketing techniques that avoid the argument are unethical. This pragmatic function of political representatives supports Jamieson's critique of campaigns that avoid argument and engagement. Engagement involves the "clash" of positions and the "extension" of responses that move the argument forward.[38] Both argument and engagement, as she uses the terms, are elements of the process of semiotic inference that constitutes argument as described by Peirce. Unfortunately, Jamieson's justification of argument is based on Enlightenment modernism, and she avoids the clash with postmodernism and the extension that would result.

Nevertheless, her critique is valid, and her studies of the present state of political discourse reveal the depth of the problem.

Both Jamieson and Bennett offer hypotheses for improving the state of our political discourse. Yet these hypotheses will not be seriously tested until politicians accept their ethical responsibilities as argumentative symbols in the community's process of semiosis and members of the news media accept their responsibility to advance the argument on behalf of the public. Furthermore, members of this public must learn to accept their ethical responsibility to balance the good of the whole ecosystem with their own personal desires in assessing the state of the argument and the legitimacy of their representatives. We can never achieve a working consensus if we do not accept ecological constraints on our own wants. Fuzzy logic requires that our opinions be included in the control system but also that no individual opinion dominates the others. No system of political communication can achieve a perfect balance, but our ethical obligation should lead us to improve what we have.

The Role of the Rhetorical Critic

One of the first steps in improving our system of political communication is effective critique of our current system. As Dewey wrote almost seventy years ago, "The essential need is the improvement of the methods and conditions of debate, discussion and persuasion. That is *the* problem of the public."[39] Rhetorical critics fulfill an ecological niche in our communicative ecosystem by providing effective critiques that improve public deliberation. The community supports intellectuals in general because they provide information that serves the community in either the long or short term. Because they are supported by the community, rhetorical critics are ethically obliged to reciprocate in teaching and research by providing information to improve public communication.

Although I have criticized some theoretical weaknesses in the works of Jamieson and Bennett, I recognize both as having fulfilled their ethical function by informing the public of the state of our political ecosystem and offering suggestions for improvement. Again, although I disagree strongly with his nominalistic postmodernism, I agree with McKerrow that rhetorical criticism should be a *critical rhetoric* that participates in public deliberation as both theory and praxis.[40] McKerrow follows Foucault in arguing for the role of the specific intellectual who uses learned expertise to produce a critical rhetoric. I differ from McKerrow and Foucault in believing that effective rhetorical criticism can truly improve our communicative ecosystem. McKerrow seeks to transform; but, because his nominalism eliminates reality, it also eliminates a reasonable hope in *real* improvement. In postmodern nominalism, concepts like justice and truth exist only as elements within a Rortian web of beliefs. Improvement is merely a refiguring of the web to emphasize some concepts and deemphasize others. Ultimately, then, improvement is not movement toward some ideal that is taken to be a real possibility of thirdness but movement driven by the libidinal desires of a particular critic shaped by that web of beliefs. A triadic perspective, on the other hand, recognizes that our understanding of ideals like justice and truth is constrained by our current semiotic system but does not give up hope that our understanding and practice can draw closer to those ideals. As Peirce pointed out, symbols grow in meaning. This triadic form of pragmatic meliorism, for example, implies that our understanding of justice has drawn closer to the real ideal of justice insofar as we have incorporated more members of the community, regardless of race and gender, under its scope. This reasonable hope in real progress makes less likely the possibility that skepticism will turn into cynicism as it did in the case of the comic-book author Morrison. Pragmatic realism can better sustain the practice of a critical rhetoric in the long run.

Jamieson and Bennett's works function differently from McKerrow's theoretical works (and my own present work) in reaching different audiences for different purposes. In calling for greater engagement by the social sciences, Dewey recognized the need for different types of research:

[A] genuine social science would manifest its reality in the daily press, while learned books and articles supply and polish tools of inquiry. . . . Even if social sciences as a specialized apparatus of inquiry were more advanced than they are, they would be comparatively impotent in the office of directing opinion on matters of concern to the public as long as they are remote from application in the daily and unremitting assembly and interpretation of "news." On the other hand, the tools of social inquiry will be clumsy as long as they are forged in places and under conditions remote from contemporary events.[41]

Theoretical arguments are important because they affect the actual practice of rhetorical criticism, which, in turn, should affect the practice of public communication. So both theorists and critics fulfill an ecological function in our communicative ecosystem.

Overall, theory and criticism should be public-centered rather than rhetor-centered. The tradition of neo-Aristotelian criticism has been almost exclusively rhetor-centered, focusing on the achievement of the rhetor's purpose. The term *good* is reduced to mean *effective*, which is reduced to mean *achieving the effects desired by the rhetor*. The clearest example of this rhetor-centered approach is Hill's analysis of Nixon's speech on Southeast Asia.[42] Hill argues that the speech should be evaluated only in terms of how it achieved Nixon's purpose with his target audience regardless of its other consequences for the public. Neo-Aristotelian criticism, as Hill presents it, seems to be far removed from Aristotle's idea of the function of rhetoric in the polis. In the first chapter of his *Rhetoric*, Aristotle argues that the usefulness of rhetoric is to ensure that public judgments are made on the basis of truth and justice (1355a) and that rhetoric is an offshoot of dialectic and ethics, which in his system is closely related to politics (1356a). Aristotle would likely agree with Hill that criticism of the truth of certain specific propositions in the speech belongs to other areas of study. This view, however, does not preclude a public-centered criticism of the invention, arrangement, and style of the speech. It seems to me that Aristotle's polis-centered practical philosophy would require such an approach.

As I have argued in chapter 4, of course, Aristotle's solutions to the problems of the public tended to be elitist. That elitism has been further exacerbated by being interpreted through the lens of Enlightenment individualism by the neo-Aristotelians. These critics in effect serve the oligarchs as Machiavelli did by showing them how better to achieve their purposes as rhetors with little regard for the good of the community. This rhetor-centered approach, bequeathed by the neo-Aristotelians, continues to influence the practice of rhetorical criticism even by those who consider themselves to be much more contemporary in their approach. In her book on rhetorical criticism, for example, Foss lists fantasy-theme analysis and Burkean analyses as ways to focus on the rhetor.[43] The fact that fantasies and dramas influence audience's motives and so have public consequences is lost in this rhetor-centered approach. The result is that the elitist tendency is carried into contemporary modes of analysis.

Bitzer's situational analysis reflects a generally pragmatic outlook on rhetoric that would allow for criticism on the basis of the appropriateness of the rhetoric as a response to a public problem.[44] Most of Bitzer's examples of rhetorical situations describe communal problems. The situational perspective, however, is often distorted by the rhetor-centered tradition. Instead of considering how the rhetoric responds to a public exigence, rhetor-centered critics focus on how the rhetoric responds to the rhetor's personal exigence. Elements in the situation are then seen as problems and possibilities for the rhetor to work his will, just as in the neo-Aristotelian approach. In their textbooks on rhetorical criticism, for example, both Hart and the Rybackis address situational elements primarily as constraints on the rhetor.[45] In contrast, the situational approach from an ecological perspective would consider how the rhetoric responds to the public exigence. The rhetor's personal exigence is simply another variable in the situation constraining the rhetoric. The ecologically minded critic would attempt to analyze what was possible within the constraints of the situation and compare that to what was actually achieved.

Public-centered rhetorical criticism would be a type of critical rhetoric because the critic seeks to contribute to the public argument by showing how the rhetoric used is or is not likely to achieve truth and justice. The rhetorical critic may not be particularly qualified at verifying the truth of particular propositions; but as with logical criticism, the critic should be qualified at analyzing the rhetorical principles being used and the likelihood that such principles will lead to truth. Furthermore, by considering a particular message as part of an ongoing argument, the critic can evaluate its contributions to the quality of that argument in a given rhetorical situation. In doing so, the critic is attempting to speak on behalf of the public, especially those elements of the public that are neglected in the argument, and so the critic operates as rhetor. The object of the critic's rhetoric, however, is the quality of the argument as a response to the public exigence, not the quality of the policy (or other object) discussed by the original rhetor. A public-centered critic seeks to improve the overall quality of public argument.

My point is not that all communication scholars should be writing public-centered criticism. As in all disciplines, scholars must work at various levels of analysis to improve the knowledge of leading principles, which are the scholar's tools for understanding how discourse works and how it could work better. My point is that the field of communication as a whole is obliged to keep the various levels of community informed about the quality of public argument. Granted that the tenure system does not encourage scholars to publish in popular media, scholars are nevertheless ethically obligated to use their expertise to support the larger communicative ecosystem by educating the general public. At different types of educational institutions and at different times in their careers, scholars can fulfill this function in different ways. Overall, however, we should recognize that currently we are not contributing enough to our community's political discourse. We scholars of rhetoric, together with members of the media and politicians, share ethical responsibility for the way we deliberate as a community. If we do not accept our responsibility, we act as parasites on our communicative ecosystem.

8

Retrospect and Prospect

I began this book by asserting my belief that most people still care about communicative ethics. This commonsense belief in ethics deserves our critical respect. My purpose here has been to clarify this belief in ethics by putting it into an ecological framework. My critical modification of the hypotheses of common sense is consistent with pragmatic realism, which Peirce called "critical common-sensism."[1] Pragmatic realism is forward looking, considering correspondence with anticipated consequences rather than with an antecedent origin to be the only practical measure of truth. As long as our hypotheses continue to be supported by their correspondence with consequences in experience, what reason besides obstinacy do we have for not calling them true? If they are true, then the relations they represent are real. Truth, however, is a fuzzy category: our hypotheses are likely to be true to some degree, not totally true or totally false. Abductive and inductive inference should be used to modify hypotheses as deductive inference is used to clarify the consequences implicit in them. My insistence that communities are real, as real as so-called individuals, should be understood in this context of fallibilism. Our hypotheses about our communities require continued testing, revision, and refinement. This fallibilism as a general principle, however, does not justify the conclusion that community as a concept is a mere positivity of our discursive regime.

The leap from fallibilism to cynicism seems to result from the disappointment of idealism. The case of the comic-book rhetor Morrison, with which we began, illustrates how postmodernism can lead to loss of hope when the real world fails to live up to idealistic expectations. If Morrison had been a pragmatic realist, he might still have suffered from burnout; but in withdrawing temporarily from the struggle, he would not have argued against the very possibility of improving the ecosystem. He would instead have recognized that his comic book was a form of public address giving him a role in public deliberation and that if he could not fill that role he should resign so that another could take his place. Then he would have sought another niche in the ecosystem in which he could better satisfy his own needs and the needs of the system. Perhaps he has now done that. Often our practice of living our lives is better than the theory we use to explain this practice.

I have, in fact, argued that the practice of postmodern theorists like Lyotard, Foucault, and Derrida is better than their theories justify. They seek after justice and truth in practice while their theories imply that *justice* and *truth* are merely names for libidinal urges, positivities of the discursive regime, or metaphysical concepts depending upon an illusory presence. They have deconstructed humane values without reconstructing alternatives that would make our lives better. At its best, postmodernism is parasitic upon those traditional values of justice and truth as it exposes hidden systems of power and privilege. At its worst, postmodernism undermines the possibility of achieving greater degrees of truth and justice in practice because it ends in nihilistic cynicism in theory. Lyotard, Foucault, and Derrida are not nihilistic cynics but only because they do not extend their theories to apply to the values that undergird their own practice. Succeeding generations of postmodernists are less likely to show such sentimentality; their own libidinal urges may lead them to carry the project out to completion. After all, the ability to deconstruct commonsense beliefs is taken as a sign of sophistication in some circles. One can achieve the pleasant feeling of sophisticated superiority by assuming that all of common sense is erroneous. Unfortunately, the final feeling will be depressed disillusion as one realizes there is no place left to stand.

We cannot escape the postmodern age in which we find ourselves, but we need not wholly embrace postmodernism as theory. Postmodern theorizing is an outgrowth of nominalism and dyadic semiology. The ecological ethic I offer here grows out of pragmatic realism and triadic semiotic. I believe it offers a better alternative to the problems of modernism. Pragmatic realism recognizes all the difficulties involved in signifying real objects, but it also recognizes that we have achieved some success in signifying or else we wouldn't be here to discuss the problem. We tend to take our successes for granted. Modernism was too optimistic about our success in reducing the manifold of experience to unity in totalizing theories; postmodernism is too pessimistic about our success in making true general statements of any kind in the chaos of diversity. Pragmatic realism recognizes that our world consists of both regularity and chaos. Regularity accounts for the ability to perceive real relations in a triadic semiotic; chaos accounts for new possibilities and true change.

Applied to our social relations, pragmatic realism engages the difficult problem of achieving community with diversity. We cannot begin to address this problem if we do not recognize that community is real, that our real relations with each other result in shared interests and common objectives. Ontological relations are real even if the object of a relation no longer exists physically. As Thirdnesses, such relations help determine our actions. Furthermore, our understanding of ourselves as individuals requires us to understand our transcendental relations to our ecosystems. To know thyself is to know ecologically. The community is a system of real relations just as the individual is. The art of communicative ethics requires us to perceive the relationship between our individual lives and our communities (as communicative ecosystems) and then to act so as to balance the needs of both. This ethical art makes great demands of practical wisdom, and we will not always succeed. Our perception of consequences is often mistaken because of semiotic errors or because random chance enters in. Nevertheless, we have the ethical obligation to try to support the ecosystem that supports us.

My argument calls for a partial return to the Aristotelian understanding of the relationship between ethics, politics, and rhetoric, especially as further developed by MacIntyre. This calls for a transformation of our current habits of privileging production over practice. The most important individual practice is the narrative quest for the good life. This quest will provide the internal goods that constitute happiness for the individual. But the quest must also take into account the practices of the various levels of the ecosystem in supporting all of its members in their individual quests. Supporting and reforming the ecosystem then become practices providing internal goods to the individual as well as the ecosystem. We cannot neglect production, but we must consider our communicative acts to be fuzzy hybrids of production and practice. In the long run, practice determines the quality of our lives and our communities. An ecological ethic calls for better understanding of the systemic effects of our communicative acts. The nature of our community depends upon the ontological relations established by our habits of communication.

The ability of the community to respond effectively within its environment depends upon the epistemic quality of our communication. Our habits of communication have important consequences for our communities both ontologically and epistemically.

Because our habits of communication have such important consequences, I have called for a return to the Aristotelian concept of virtue as habits that lead to happiness for both the individual and the community. I have, however, qualified the return to Aristotle by calling for a more pragmatic, process-oriented conception of reasoning. This shift will require an understanding of Peirce's logic of vagueness and more recent theories of fuzzy logic. I use fuzzy logic as the model of practical wisdom in deliberation. Effective deliberation requires the virtue of truthfulness to predominate, although I grant that, at times, telling the truth may not be the wisest course. All exceptions to the principle of honesty, however, rely on the justification that the act will, in the long run, promote better consequences for the ecosystem. In addition, fuzzy logic calls for systemic openness so that all inputs are incorporated into deliberation. Toleration is therefore an ecological virtue.

These ecological principles apply at all levels of our communicative ecosystem. Interpersonal communication, even between only two people, shapes an ontological relation that is a real community. This community may be just or unjust, depending upon how it supports its members in their quest for the good. Theories of competence in communication require a conception of what the good is in interpersonal communication. I suggest that interpersonal competence requires ecological wisdom and its concomitant virtues that would combine an ethic of justice with an ethic of care. We are not responsible for another person's achievement of happiness, but we are responsible for the condition of the ecosystem within which that person seeks happiness.

Business organizations are also communicative ecosystems, not simple mechanistic productive systems. Systems theory in the field of organizational communication requires a major perspective shift in the direction of practice rather than production. The tendency in our society to idolize production reduces our ability to improve the practice of our systems. We ignore the lessons of common sense that our relationships are more important than our products in the long run. The tendency of organizational theorists to equate the goals of the organization with the goals of management is an oligarchic, not an ecological, approach. Recent attempts to develop solidarity in organizations, such as Theory Z, have tendencies toward fascism because they do not account for real diversity. Weick's process-oriented theory is a significant improvement on traditional systems approaches. Weick's nominalism, however, fails to take into account the real ontological relations that develop. He can account for diversity and fragmentation but not for real community. An ecological perspective treats deliberation under the model of fuzzy logic as the epistemic source of sensus communis and the patterns of communication as the ontological source of the organizational community. The goals of the oligarchy are merely a part of the overall telos of this community. A reformed systems theory, therefore, should account for the communicative system's consequences on all members of that system and on the other systems that constitute its environment.

In representative politics, an ecological perspective considers the systemic function of the politician to be semiotic in nature. Political representatives serve us as symbols belonging to that class of symbols called arguments. The will of the people is not an a priori object but the a posteriori outcome of argumentation. Our political processes should be fuzzy logic controllers that follow leading principles of abductive, inductive, and deductive logic. Politicians are ethically obligated to fulfill their argumentative function well. All of us are ethically obligated to recognize that our will is merely an element in the working out of the communal will. We should take our opinions seriously but recognize the fallibilism of our partial perspective. The media should recognize its ethical obligation to support the ecosystem that supports it by communicating information relevant to the process of public argumentation. Finally, academics, especially rhetorical critics, have an obligation to improve the system of political argumentation so that it better follows the leading principles of fuzzy logic. Doing so requires more public-centered, rather than rhetor-centered, rhetorical criticism.

The ecological approach to ethics in some ways parallels the communicative ethics of Habermas. Habermas has also argued against the implications of postmodernism. He too has drawn upon Peirce's idea of the unlimited communication community in developing his own concept of society grounded in communicative action, since communicative interactions are regulated by intersubjectively recognized validity claims.[2] Habermas's well-known but often misunderstood *ideal speech situation* is, in his use, an attempt to deduce the consequences of the concept of an unlimited communication community in accordance with the pragmatic maxim. He has recently acknowledged that the terminology "ideal speech situation" has "concretistic connotations" that are "misleading." What he intended was a counterfactual ideal "that we can approximate in real contexts of argumentation." "At any given moment we orient ourselves by this idea when we endeavor to ensure that (1) all voices in any way relevant get a hearing, (2) the best arguments available to us given our present state of knowledge are brought to bear, and (3) only the unforced force of the better argument determines the 'yes' and 'no' responses of the participants."[3] As I have argued throughout, an ethic of this sort is presumed in the principles of logic and in the speech act of asserting truth. The degree to which we fall short of these conditions constitutes a flaw in our deliberative logic. Practical wisdom requires us to achieve these conditions as best we can. In this I concur with Habermas.

Where I disagree with Habermas is that point where he reverts to Kantian notions of morality and autonomy. Habermas distinguishes between "pragmatic, ethical, and moral" uses of practical reason.[4] The pragmatic use occurs "within the horizon of purposive rationality" in which values are taken for granted and appropriate means are deliberated. The ethical use occurs when values are questioned and justified on the Aristotelian basis of the "good life." This usage is consistent with Foucault's final project of ethics as the aesthetic of living. The moral use occurs when we must examine our pragmatic and ethical maxims because of their potential conflict with others. Morality questions whether such maxims are "suitable to regulate our communal existence." Habermas follows Kant in asserting that "moral commands are categorical or unconditional imperatives."[5] He follows Kant further in associating the moral with free will:

The categorical "ought" of moral injunctions, finally, is directed to the *free will (freien Willen)*, emphatically construed, of a person who acts in accordance with self-given laws; this will alone is autonomous in the sense that it is completely open to determination by moral insights. In the sphere of validity of the moral law, neither contingent dispositions nor life histories and personal identities set limits to the determination of the will by practical reason. Only a will that is guided by moral insight, and hence is completely rational, can be called autonomous. All heteronomous elements of mere choice or commitment to an idiosyncratic way of life, however authentic it may be, have been expunged from such a will.[6]

The ecological ethic challenges this trichotomy of practical reason. All our prudential decisions have potential impact on our ecosystem. A manufacturer's decision about how to make widgets, for example, should not be made without considering how the techniques of manufacture will affect the ecosystem. Ecologically, other levels of community should always be part of our decisions. Granted, we often do not consider the larger community in our practical decisions. The reason, however, is simply that we assume this particular decision does not have important affects on the ecosystem beyond ourselves. This assumption should be considered a hypothesis that is open to challenge—and we should remember, of course, that we must have good reason to challenge it. When we learn that our supposedly private actions have public consequences, those consequences become part of our deliberation. This approach incorporates a Deweyan conception of the public that results in a polymorphous understanding of the public sphere. In the ecological ethic, the "good life," that is, the good life narrative, must incorporate responsibility to the ecosystem that supports us. For this reason Foucault's ethic is insufficient for achieving a happy life narrative. We do not exist as individuals apart from our ecosystem. Pragmatic decisions are also ethical and moral decisions. As Dewey pointed out, ends and means are a continuum.

Habermas has simply abstracted elements of practical decisions and deliberation and made them into crisp categories unrealistically. I have emphasized the role of fuzzy logic in practical reasoning because it better captures our actual experience. If we take "rule" to mean, in the Peircean sense, an understanding of regularities of antecedent-consequent relations that guide our behavior, we do not make decisions simply from one type of rule as Habermas implies. Practical wisdom (phronēsis) in an ecological ethic requires deliberation in a fuzzy system that uses all the rules all the time. Kosko, the foremost proponent of fuzzy logic, explains how fuzzy systems deliberate: "In a fuzzy system which rule 'fires' or activates at which time? They all fire all the time. They fire in *parallel*. And all rules fire to some degree. Most fire to zero degree. They fire *partially*. Parallel and partially. That's how *associative* memory works. The result is a fuzzy weighted average."[7]

Habermas is stuck in two-valued logic when he treats the pragmatic, the ethical, and the moral as distinctive categories. In practical deliberation, these rules are used together. In different cases, some rules weigh more than in other cases. The purpose in abstracting rules is to correct errors in the process of deliberation; for example, when we find our interpersonal communication is not maintaining a good relationship, we may need consciously to correct our rules by abstracting them. Our decisions do not belong to one category, however. All of our decisions are ethical to some degree. The a priori category of the moral is transformed in the ecological ethic to a posteriori rules derived by abduction and tested in induction.

Autonomy is also a matter of degree. Some of our decisions are virtually compelled by circumstances. In others we have more choices, but we are never totally free of our circumstances and our libido. Practical wisdom involves balancing multiple desires. Our historical development has provided us with the opportunity to reason about our desires. Moral reasoning does not escape history. When we say our ethical decision was right, we are simply claiming that the unlimited community of ethical inquiry would agree with our decision in those circumstances because it strikes the right balance between our life narrative and the ecosystem. We cannot know that the claim is true; but this claim is what we aim for in our ethical decisions, just as truth is what we aim for in our logical decisions. In both cases, we learn to correct ourselves through experience. Autonomy is more a matter of self-correction than of escape from our historical circumstances.

Critical thinking increases autonomy by enabling us to correct our habits and improve our life narratives and the ecosystem supporting those narratives. Lyotard was right in criticizing much of systems theory for its production orientation; unfortunately, his agonistic libidinal economy was not a better alternative. When we fail to examine our dedication to production critically, we are less free to improve the quality of our lives. The practice-production distinction, of course, is not an either-or choice. Happiness in practice requires some degree of successful production in order to sustain our ecosystem. Again the problem is a matter of balancing differing demands using practical wisdom. Our reasoning has suffered because we have tended to reduce the idea of *logical* to the quantifiable, limited to crisp categories and mathematical probabilities. This tendency has biased us toward production rather than practice in our models of communicative competence at the interpersonal, organizational, and political levels of the ecosystem. This limited notion of rationality also contributes to the devaluing of the feminine in our deliberation. I believe that an ecological perspective emphasizing practice and employing multivalued logic in deliberation will increase our actual autonomy in our real historical circumstances. Better deliberation will allow us all to create better life narratives in better communities.

Better deliberation at the individual and the communal level can take place only when we develop the virtues of openness and honesty in our communication. Fuzzy control systems must be open to all inputs, and those inputs must adequately represent their sources. As with all logical systems, "garbage in: garbage out." Even aristocrats in the Aristotelian sense have no a priori right to dominate communicative channels. Such domination would unnecessarily limit the abductive process of hypothesis formation and would distort the inductive process of testing hypotheses in communal deliberation. In fact, most oligarchies are not aristocratic but plutocratic, based in that sardonic version of the Golden Rule: the one with the gold rules. Plutocratic distortion of practical reasoning occurs at all levels of the communicative ecosystem. A plutocratic husband makes decisions without listening to his wife because she doesn't provide as much income as he does. Hierarchical decision making in many organizations is plutocratic. Plutocratic elements that control campaign pursestrings maintain excessive influence over our political deliberations from the local to the international. This imbalance distorts the deliberative process, resulting in a communicative ecosystem that does not nurture all of its members. Foucault, Lyotard, Derrida, and other postmodernists have helped show us how marginalized voices are lost in our communal deliberation. It does not follow that the marginalized voices are necessarily right, but good deliberation would give weight to their inputs. We must continually work toward greater openness in our communicative systems.

Dishonesty makes deliberation less reliable by increasing chaos unnecessarily. Misinformation creates more problems than lack of information because that lack is a stimulus to inquiry but misinformation blocks the path of inquiry. In those rare cases where lying is justified as the lesser evil, the consequences of dishonesty must still be addressed. Like fuzzy controllers, we must compensate and adjust for the changes our own actions have caused. We must act like responsible factories that minimize their pollution of the ecosystem and also work to reduce the consequences of the unavoidable remnant of pollution. The communicative ecosystem can tolerate a minimal level of misinformation, especially if the system is truly open. The large number of inputs will compensate for those misleading inputs. The greater the power of the communicator within a particular level of the ecosystem, however, the greater the damage done by dishonesty. Honesty must be a virtue of all individuals but especially the powerful so that the ecosystem as a whole remains reliable.

If we come to accept the reality of our communal relations and our responsibility to the communicative ecosystem that sustains them, we will improve our own life narratives and make it possible for others to improve theirs. We can make our communities better by communicating more ethically. The ecological model, when interpreted through Peircean semiotic theory, offers the real possibility of achieving community with diversity. How much of that possibility can be made concrete depends, first, on our recognizing that possibility and, second, on our acting in accordance with it. Our wisdom doesn't have to be perfect for us to improve the situation we find ourselves in. Together we could make real progress. The purpose of this book is to show the possibility of living a better life in a better community. Ethical theory alone, however, cannot make the possibility an actuality. The actuality depends on all of our actions. What kind of future are we creating with our actions?

Ethics on the Infobahn

Lyotard, like many others, is fascinated with the possibilities of computer communication, what politicians have labeled the information superhighway to build an analogy with the interstate highway system. Lyotard argued somewhat reductively that the computerization of society could proceed in either of two paths:

It could become the "dream" instrument for controlling and regulating the market system, extended to include knowledge itself and governed exclusively by the performativity principle. In that case, it would inevitably involve the use of terror. But it could also aid groups discussing metaprescriptives by supplying them with the information they usually lack for making knowledgeable decisions. The line to follow for computerization to take the second of these two paths is, in principle, quite simple: give the public free access to the memory and data banks. Language games would then be games of perfect information at any given moment. But they would also be non-zero-sum games. . . . For the stakes would be knowledge (or information, if you will), and the reserve of knowledge—language's reserve of possible utterances—is inexhaustible. This sketches the outline of a politics that would respect both the desire for justice and the desire for the unknown.[8]

For Lyotard, of course, the libidinal desire is the important factor, and so any utterance counts as information. Furthermore, as we have seen, Lyotard's theory is based on conflict. In a provocative essay, Galison has argued that Lyotardian postmodernism is continuous with Wiener's cybernetic theories based on wartime experience.[9] Wiener developed his cybernetic theory during World War II as a means of shooting down enemy airplanes. Wiener then extended cybernetic theory into a "quasi-solipsistic" ontology in which we are all monads in opposition—an ontology that prefigures Lyotard's opposing, fragmented language games.[10] The Lyotardian approach to language games emphasizes the competitive, agonistic aspect to the neglect of the cooperative. To be truly reformed, systems theory and cybernetics must dissociate themselves from their original connection with wartime origins. For a pragmatic realist, the real possibility of justice and truth requires real community; and that factor should also guide our understanding of systems and our policy decisions. I share Lyotard's desire for justice and for openness of information. The choice, however, is not simply between the paths of terrorizing control or agonistic language games. Our system of computerized information networks should not fit neatly into either category. The totalitarian and fragmentary models are extreme possibilities that an ecological ethic would seek to avoid.

On the other hand, the range of possibilities for the public information system is in danger of being narrowed radically. Some fifty cities now offer Free-Net services, which are community computer networks that give the public free access to data banks from business, government, and educational sources as Lyotard suggested. The National Public Telecomputing Network, which coordinates many of these community Free-Nets, is now asking for national funding from Congress, using the model of the Corporation for Public Broadcasting.[11] This very system of funding for public broadcasting, however, is currently under attack. The conservative majority in Congress has shown displeasure at the content of public broadcasting because it does not reflect what conservative members assume to be majority public opinion. In stark contrast with my argument for openness in our communicative systems, these representatives seem to be arguing for increased redundancy. Since redundancy reinforces the status quo, these arguments serve their own interests in that their positions are dependent upon the current plutocratic system of communication. For the same reason, they are not likely to support a more democratic system of computerized communication. As a computer magazine has observed, the Republican Congress supports legislation for an information superhighway but with two major changes: "Dole will insist on a more market-driven bill, which is likely to give existing communications and media giants advantages over smaller concerns. And the revised bill will make no provisions for a universal-service fund, which Republicans view as an unjustifiable tax but which Democrats argue would ensure basic information access for those who can't afford the technology."[12] In both cases, the Republican approach reinforces the plutocracy. The plutocrats are not likely to encourage a Free-Net system that undermines their communicative power. The distortion of political deliberation discussed in chapter 7 is evident in the influence of corporate money on the debate about public access. Although a weakened system of Free-Nets is likely to survive, at least for a while, we are in real danger of moving toward the totalizing pole of possibilities by increasing the communicative power of the already privileged.

All of us who have access to the Internet, of course, are now in a certain position of privilege. A recent study by the Times Mirror Center for the People and the Press shows that access to personal computing equipment correlates more with income level than does access to other types of electronic equipment. The difference in access becomes startling when education is included. "Households in which the adults earn $50,000 or more a year and at least one adult has a college education are *five times* more likely to own a PC and *ten times* more likely to go online."[13] The infobahn is, for the most part, a private road for the elite. It is a place where that elite can convince themselves that they deserve their privilege because it requires some technical expertise. The Internet creates an illusion of community and diversity because the discussions seem to be open to anyone. In fact, many discussion groups on the net simply reinforce already accepted opinions and avoid real engagement with dissenting opinions. People tend to gravitate toward discussion groups that share their opinions. Argument that might actually change opinions is avoided. Occasionally a dissenting opinion may be heard. Often, however, dissent takes the form of a "flame"—an ad hominem attack that blocks real argument; if not, the dissent is often responded to with flames by those whose current opinions have been challenged. Where effective argument takes place is normally within narrow, technical domains of discourse. The online networks do not often effectively discuss general communal issues. On those topics, the information superhighway transports redundant ideas better than informative ideas. It is a place where we the advantaged can take a Sunday drive that confirms us in our advantage because the disadvantaged cannot be seen.

The disadvantaged are not only the poor but also women. Although access for women is increasing, online computing continues to be dominated by men. The tendency to make more and more organizational and political communication computerized may appear to be neutral, but under current circumstances this tendency is likely to reinforce male hegemony in those areas of communication. Ebben studied the discourse on the soc.women discussion group, a Usenet news group formed by women to discuss women's issues, and found that male participants tended to dominate the message traffic.[14] In a sample one-month period 148 men and 86 women participated, and men were responsible for more than 63 percent of the messages sent. Given that more men than women have access to the Internet, this might simply indicate that some men are sincerely interested in hearing and understanding women's perspectives. Male participation that seriously engaged in questioning and argument with women about concerns that women have certainly would not be an ethical problem. Ebben found, however, that very little serious confrontation with women's issues took place. The topic that generated the most discussion (eighty-two messages) was titled "Take back the dildo," a hostile message from a man that initiated a "flame war." The topic in distant second place (twenty-eight messages) was a woman-initiated discussion of women's problems with technology. Ebben reports that this thread degenerated into sarcastic rejection of women's reports of their own experience by some men. The topic that was a close third (twenty-six messages) was another flame war initiated by a male with a message labeled "Quote Feminazi unquote." In general, Ebben's study showed that the hostile atmosphere generated primarily by men on a group dedicated to women's issues tended to reduce women's participation. Some men who were hoping for a serious discussion of women's issues also gave up. The supposed liberating power of unmoderated discussion turned out to be a demonstration of masculine power within the discursive regime of the Internet. In this case, the ethical problems of access were compounded by acts of verbal aggression on behalf of the status quo. Our information systems continue to operate on the wartime model of cybernetics.

From the perspective of an ecological ethic, to maintain the limited access of the status quo is unethical. We are now at a critical moment in the evolution of our computer information network. We have the opportunity to make this subsystem that is growing in importance more just. Given this ecological crisis of computer communication, the individual actions of those with current access to the Internet have increased importance. We have seen the problems caused by acts of chauvinistic verbal aggression. The Internet has also attracted a number of libertines who do not accept any responsibility for the consequences of their communication. In addition to the damage caused by their irresponsible acts of communication, these Internet libertines make public access to the Internet less likely; they provide ammunition for the opponents of public access. They undermine the system that makes their communication possible.

A University of Michigan student posted a story to the Usenet news group alt.sex.stories that described the kidnap, rape, and murder of a fellow student, whom he named. He then exchanged e-mail messages with another man about how to carry out such a macabre adventure.[15] Discussions of this case on the Internet generally concerned themselves only with the issue of free speech and have avoided confronting the ethical issues, perhaps under the impression that ethics is a matter of personal taste but freedom of speech is somehow absolute. As a society, we have chosen to limit government censorship of communication except in cases of egregious harm. But communicative libertarianism is not libertinism. The degree of free speech that we have in our communicative ecosystem depends in part upon the exercise of ethical responsibility by communicators. Regardless of the legality of what this student did, his actions were unethical. Those actions are likely to result in a diminution of the ecosystem's ability to support others in their freedom to communicate. Access to discussion groups on controversial topics is likely to be limited by institutions that require public support. Given the current mood of Congress, attempts at outright censorship of discussion groups might ensue. At the very least, the Internet will not be associated with "family values," and so public access will be discouraged.

I am not arguing that ethical responsibility requires prudishness in communication. Nor is the problem simply offensiveness. The stories that the student posted had disclaimers warning those who might be offended not to read any further. One is not likely to stumble into one of these stories by accident, so the claim of offensiveness is weak. Nevertheless, some types of stories are unethical because of their likely consequences on the communicative ecosystem. Stories that associate the sexual drive with domination of others as nonconsensual objects can do real damage to the semiotic systems of those who read them and are not offended. This habit of association can ultimately change the behavior of these readers because such behavior is itself the energetic interpretant of the way we combine signs to signify complex objects such as sexual satisfaction. Labeling the stories as fantasies does not prevent such patterns of association unless the fantasies totally lack realism, which is not true in most cases. In this student's case, the story was so realistic it included the name of a real student as the intended victim. As a result, she reportedly considered dropping out of school. His abuse of the communicative system has made it less nurturing for her. But even if her name had not been used, he and others who have posted stories glamorizing nonconsensual sex have distorted the semiotic systems of their readers. In a violent society like ours, these distortions are dangerous. Even if most readers would not act out the extreme cases of nonconsensual sex—violent rape and murder—they have been rendered more susceptible to committing date rape if they read these stories habitually. Regular readers are also likely to have difficulty expressing love through sex when sexual excitement has become semiotically connected with power. Considering the damage that stories celebrating nonconsensual sex can do to many levels of the ecosystem, I consider both the posting and the reading for enjoyment of these stories to be unethical communicative acts.

On the other hand, I do not consider stories or discussions of consensual sexual behavior, no matter how offensive others may find them, to be unethical in general. I don't think that our communicative ecosystem and our life narratives are threatened by an association of caring and sex, even if the sex is unconventional. Homogeneity in sexual activity is not a public exigence. Frank discussions of sexual alternatives may improve some people's life narratives. Improved sexual satisfaction could lead to stronger families. Perhaps free and open discussion of sex on the Internet should be treated as a "family values" issue. Unfortunately, the actual discussions of sex on the Internet tend to stay at the adolescent level, which may be an indicator of who the majority of participants are.

Participation by trained sexologists to raise the informational content of the message traffic would certainly be desirable. The major ethical problem with discussions of consensual sex on the Internet, other than the general tendency to flame those who are different, is the willingness of many to assert untested opinion as verified fact. But this is also a general problem: much of what is transported on the information superhighway is not information at all unless one follows Lyotard in labeling any possible utterance as information. The simplest way to improve the Internet's ability to carry real information would be for all of us to accept responsibility for our assertions of truth, whether on sexual matters or any other issue. That improvement, of course, could take place in all of our communicative systems, not just the computerized versions.

Conclusion

The information superhighway is not a panacea for the ills of our communicative ecosystem. The infobahn simply reflects and intensifies the problems that exist. If we do not consider its ecological implications, it will make the environment worse, as many physical highways have. Considering the agonistic origins of cybernetics, that technology alone will not help us improve our communication unless we first work on our *technē ethikē,* our art of ethics. This book makes no pretense at being a full discussion of such an art. I offer it simply as a step in that direction—an attempt to rethink the theory of communicative ethics in order to develop better praxis. The meaning of this theory is to be found in its consequences in practice.

Our future is neither necessarily bleak nor bright. It depends in large part on whether we take seriously the demands of community and diversity as necessary complements. Our happiness also depends in part on chance; chaos is all around us. Our responsibility is to deal with regularities, however, with likely consequences of our actions, while being open to the changes wrought by chaos. As in the process of evolution, some of these changes will be fortuitous. Still, our ability to argue and deliberate should help us anticipate the consequences of those mutations and avoid some of the wastefulness of natural selection. We cannot anticipate these chaotic elements until they become regular to some extent; then our ability to make abductive and inductive inferences will allow us to manage the new. As I have argued, of course, abductive and inductive inference are dependent upon open and honest communities of inquiry. Our ability to deliberate about communicative ethics itself depends upon the state of ethics of the communicative ecosystem. Before we concern ourselves with the details about exceptions to our ethical maxims, we ought to ensure that as individuals and communities we practice the basic virtues.

We must teach ethics—not as absolute principles based in a priori metaphysics but as virtues learned through communal experience. The working out of these virtues in practical maxims is always subject to revision by the facts of experience. The possibility of future revision, however, should not prevent us from teaching what we believe to be correct. We are not imposing a religious value system on others by teaching them that they must be responsible to the ecosystem that supports them; we are teaching common sense. In our families, schools, and professional groups, we should teach ecological responsibility. We should demand commonsense ethical behavior from our politicians. Those who refuse to accept their responsibilities to the communicative ecosystem that nurtures them are effectively ostracizing themselves. We should not encourage parasitic, self-centered behavior. Ecological responsibility should be part of everyone's narrative pursuit of the good, no matter how diverse their other desires.

At the same time, we must be critical of our ecosystem as it exists, seeking to improve its ability to nurture all of its members. This criticism, however, must also be realistic in considering the consequences of changes to the system. Our current system is a mixture of vices and virtues. Suggestions for change are abductive hypotheses that should be examined deductively for their likely consequences and then tested inductively. We should not ruin what is good in a vain chase after what is perfect. On the other hand, we cannot let pure self-interest determine what changes are desirable. None of us has an a priori right to greater communicative power. If we want better communities, we must share communicative power.

The title of this book is *Community over Chaos* but not because an ecological ethic would lead to the victory of some communal metanarrative over individual freedom. An effective community provides the umbrella for diversity, balancing justice and freedom. The more its members recognize their responsibilities to the ecosystem, the stronger that ecosystem becomes, and the more able it is to support individual diversity. Failure to recognize responsibilities results in increasing chaos that will, in the long run, reduce the ability of individuals to control their own life narratives. I offer the ecological model of communicative ethics as my hypothesis for achieving an effective synthesis of community and diversity in this postmodern world. I offer it with the reasonable hope that it will be thoroughly examined in theoretical argument, amplified, modified, and tested in practice. I am convinced that somewhere along that path we'll find the possibility of happier lives in happier communities.

Notes

---

1. Our Postmodern Ethical Quandary

1. Kenneth Burke, *Permanence and Change: An Anatomy of Purpose*, 3d ed. (Berkeley: University of California Press, 1984), 175.

2. Thomas B. Farrell, *Norms of Rhetorical Culture* (New Haven: Yale University Press, 1993).

3. Grant Morrison, Charles Truog, and Mark Farmer, "Deus ex Machina," *Animal Man* 26 (August 1990). All quotations of Morrison's text come from this edition.

4. Jean-François Lyotard, *The Postmodern Condition: A Report on Knowledge*, trans. Geoff Bennington and Brian Massumi (Minneapolis: University of Minnesota Press, 1984), xxiii–xxiv.

5. Ibid., 31.

6. Ibid., 33.

7. Ibid., 34.

8. Ibid., 36.

9. Immanuel Kant, "Metaphysical Foundations of Morals," in *The Philosophy of Kant*, ed. Carl J. Friedrich (New York: Random House, 1949), 140–208.

10. Lyotard, *Postmodern Condition*, 11.

11. Ibid.

12. Harold Lasswell, "The Structure and Function of Communication in Society," in *The Communication of Ideas*, ed. Lyman Bryson (New York: Harper, 1948), 37–51.

13. Lyotard, *Postmodern Condition*, 37.

14. Ibid., 10–11.

15. Ibid., 39.

16. Immanuel Kant, "Critique of Judgment," in *Philosophy of Kant*, 300.

17. Ibid., 307.

18. Lyotard, *Postmodern Condition*, 81–82.

19. Kant, "Judgment," 282–83.

20. Ibid., 305.

21. Julian Pefanis, *Heterology and the Postmodern* (Durham: Duke University Press, 1991), 90.

22. Jean-François Lyotard, *Driftworks*, endnotes, cited in Pefanis, 91.

23. Jean-François Lyotard, *Libidinal Economy*, trans. Iain Hamilton Grant (Bloomington: Indiana University Press, 1993).

24. Lyotard, *Postmodern Condition*, 66.

25. "Professional-Style Taunting Led to Brawl, Death," *New Orleans Times-Picayune*, 20 May 1993.

26. Aristotle, *Nichomachean Ethics*, 1131a (hereafter cited as *EN*).

27. Aristotle, *Politics*, 1253a6–35.

28. Kenneth Burke, *A Rhetoric of Motives* (Berkeley: University of California Press, 1969), 20.

29. John M. Ellis, *Against Deconstruction* (Princeton: Princeton University Press, 1989), 35.

30. Christopher Norris, *Deconstruction: Theory and Practice* (London: Methuen, 1982), 128.

31. Irene E. Harvey, *Derrida and the Economy of "Différance"* (Bloomington: Indiana University Press, 1986), 44ff.

32. Jacques Derrida, *Of Grammatology*, trans. Gayatri Chakravorty Spivak (Baltimore: Johns Hopkins University Press, 1976), 24.

33. Alan D. Schrift, *Nietzsche and the Question of Interpretation: Between Hermeneutics and Deconstruction* (New York: Routledge, 1990), 116.

34. Derrida, *Grammatology*, 7.

35. Ibid., 158.

36. Ibid., 9.

37. Ibid., 44.

38. Ibid., 56.

39. Ibid., 7–8.

40. Ibid., 14.

41. Ibid., 23–24.

42. Martin Heidegger, *The Basic Problems of Phenomenology*, rev. ed., trans. Albert Hofstadter (Bloomington: Indiana University Press, 1982), 227.

43. John D. Caputo, "Mysticism and Transgression: Derrida and Meister Eckhart," in *Derrida and Deconstruction*, ed. Hugh J. Silverman (New York: Routledge, 1989), 26.

44. Derrida, *Grammatology*, 61.

45. Ibid., 62.

46. Ibid., 63.

47. Ibid., 65.

48. Jacques Derrida, "Differance," in *Speech and Phenomena and Other Essays on Husserl's Theory of Signs*, trans. David Allison (Evanston: Northwestern University Press, 1973), 142.

49. Irene E. Harvey, *Derrida and the Economy of "Différance"* (Bloomington: Indiana University Press, 1986), 120.

50. Derrida, *Grammatology*, 166.

51. Harvey, *Economy of "Différance,"* 124.

52. Robert Bernasconi, "Deconstruction and the Possibility of Ethics," in *Deconstruction and Philosophy: The Texts of Jacques Derrida*, ed. John Sallis (Chicago: University of Chicago Press, 1987), 135.

53. Jacques Derrida, Afterword, *Limited Inc*, trans. Samuel Weber (Evanston: Northwestern University Press, 1988), 151.

54. Caputo, "Mysticism and Transgression," 30.

55. Eugene Goodheart, *The Skeptic Disposition in Contemporary Criticism* (Princeton: Princeton University Press, 1984), 177.

56. David Hume, *An Inquiry Concerning Human Understanding* (Indianapolis: Bobbs-Merrill, 1955), 168.

57. Michel Foucault, *The Order of Things: An Archaeology of the Human Sciences* (*Les mots et les choses*) (New York: Random House, 1970), xxiii.

58. Immanuel Kant, "Prolegomena to Every Future Metaphysics That May Be Presented as a Science," in *Philosophy of Kant*, 98–115.

59. Foucault, *Order of Things*, 313.

60. Michel Foucault, "From *The Archaeology of Knowledge*," in *The Rhetorical Tradition: Readings from Classical Times to the Present*, ed. Patricia Bizzell and Bruce Herzberg (Boston: St. Martin's, 1990), 1138.

61. Foucault, "Archaeology," 1148.

62. Friedrich Nietzsche, *On the Genealogy of Morals and Ecce Homo*, trans. Walter Kaufmann and R. J. Hollingdale (New York: Random House, 1967), 21.

63. Foucault, *Order of Things*, 157–58.

64. Ibid., 168.

65. Michel Foucault, *The Foucault Reader*, ed. Paul Rabinow (New York: Pantheon, 1984), 54–55.

66. Tom McArthur, ed., *The Oxford Companion to the English Language* (Oxford: Oxford University Press, 1992), s.v. *structuralism*.

67. Foucault, *Order of Things*, xiv.

68. Foucault, "Archaeology," 1135.

69. Foucault, *Order of Things*, 365.

70. Foucault, *Foucault Reader*, 199.

71. Ibid., 56.

72. Ibid., 174.

73. Charles Taylor, "Foucault on Freedom and Truth," in *Foucault: A Critical Reader*, ed. David Couzens Hoy (Oxford: Basil Blackwell, 1986), 87–88.

74. Nietzsche, *Genealogy of Morals*, 107.

75. Barbara Biesecker, "Michel Foucault and the Question of Rhetoric," *Philosophy and Rhetoric* 25 (1992): 362.

76. Ibid., 357.

77. Ibid., 359.

78. Edward W. Said, "Foucault and the Imagination of Power," in *Foucault: A Critical Reader*, 151.

79. Foucault, *Foucault Reader*, 193.

80. John E. Grumley, *History and Totality: Radical Historicism from Hegel to Foucault* (London: Routledge, 1989), 205.

81. Foucault, *Foucault Reader*, 362.

82. Michel Foucault, *The Use of Pleasure*, vol. 2 of *The History of Sexuality*, trans. Robert Hurley (New York: Pantheon, 1985), 26.

83. Michel Foucault, *Politics, Philosophy, Culture: Interviews and Other Writings*, ed. Lawrence D. Kritzman (New York: Routledge, 1988), 50–51.

84. Foucault, *Foucault Reader*, 381.

85. Foucault, *Order of Things*, 328.

86. Ibid., 386–87.

87. Carole Blair and Martha Cooper, "The Humanist Turn in Foucault's Rhetoric of Inquiry," *Quarterly Journal of Speech* 73 (1987): 151–71.

88. Hume, *Human Understanding*, 169.

89. Charles Sanders Peirce, *Philosophical Writings of Peirce*, ed. Justus Buchler (New York: Dover, 1955), 290–301.

90. John R. Lyne, "Rhetoric and Semiotic in C. S. Peirce," *Quarterly Journal of Speech* 66 (1980): 159.

2. The Pragmatic Alternative

1. Charles Sanders Peirce, "A Guess at the Riddle," in *Peirce on Signs*, ed. James Hoopes (Chapel Hill: University of North Carolina Press, 1991), 197.

2. Umberto Eco, *A Theory of Semiotics* (Bloomington: Indiana University Press, 1976).

3. Lyotard, *Postmodern Condition*, 65.

4. Charles S. Peirce, "A Neglected Argument for the Reality of God," in *Selected Writings (Values in a Universe of Chance)*, ed. Philip P. Wiener (New York: Dover, 1966), 358.

5. Peirce, Review of Fraser's *The Works of George Berkeley*, in *Peirce on Signs*, 121.

6. Ibid., 122.

7. Peirce, "How to Make Our Ideas Clear," in *Selected Writings*, 120.

8. Ibid., 124.

9. Charles Sanders Peirce, "The Fixation of Belief," in *Philosophical Writings of Peirce*, ed. Justus Buchler (New York: Dover, 1955), 18.

10. Peirce, "How to Make Our Ideas Clear," 133.

11. Peirce, "Neglected Argument," 378.

12. Peirce, "The Scientific Attitude and Fallibilism," in *Philosophical Writings*, 54.

13. Richard Rorty, "Pragmatism, Davidson, and Truth," in *Objectivity, Relativism, and Truth* (New York: Cambridge University Press, 1991), 126–50.

14. Ibid., 139.

15. Rorty, "Science as Solidarity," in *Objectivity, Relativism, and Truth*, 39.

16. Janet Horne, "Rhetoric after Rorty," *Western Journal of Speech Communication* 53 (1989): 247–59.

17. Peirce, "Fixation of Belief," in *Selected Writings*, 91–112.

18. Ibid., 99–100.

19. Ibid., 103.

20. Ibid.

21. Ibid., 104.

22. Rorty, *Objectivity, Relativism, and Truth*, 14.

23. Peirce, "Fixation of Belief," 106.

24. Cited in Horne, "Rhetoric after Rorty," 251.

25. Peirce, "Fixation of Belief," 108.

26. Lyne, "Rhetoric and Semiotic," 161.

27. Rorty, "Pragmatism, Davidson, and Truth," 131.

28. Karl-Otto Apel, *Charles S. Peirce: From Pragmatism to Pragmaticism* (Amherst: University of Massachusetts Press, 1981), 36.

29. Peirce, "Neglected Argument," 374–75.

30. Peirce, "Grounds of Validity of the Laws of Logic," in *Peirce on Signs*, 113.

31. James O'Byrne, "Scientific Methods Colored by Bias," *New Orleans Times-Picayune*, 15 August 1993.

32. Peirce, Review of Fraser's *Berkeley*, 128.

33. Raymie E. McKerrow, "Critical Rhetoric: Theory and Praxis," *Communication Monographs* 56 (1989): 91–111.

34. Rorty, "Inquiry as Recontextualization: An Anti-dualist Account of Interpretation," in *Objectivity, Relativism, and Truth*, 93.

35. Peirce, "Lectures on Pragmatism," in *Peirce on Signs*, 244. The first quoted sentence appeared in boldface in this version of the text.

36. Peirce, "Letters to Lady Welby," in *Selected Writings*, 420.

37. Lyne, "Rhetoric and Semiotic," 166.

38. Peirce, "The Basis of Pragmaticism," in *Peirce on Signs*, 256.

39. Peirce, "Critical Common-Sensism," in *Philosophical Writings*, 295.

40. Ibid., 295.

41. Ibid.

42. Peirce, "The Basis of Pragmaticism," 257–58.

43. Peirce, "Neglected Argument," 365.

44. Ibid., 370.

45. John Deely, *Basics of Semiotics* (Bloomington: Indiana University Press, 1990), 23.

46. Peirce, "The Principles of Phenomenology," in *Philosophical Writings*, 75.

47. Ibid.

48. Douglas Greenlee, *Peirce's Concept of Sign* (The Hague: Mouton, 1973), 41–42.

49. Peirce, "One, Two, Three: Fundamental Categories," in *Peirce on Signs*, 185.

50. Peirce, "Principles of Phenomenology," 76.

51. Peirce, "One, Two, Three: Fundamental Categories," 185.

52. Peirce, "Principles of Phenomenology," 77.

53. Peirce, "One, Two, Three: Fundamental Categories," 182.

54. Robert W. Burch, *A Peircean Reduction Thesis: The Foundations of Topological Logic* (Lubbock: Texas Tech University Press, 1991).

55. Peirce, "Logic as Semiotic: The Theory of Signs," in *Philosophical Writings*, 100.

56. Deely, *Basics of Semiotics*, 50–89.

57. Peirce, "Logic as Semiotic," 107.

58. Greenlee, *Peirce's Concept of Sign*, 89.

59. Peirce, "Perceptual Judgments," in *Philosophical Writings*, 302–305.

60. Peirce, "Grounds of Validity of the Laws of Logic," 99.

61. Peirce, "Perceptual Judgments," 304.

62. Deely, *Basics of Semiotics*, 59–60.

63. Peirce, "Letters to Lady Welby," 390–91 and 426.

64. Deely, *Basics of Semiotics*, 55.

65. Martin Heidegger, *The Basic Problems of Phenomenology*, rev. ed., trans. Albert Hofstadter (Bloomington: Indiana University Press, 1982), 280–86.

66. Deely, *Basics of Semiotics*, 37.

67. Ibid., 38.

68. Ibid., 38–39.

69. Vincent M. Colapietro, *Peirce's Approach to the Self: A Semiotic Perspective on Human Subjectivity* (Albany: SUNY Press, 1989), 91.

70. Deely, *Basics of Semiotics*, 41–44.

71. Ibid., 45.

72. Ibid., 52.

73. Ibid.

74. Peirce, "Logic as Semiotic," 99.

75. Peirce, "Letters to Lady Welby," 406 and 415.

76. Apel, *Charles S. Peirce*, 163.

77. Cited in James Campbell, *The Community Reconstructs: The Meaning of Pragmatic Social Thought* (Urbana: University of Illinois Press, 1992), 28.

78. John Dewey, *Experience and Nature*, 2d ed. (La Salle, Ill.: Open Court, 1971), 134.

79. Ibid., 138.

80. Ibid., 141.

81. Ibid., 151.

82. Ibid., 81–82.

83. John Dewey, *Theory of Valuation* (Chicago: University of Chicago Press, 1939), 18.

84. Ibid., 21.

85. Ibid., 25.

86. Ibid., 43.

87. John Dewey, *The Public and Its Problems* (Athens, Ohio: Swallow, 1954), 34.

88. Ibid., 25.

89. Ibid., 126–27.

90. Ibid., 116.

91. Ibid., 131.

92. Jürgen Habermas, *The Structural Transformation of the Public Sphere: An Inquiry into a Category of Bourgeois Society*, trans. Thomas Burger and Frederick Lawrence (Cambridge, Mass.: MIT Press, 1989).

93. Nancy Fraser, "Rethinking the Public Sphere: A Contribution to the Critique of Actually Existing Democracy," in *The Phantom Public Sphere*, ed. Bruce Robbins (Minneapolis: University of Minnesota Press, 1993), 1–32.

94. Ibid., 21.

3. From the Archaic to the Ecological

1. Aristotle, *EN*, 1098a.

2. Alasdair MacIntyre, *After Virtue: A Study in Moral Theory* (Notre Dame: University of Notre Dame Press, 1984), 205.

3. Ibid., 211.

4. Ibid., 213–14.

5. Ibid., 219.

6. Ibid.

7. Ibid., 187.

8. See, for example, Aristotle, *EN*, 1094a.

9. MacIntyre, *After Virtue*, 187–88.

10. Farrell, *Norms of Rhetorical Culture*, 76.

11. MacIntyre's own version can be found in *After Virtue*, 191.

12. In some theologies, of course, life on earth is poiesis, not praxis, because its purpose is to earn eternal reward. In this case, life on earth is not the completed narrative but merely an episode, comparable to a career; eternal life is the praxis.

13. Farrell, *Norms of Rhetorical Culture*, 230–57.

14. Allyn Fisher, "Hate Fueled Gunman's Spree," *New Orleans Times-Picayune*, 26 February 1994.

15. MacIntyre, *After Virtue*, 222.

16. Alasdair MacIntyre, *Whose Justice? Which Rationality?* (Notre Dame: University of Notre Dame Press, 1988), 398.

17. John Dewey and James H. Tufts, *Ethics*, rev. ed. (New York: Henry Holt, 1932), 66–67.

18. MacIntyre, *Whose Justice?* 356.

19. Ibid., 356–57.

20. Ibid., 358.

21. Ibid., 368–69.

22. Ibid., 368.

23. Kenneth Burke, "Auscultation, Creation, and Revision," in *Extensions of the Burkeian System*, ed. James W. Chesebro (Tuscaloosa: University of Alabama Press, 1993), 112.

24. MacIntyre, *Whose Justice?* 351.

25. Ludwig von Bertalanffy, *A Systems View of Man*, ed. Paul A. LaViolette (Boulder, Colo.: Westview, 1981), 109.

26. Peter L. Berger and Thomas Luckmann, *The Social Construction of*

Reality: A Treatise in the Sociology of Knowledge (1966; Garden City, N.Y.: Anchor, 1967), 125.

27. Richard Harvey Brown, *Society as Text: Essays on Rhetoric, Reason, and Reality* (Chicago: University of Chicago Press, 1987), 118. Brown uses the metaphor of text—"a structure or grammar of rules and communications" (119). Text as metaphor, however, carries a connotation of fixity that I wish to avoid. *System,* as I use the term, is not just structure but structure in process.

28. Fred R. Dallmayr, *Polis and Praxis: Exercises in Contemporary Political Theory* (Cambridge, Mass.: MIT Press, 1984), 192–223.

29. Ludwig von Bertalanffy, *General System Theory: Foundations, Development, Applications* (New York: George Braziller, 1968), chap. 2.

30. Ibid., 142.

31. The difference is the difference between *stasis,* standing or position, and *rhesis,* flow or movement through time. *Homeostasis* is a term of cybernetic regulation, for which *homeorhesis* is the ecological correlate. See David Conrad Steffenson, "A Foundational Model for an 'Ecological Social Ethic' " (Ph.D diss., Union for Experimenting Colleges and Universities, 1984), 238–42.

32. Aristotle, *EN,* 1106b and 1109b.

33. Ibid., 1144b.

34. Magoroh Maruyama, "The Second Cybernetics: Deviation-Amplifying Mutual Causal Processes," *American Scientist* 51 (1963): 164–79. See also Ervin Laszlo, *Introduction to Systems Philosophy: Toward a New Paradigm of Contemporary Thought* (New York: Gordon and Breach, 1972), 88–94 and 102–12.

35. Laszlo, *Introduction to Systems Philosophy,* 91.

36. Ibid., 131.

37. John Y. Kim, "Feedback in Social Sciences: Toward a Reconceptualization of Morphogeneses," in *General Systems Theory and Human Communication,* ed. Brent D. Ruben and John Y. Kim (Rochelle Park, N.J.: Hayden, 1975), 207–21.

38. Ibid., 214.

39. Dewey and Tufts, *Ethics,* 66–67.

40. Hugh Dalziel Duncan, *Communication and Social Order* (London: Oxford University Press, 1962), 265.

41. Laszlo, *Introduction to Systems Philosophy,* 47–53 and 112–17.

42. Hierarchy in this sense does not include the notion of authority or rule but simply describes the relationship of systems in constituting larger systems. In social relations, confusion of the constitutive nature of this hierarchy with the authoritative sense of hierarchy results in a Fascist notion of the state.

43. For a more detailed discussion of coupling in systems, see Karl E. Weick, "Educational Organizations as Loosely Coupled Systems," *Administrative Science Quarterly* 21 (1976): 1–18.

44. In the differential equations Bertalanffy uses to model systems, he notes that the coefficients of one element may be large in all equations while the coefficients of other elements are much smaller and even approach zero.

See Bertalanffy, *General System Theory,* 71. From a rhetorician's standpoint, *ethos* seems to be a qualitative counterpart to the quantitative concept of coefficient.

45. Farrell, *Norms of Rhetorical Culture,* 288–93.

46. Genesis 11. The myth actually begins with a highly centripetal system that is portrayed as arrogant in its unity. God disintegrates the system by confounding the communicative links; its members are dispersed across the entire earth. The rhetorical effectiveness of the story lies in the implied threats to the community: organize apart from God (or the authority of the priesthood), and the entire community will disintegrate. For the Jewish exiles in Babylon (Babel), loss of community meant loss of self-identity (transcendental relations).

47. Kenneth Burke, *The Philosophy of Literary Form: Studies in Symbolic Action,* 3d ed. (Berkeley: University of California Press, 1973), 200.

48. Ibid., 207.

49. Aristotle, *EN,* 1159b25–60a30.

50. Kenneth Burke, *A Grammar of Motives* (Berkeley: University of California Press, 1969), 57.

51. Burke, *Rhetoric,* 21 and 55–59.

52. *Pistis* is a polysemic term. For an explanation of Aristotle's uses of the term, see William M. A. Grimaldi, *Studies in the Philosophy of Aristotle's Rhetoric, Hermes: Zeitschrift für klassische Philologie,* Einzelschriften, vol. 25 (Wiesbaden: Franz Steiner Verlag, 1972), 58–59.

53. Aristotle, *Rhetoric,* 1356a1–3. See also Grimaldi, *Studies,* 60–63. Grimaldi would prefer to substitute *to pragma* (the subject matter of the speech in its logical aspect appealing to the intellect of the listener) for the highly ambiguous term *logos.* What is important to remember is that the term stands not for pure logic but for an appeal to what the listener counts as logical.

54. James L. Kinneavy, *A Theory of Discourse: The Aims of Discourse* (New York: Norton, 1980), 225.

55. Aristotle, *Rhetoric,* 1377b20–30.

56. Ibid., 1367b10–25.

57. Ibid., 1381a1–15.

58. Ibid., 1382a.

59. *Ad Herennium,* 1.5.

60. This strategy can backfire when the audience perceives the attack by one candidate on another's character to be unfair. The audience dissociates itself from the character of the attacking candidate because his or her action demonstrates an unacceptable moral difference from the audience.

61. Clancy DuBos, "Returning Fire on the Flyers Issue," *New Orleans Weekly Gambit,* 1 March 1994, p. 13.

62. Malcolm X and Alex Haley, *The Autobiography of Malcolm X* (New York: Ballantine, 1973), 283.

63. Plato, *Phaedrus,* 270.

64. Aristotle, *Rhetoric,* 1378a–1391b.

65. Aristotle, *Rhetoric,* 1380a and 1380b, for example.

66. Donald C. Bryant, "Rhetoric: Its Function and Its Scope," *Contempo-*

rary Rhetoric: A Coursebook, ed. Douglas Ehninger (Glenview, Ill.: Scott, Foresman, 1972), 26.

67. Ibid., 26.

68. See, for example, Roderick P. Hart, "An Unquiet Desperation: Rhetorical Aspects of 'Popular' Atheism in the United States," *Quarterly Journal of Speech* 64 (1978): 33–46; Theodore Otto Windt, Jr., "The Diatribe: Last Resort for Protest," *Quarterly Journal of Speech* 58 (1972): 1–14; and Richard B. Gregg, "The Ego-Function of the Rhetoric of Protest," *Philosophy and Rhetoric* 4 (1971): 71–91.

69. Yet in the larger scene, the system of logic itself is a unifying factor. Formal logic compels assent because it is agreed to by the community of inquiry.

70. E. M. Cope, *An Introduction to Aristotle's Rhetoric* (London: Macmillan, 1867), 93.

71. Agreement is necessary, but supplying of missing premises is not necessary. Normally, the audience simply agrees that C follows from A without necessarily supplying B. Only upon critical reflection would a listener notice the premise necessary to move from A to C. Consubstantiality may come from the simple habit of moving from A to C without considering B.

72. Lloyd F. Bitzer, "Aristotle's Enthymeme Revisited," *Quarterly Journal of Speech* 45 (1959): 408.

73. Gerard A. Hauser, "The Example in Aristotle's Rhetoric: Bifurcation or Contradiction?" *Philosophy and Rhetoric* 1 (1968): 88.

74. For an opposing view of the logical nature of Aristotle's *Rhetoric,* see Edwin Black, *Rhetorical Criticism: A Study in Method* (Madison: University of Wisconsin Press, 1978), 91–131. Black's approach contrasts sharply with that of other commentators, especially Grimaldi. See, for example, Grimaldi, *Studies,* 136–51.

75. Chaim Perelman, *The Realm of Rhetoric,* trans. William Kluback (Notre Dame: University of Notre Dame Press, 1982), 23.

76. Ibid., 24.

77. Ibid., 19–20.

78. Ernest Bormann, "Fantasy Theme Analysis and Rhetorical Theory," *The Rhetoric of Western Thought,* ed. James L. Golden, Goodwin F. Berquist, and William E. Coleman, 3d ed. (Dubuque: Kendall/Hunt, 1983), 434.

79. Ibid., 436.

80. Ibid., 437.

81. The theme underlies much of twentieth-century theory. Weaver, for example, saw in "charismatic terms" "something like the creation of a spontaneous general will." Richard Weaver, *The Ethics of Rhetoric* (South Bend, Ind.: Regnery/Gateway, 1953), 230.

82. Burke, *Rhetoric,* 20–21.

83. Burke, *Grammar,* 23.

84. Ibid., 24.

85. Ibid., 34.

86. Ibid., 26.

87. Ibid., 26–27.

88. Robert Ornstein, *The Evolution of Consciousness* (New York: Prentice Hall, 1991), 73.

89. George L. Mosse, "The Genesis of Fascism," in *Fascism: An Anthology,* ed. Nathanael Greene (Arlington Heights, Ill.: AHM Publishing, 1968), 6–8.

90. Denis Mack Smith, "The Theory and Practice of Fascism," in *Fascism,* 73–112.

91. Alan Bullock, "The Dictator," in *Fascism,* 234.

92. Mosse, "Genesis of Fascism," 4–5.

4. The Cardinal Virtues of the Communicative Ecosystem

1. Aristotle, *EN,* 1139a31.

2. Ibid., 1139b6.

3. Ibid., 1140a24–b7.

4. Ibid., 1141b24–35.

5. Raymie E. McKerrow, "The Repressive Voice of Modernity in a Postmodern Rhetoric" (paper presented at the annual meeting of the Southern States Communication Association, Norfolk, Va., April 1994).

6. Ibid., 2–3.

7. Ellen Meiksins Wood and Neal Wood, *Class Ideology and Ancient Political Theory: Socrates, Plato, and Aristotle in Social Context* (Oxford: Basil Blackwell, 1978), p. 209.

8. Kenneth Burke, *A Grammar of Motives* (Berkeley: University of California Press, 1962), 227.

9. Ibid., n. 7.

10. Aristotle, *Metaphysics,* 1048a25–b17, cited and translated in George A. Blair, *Energeia and Entelecheia: "Act" in Aristotle* (Ottawa: University of Ottawa Press, 1992), 35–37.

11. Aristotle, *Rhetoric,* 1411b20–12a10.

12. Blair, *Energeia and Entelecheia in Aristotle,* 80–81.

13. Aristotle, *De Interpretatione,* 16a3–8.

14. Charlotte Witt, *Substance and Essence in Aristotle: An Interpretation of Metaphysics VII–IX* (Ithaca: Cornell University Press, 1989), 173–74.

15. Ibid., 180–97.

16. Aristotle, *EN,* 1177a13–b30.

17. Ibid., 1177b27–32.

18. Ibid., 1099b3–8.

19. Aristotle, *Politics,* 1254a20–55a30.

20. Ibid., 1260a10–25.

21. Ibid., 1278a1–10.

22. Ibid., 1279a20–b10.

23. Ibid., 1283a10–25.

24. Ibid., 1280a10–20.

25. John Dewey, *Reconstruction in Philosophy* (Boston: Beacon, 1948), xi.

26. Bertrand P. Helm, "The Nature and Modes of Time," in *The Relevance of Charles Peirce*, ed. Eugene Freeman (LaSalle, Ill.: Hegeler Institute, 1983), 181.

27. Ibid., 184.

28. Ibid., 185–87.

29. Aristotle, *Politics*, 1259b25–30.

30. Ornstein, *Evolution of Consciousness*, 126–27.

31. C. S. Peirce, Manuscript L75, ed. Joseph Ransdell, Peirce Telecommunity Project, Electronic Peirce Consortium, memoir 8; available on Internet via Gopher from Georgetown University.

32. Kenneth Burke, *The Rhetoric of Religion* (Berkeley: University of California Press, 1970), 33.

33. Walter R. Fisher, *Human Communication as Narration: Toward a Philosophy of Reason, Value, and Action* (Columbia: University of South Carolina Press, 1987), 88–89.

34. Ibid.

35. The ethical debate is summarized in Paul Ricoeur, "Ethics and Culture: Habermas and Gadamer in Dialogue," *Philosophy Today* 17 (1973): 153–65.

36. Ibid., 163.

37. Ibid., 165.

38. Barbara Warnick, "The Narrative Paradigm: Another Story," *Quarterly Journal of Speech* 73 (1987): 172–82.

39. Fisher, *Human Communication as Narration*, 66.

40. Ibid., 88.

41. Peirce, "Logic as Semiotic," 99.

42. Daniel McNeil and Paul Freiberger, *Fuzzy Logic* (New York: Touchstone, 1993), 28.

43. Jarrett E. Brock, "C. S. Peirce's Logic of Vagueness" (Ph.D. diss., University of Illinois, 1969; Ann Arbor: University Microfilms, 1978). Mihai Nadin, "The Logic of Vagueness and the Category of Synechism," in *The Relevance of Charles Peirce*, 154–66.

44. *Collected Papers* 2.418, cited in Brock, *Logic of Vagueness*, 26.

45. *Collected Papers* 2.410, cited in Brock, *Logic of Vagueness*, 28.

46. *Collected Papers* 3.93–94, 8.208, cited in Brock, *Logic of Vagueness*, 339.

47. Brock, *Logic of Vagueness*, 184.

48. Ibid., 344.

49. Ibid., 346.

50. Heinz R. Pagels, "Uncertainty and Complementarity," in *The World Treasury of Physics, Astronomy, and Mathematics*, ed. Timothy Ferris (Boston: Little, Brown, 1991), 101.

51. Nadin, "Logic of Vagueness," 163.

52. McNeil and Freiberger, *Fuzzy Logic*, 113–14. They use the analogy of a committee deliberating.

53. Ibid., chap. 9.

54. Michael Calvin McGee, "Text, Context, and the Fragmentation of

Contemporary Culture," *Western Journal of Speech Communication* 54 (1990): 278.

55. Actually, the issue is broader than fuzzy logic and includes other multivalued logics such as the Extended Post system. See, for example, Silvano Di Zenzo, "A Many-Valued Logic for Approximate Reasoning," *IBM Journal of Research and Development* 32 (1988): 552–65.

56. Eco, *Theory of Semiotics*, 7.

57. The term *encyclopedia* contrasts with the term *dictionary* in semiotic theory. See Umberto Eco, *Semiotics and the Philosophy of Language* (Bloomington: Indiana University Press, 1984), chap. 2.

58. Peirce defines truth as "the opinion which is fated to be ultimately agreed to by all who investigate." We have no way of knowing, however, that we have reached the ultimate stage of our inquiry. C. S. Peirce, *Philosophical Writings of Peirce*, ed. Justus Buchler (New York: Dover, 1955), 38.

59. Søren Kierkegaard, *The Point of View, Etc.*, trans. Walter Lowrie (London: Oxford University Press, 1939), 39–40.

60. Rorty, *Objectivity, Relativism, and Truth*, 15 and 197–210.

61. John Locke, "An Essay Concerning the True Original, Extent and End of Civil Government," in *Social Contract: Essays by Locke, Hume, and Rousseau*, ed. Ernest Barker (London: Oxford University Press, 1947), 4.

62. J.-J. Rousseau, "The Social Contract," in *Social Contract*, 169.

63. Contemporary defenses of the Enlightenment concept of tolerance normally rely less on the notion of natural rights and more on the pragmatic consequences of a policy of tolerance. See, for example, Hans-Martin Sass, "Ideational Politics and the Word 'Tolerance,' " *Philosophy and Rhetoric* 11 (1978): 98–113.

64. Paul Berman, Introduction to *Debating P. C.: The Controversy over Political Correctness on College Campuses*, ed. Paul Berman (New York: Dell Laurel, 1992).

65. Joan Wallach Scott, "The Campaign Against Political Correctness: What's Really at Stake," *Radical History Review* 54 (1992): 67.

66. Christopher Newfield, "What Was Political Correctness? Race, the Right, and Managerial Democracy in the Humanities," *Critical Inquiry* 19 (1993): 308–36.

67. Cited in Colapietro, *Peirce's Approach to the Self*, 96–97.

68. Aristotle, *Rhetoric*, 1367b.

5. Ethics in Interpersonal Communication

1. Ralph E. Cooley and Deborah A. Roach, "A Conceptual Framework," in *Competence in Communication: A Multidisciplinary Approach*, ed. Robert N. Bostrom (Beverly Hills: Sage, 1984), 27.

2. Aristotle, *Rhetoric*, 1354a1–15.

3. This is Socrates' criticism of rhetoric in Plato's *Gorgias*, 465a2–b1.

4. Aristotle, *Rhetoric*, 1355b25–30. Estō dē rhētorikē dunamis peri ekaston tou theōrēsai to endekhomenon pithanon.

5. Ibid., 1403b3–1404b1.

6. Aristotle, *Rhetoric*, 1355a; *Politics*, 1288a33–b1.

7. Aristotle, *Rhetoric*, 1356a; *EN*, 1094a25–b4.

8. Isocrates, *Antidosis*, 187–93.

9. Isocrates, *Panathenaicus*, 12.

10. Isocrates, *Antidosis*, 254; Aristotle, *Politics*, 1253a7–20.

11. Brian H. Spitzberg and William R. Cupach, *Interpersonal Communication Competence* (Beverly Hills: Sage, 1984), 15. The authors recognize a "new" strain of cooperative rhetoric in Richards and Burke. This recognition may be why they include standards of appropriateness in their idea of competence.

12. Malcolm R. Parks, "Interpersonal Communication and the Quest for Personal Competence," in *Handbook of Interpersonal Communication*, ed. Mark L. Knapp and Gerald R. Miller (Beverly Hills: Sage, 1985), 175.

13. Ibid., 177–86.

14. Ibid., 181.

15. Ibid., 193.

16. Ibid., 194.

17. Spitzberg and Cupach, *Interpersonal Communication Competence*, 68.

18. Ibid., 106.

19. Ibid., 115.

20. Ibid., 94–97.

21. Stanley Deetz, "Reclaiming the Subject Matter as a Guide to Mutual Understanding: Effectiveness and Ethics in Interpersonal Interaction," *Communication Quarterly* 38 (1990): 229.

22. Ibid., 228.

23. William G. Powers and David N. Lowry, "Basic Communication Fidelity: A Fundamental Approach," in *Competence in Communication*, 57–71.

24. Deetz, "Effectiveness and Ethics in Interpersonal Interaction," 232.

25. Ibid., 233.

26. Ibid., 236.

27. Ibid., 237.

28. Ibid., 238.

29. Ibid.

30. Dominic A. Infante, "Aggressiveness," in *Personality and Interpersonal Communication*, ed. James C. McCroskey and John A. Daly (Beverly Hills: Sage, 1987), 157–92.

31. See, for example, Albert O. Hirschman, *The Rhetoric of Reaction* (Cambridge, Mass.: Belknap Press of Harvard University Press, 1991).

32. Deetz, "Effectiveness and Ethics in Interpersonal Interaction," 240; Roderick P. Hart and Don M. Burks, "Rhetorical Sensitivity and Social Interaction," *Communication Monographs* 39 (1972): 75–91.

33. Deetz, "Effectiveness and Ethics in Interpersonal Interaction," 240.

34. Cheris Kramarae, *Women and Men Speaking: Frameworks for Analysis* (Rowley, Mass.: Newbury House Publishers, 1981), 1.

35. Dale Spender, *Man Made Language*, 2d ed. (London: Routledge and Kegan Paul, 1985), 140.

36. Donald G. MacKay, "Prescriptive Grammar and the Pronoun Problem," in *Language, Gender, and Society,* ed. Barrie Thorne, Cheris Kramarae, and Nancy Henley (Rowley, Mass.: Newbury House Publishers, 1983), 38–53.

37. See the annotated bibliography in *Language, Gender, and Society,* 151–331.

38. Kramarae, *Women and Men Speaking,* 29.

39. Jack W. Sattel, "Men, Inexpressiveness, and Power," in *Language, Gender, and Society,* 120.

40. Carol Gilligan and Jane Attanucci, "Two Moral Orientations," in *Mapping the Moral Domain: A Contribution of Women's Thinking to Psychological Theory and Education,* ed. Carol Gilligan, Janie Victoria Ward, and Jill McLean Taylor, with Betty Bardige (Cambridge, Mass.: Harvard University Press, 1988), 73.

41. Carol Gilligan, "Remapping the Moral Domain: New Images of Self in Relationship," in *Mapping the Moral Domain,* 3–19.

42. Gilligan, "Two Moral Orientations," 73–86; and Nona Plessner Lyons, "Two Perspectives: On Self, Relationships, and Morality," in *Mapping the Moral Domain,* 21–48.

43. Melanie M. Bloom, "Sex Differences in Ethical Systems: A Useful Framework for Interpreting Communication Research," *Communication Quarterly* 38 (1990): 252.

44. Carol Gilligan and Grant Wiggins, "The Origins of Morality in Early Childhood Relationships," in *Mapping the Moral Domain,* 121.

45. Julia T. Wood, *Gendered Lives: Communication, Gender, and Culture* (Belmont, Calif.: Wadsworth, 1994), 64.

46. Spender, *Man Made Language,* 82–83.

47. Deborah Tannen, "The Relativity of Linguistic Strategies: Rethinking Power and Solidarity in Gender and Dominance," in *Gender and Conversational Interaction,* ed. Deborah Tannen (New York: Oxford University Press, 1993), 165–88.

48. Maurice Natanson, "The Arts of Indirection," in *Rhetoric, Philosophy, and Literature: An Exploration,* ed. Don M. Burks (West Lafayette, Ind.: Purdue University Press, 1978), 35–47.

49. Tannen, "The Relativity of Linguistic Strategies," 175.

50. See, for example, Richard L. Johannesen, *Ethics in Human Communication,* 3d ed. (Prospect Heights, Ill.: Waveland, 1990), 139–49.

51. Gayatri Chakravorty Spivak, "Subaltern Studies: Deconstructing Historiography," in *In Other Worlds: Essays in Cultural Politics* (New York: Methuen, 1987), 209.

52. Gayatri Chakravorty Spivak, "A Literary Representation of the Subaltern: A Woman's Text from the Third World," in *In Other Worlds,* 253–54.

6. Organizational Ecology

1. Max Weber, *The Theory of Social and Economic Organization,* trans. A. M. Henderson and Talcott Parsons (Glencoe, Ill.: Free Press, 1947);

Frederick W. Taylor, *Principles of Scientific Management* (New York: Harper and Row, 1911).

2. Chester I. Barnard, *The Functions of the Executive* (Cambridge, Mass.: Harvard University Press, 1938), 90.

3. Although led by Elton Mayo, the studies were published by Fritz J. Roethlisberger and William J. Dickson, *Management and the Worker* (Cambridge, Mass.: Harvard University Press, 1939).

4. Daniel Katz and Robert Kahn, "Open-System Theory," in *Readings in Organization Theory: Open System Approaches*, ed. John G. Maurer (New York: Random House, 1971), 13–30.

5. Ibid., 14.

6. George Cheney, "The Rhetoric of Identification and the Study of Organizational Communication," *Quarterly Journal of Speech* 69 (1983): 143–58.

7. William M. Evan, "The Organization-Set: Toward a Theory of Interorganizational Relations," in *Readings in Organization Theory*, 33.

8. Kenneth E. Boulding, *The Organizational Revolution* (New York: Harper and Brothers, 1953), xx–xxi.

9. Evan, "The Organization-Set," 36. Evan later provides an example of civil-service unions being constrained from striking by the normative reference organization of the government. From my perspective, however, the civil servants are the government. His example again shows how he assumes that the values of the top of the hierarchy are the values of the organization.

10. Michael Burawoy, *Manufacturing Consent* (Chicago: University of Chicago Press, 1979), 15.

11. Ibid., 17.

12. Ibid., 18.

13. Ibid., 64.

14. Ibid., 81.

15. Stanley Deetz, "Keeping the Conversation Going: The Principle of Dialectic Ethics," *Communication* 7 (1983): 271.

16. Ibid., 279.

17. Peirce, "Critical Common-Sensism," in Buchler, *Philosophical Writings of Peirce*, 290–301.

18. William G. Ouchi, *Theory Z: How American Business Can Meet the Japanese Challenge* (New York: Avon Books, 1982), 8.

19. Ibid., 36.

20. Ibid., 37.

21. Ibid., 77.

22. Ibid., 78.

23. Ibid., 79.

24. Ibid., 179.

25. Katz and Kahn, "Open-System Theory," 16.

26. Ouchi, *Theory Z*, 19.

27. Katz and Kahn, "Open-System Theory," 17.

28. Foucault, *Foucault Reader*, 197.

29. Ibid., 217.

30. Ouchi, *Theory Z*, 23.

31. Ellen A. Fagenson, "Is What's Good for the Goose also Good for the Gander? On Being White and Male in a Diverse Workforce," *Academy of Management Executive* 7 (November 1993): 80–81.

32. Patricia Buhler, "Understanding Cultural Diversity and Its Benefits," *Supervision* 54 (July 1993): 17–19.

33. Tom Lester, "A Woman's Place," *Management Today* (April 1993): 46–50.

34. M. D. Cohen, J. G. March, and J. P. Olsen, "A Garbage Can Model of Organizational Choice," *Administrative Science Quarterly* 17 (1972): 1–25.

35. Mats Alvesson, *Cultural Perspectives on Organizations* (Cambridge: Cambridge University Press, 1993), 12.

36. Craig Lundberg, "Open Letter to Karl Weick," *Journal of Applied Behavioral Science* 18 (1982): 113–17.

37. Karl E. Weick, *The Social Psychology of Organizing*, 2d ed. (Reading, Mass.: Addison-Wesley Publishing, 1979), 26.

38. Ibid., 21.

39. Ibid., 133–34.

40. Ibid., 92–93.

41. Ibid., 130.

42. Ibid., 135.

43. Ibid., 201.

44. Ibid., 218–24.

45. Ibid., 8.

46. Ibid.

47. J. Vernon Jensen, "Ethical Tension Points in Whistleblowing," in *Ethics in Human Communication*, 284.

7. The Politics of Representation

1. Cited in Angus Lind, "Remembering a National Icon," *New Orleans Times-Picayune*, 4 November 1994.

2. Kathleen Hall Jamieson, *Dirty Politics: Deception, Distraction, and Democracy* (New York: Oxford University Press, 1992).

3. W. Lance Bennett, *The Governing Crisis: Media, Money, and Marketing in American Elections* (New York: St. Martin's Press, 1992), 1, 13.

4. Jamieson, *Dirty Politics*, 217.

5. Bennett, *Governing Crisis*, 189.

6. Martha Cooper, "Ethical Dimensions of Political Advocacy from a Postmodern Perspective," in *Ethical Dimensions of Political Communication*, ed. Robert E. Denton, Jr. (New York: Praeger, 1991), 23–47.

7. Ibid., 42.

8. Craig Allen Smith, *Political Communication* (San Diego: Harcourt Brace Jovanovich, 1990), 51.

9. Ibid., 133.

10. Peirce, "Logic as Semiotic," in *Philosophical Writings*, 101.

11. Ibid., 102.

12. Ibid., 108.

13. Ibid., 102.

14. Ibid., 112.

15. Ibid., 114.

16. Ibid., 102–103.

17. Ibid., 115.

18. Peirce, "How to Make Our Ideas Clear," in *Selected Writings*, 124.

19. Peirce, "Fixation of Belief," in *Selected Writings*, 107.

20. Peirce, "Critical Common-Sensism," in *Philosophical Writings*, 290.

21. Ibid., 292.

22. Ibid., 291.

23. Ibid., 290.

24. Ibid., 291.

25. Peirce, "Logic as Semiotic," 103, 117–18.

26. Peirce, "What Is a Leading Principle?" in *Philosophical Writings*, 129–34.

27. Peirce, "Grounds of Validity of the Laws of Logic," in *Peirce on Signs*, 89.

28. J. Jay Zeman, "Peirce on Abstraction," in *The Relevance of Charles Peirce*, 293–311.

29. Peirce, "Abduction and Induction," in *Philosophical Writings*, 150–56.

30. Ibid., 151.

31. Ibid., 154.

32. Peirce, "Grounds of Validity of the Laws of Logic," in *Peirce on Signs*, 112.

33. Edmund Burke, "Speech to the Electors of Bristol, On Thursday, the 3rd of November, 1774," in *The Works of the Right Honourable Edmund Burke*, vol. 2 (London: Oxford University Press, 1906), 164–65.

34. Bennett, *Governing Crisis*, 5–6.

35. Ibid., 96.

36. "Secondhand Smoke: Is It a Hazard?" *Consumer Reports* 60, no. 1 (January 1995): 29.

37. Bennett, *Governing Crisis*, 107.

38. Jamieson, *Dirty Politics*, 216.

39. Dewey, *Public and Its Problems*, 208.

40. Raymie E. McKerrow, "Critical Rhetoric: Theory and Praxis," *Communication Monographs* 56 (1989): 91–111.

41. Dewey, *Public and Its Problems*, 180–81.

42. Forbes Hill, "Conventional Wisdom—Traditional Form—The President's Message of November 3, 1969," *Quarterly Journal of Speech* 58 (1972): 373–86.

43. Sonja K. Foss, *Rhetorical Criticism: Exploration and Practice* (Prospect Heights, Ill.: Waveland Press, 1989), 286.

44. Lloyd F. Bitzer, "The Rhetorical Situation," *Philosophy and Rhetoric* 1 (1968): 1–14.

45. Roderick P. Hart, *Modern Rhetorical Criticism* (Glenview, Ill.: Scott, Foresman, 1990), 70–86; Karyn Rybacki and Donald Rybacki, *Communication Criticism: Approaches and Genres* (Belmont, Calif.: Wadsworth, 1991), 27–30.

8. Retrospect and Prospect

1. Peirce, "Critical Common-Sensism," in *Philosophical Writings*, 290–301.

2. Jürgen Habermas, "Morality, Society, and Ethics: An Interview with Torben Hviid Nielsen," in *Justification and Application: Remarks on Discourse Ethics*, trans. Ciaran P. Cronin (Cambridge, Mass.: MIT Press, 1993), 165.

3. Ibid., 163–64.

4. Jürgen Habermas, "On the Pragmatic, the Ethical, and the Moral Employments of Practical Reason," in *Justification and Application*, 1–17.

5. Ibid., 3–8.

6. Ibid., 9–10.

7. Bart Kosko, *Fuzzy Thinking: The New Science of Fuzzy Logic* (New York: Hyperion, 1993), 171.

8. Lyotard, *Postmodern Condition*, 67.

9. Peter Galison, "The Ontology of the Enemy: Norbert Wiener and the Cybernetic Vision," *Critical Inquiry* 21 (1994): 228–66.

10. Ibid., 256–59.

11. Joe Abernathy, "Creating the PBS of the Internet," *PC World* 13:2 (February 1995): 62–64.

12. "Republicans Lay Plans for the I-Way," *PC World* 13:2 (February 1995): 64.

13. Roberta Furger, "Unequal Distribution: The Information Haves and Have-Nots," *PC World* 12:9 (September 1994): 30.

14. Maureen Majella Ebben, "Women on the Net: An Exploratory Study of Gender Dynamics on the Soc.women Computer Network" (paper presented at the annual meeting of the Speech Communication Association Convention, New Orleans, La., November 1994).

15. Brian S. Akre (Associated Press), "Student Jailed in Rape Messages," *New Orleans Times-Picayune*, 12 February 1995, A-2.

Bibliography

Alvesson, Mats. *Cultural Perspectives on Organizations.* Cambridge: Cambridge University Press, 1993.

Apel, Karl-Otto. *Charles S. Peirce: From Pragmatism to Pragmaticism.* Translated by John Michael Krois. Amherst: University of Massachusetts Press, 1981.

Arnett, Ronald C. "The Practical Philosophy of Communication Ethics and Free Speech as the Foundation for Speech Communication." *Communication Quarterly* 38 (1990): 208–17.

———. "The Status of Communication Ethics Scholarship in Speech Communication Journals from 1915 to 1985." *Central States Speech Journal* 38 (1987): 44–61.

Ayer, A. J. *Philosophical Essays.* London: Macmillan, 1954.

Baier, Kurt. *The Moral Point of View: A Rational Basis of Ethics.* Ithaca: Cornell University Press, 1958.

Barker, Ernest, ed. *Social Contract: Essays by Locke, Hume, and Rousseau.* London: Oxford University Press, 1947.

Barnard, Chester I. *The Functions of the Executive.* Cambridge, Mass.: Harvard University Press, 1938.

Baynes, Kenneth, James Bohman, and Thomas McCarthy, eds. *After Philosophy: End or Transformation?* Cambridge, Mass.: MIT Press, 1987.

Bennett, W. Lance. *The Governing Crisis: Media, Money, and Marketing in American Elections.* New York: St. Martin's Press, 1992.

Berger, Peter L., and Thomas Luckmann. *The Social Construction of Reality: A Treatise in the Sociology of Knowledge.* 1966. Garden City, N.Y.: Anchor, 1967.

Berman, Paul, ed. *Debating P. C.: The Controversy over Political Correctness on College Campuses.* New York: Dell Laurel, 1992.

Biesecker, Barbara. "Michel Foucault and the Question of Rhetoric," *Philosophy and Rhetoric* 25 (1992): 351–64.

Binkley, Luther J. *Contemporary Ethical Theories.* New York: Philosophical Library, 1961.

Bitzer, Lloyd F. "Aristotle's Enthymeme Revisited." *Quarterly Journal of Speech* 45 (1959): 399–408.

———. "The Rhetorical Situation." *Philosophy and Rhetoric* 1 (1968): 1–14.

Bizzell, Patricia, and Bruce Herzberg, eds. *The Rhetorical Tradition: Readings from Classical Times to the Present.* Boston: St. Martin's Press, 1990.

Black, Edwin. Rhetorical Criticism: A Study in Method. 1965. Madison: University of Wisconsin Press, 1978.

Blair, Carole, and Martha Cooper. "The Humanist Turn in Foucault's Rhetoric of Inquiry." *Quarterly Journal of Speech* 73 (1987): 151–71.

Blair, George A. *Energeia and Entelecheia: "Act" in Aristotle.* Ottawa: University of Ottawa Press, 1992.

Bloom, Melanie M. "Sex Differences in Ethical Systems: A Useful Framework for Interpreting Communication Research." *Communication Quarterly* 38 (1990): 244–54.

Bostrom, Robert N. *Competence in Communication: A Multidisciplinary Approach.* Beverly Hills: Sage, 1984.

Boulding, Kenneth E. *The Organizational Revolution.* New York: Harper and Brothers, 1953.

Brock, Jarrett E. "C. S. Peirce's Logic of Vagueness." Ph.D. diss., University of Illinois, 1969. Ann Arbor: University Microfilms, 1978.

Brown, Richard Harvey. *Society as Text: Essays on Rhetoric, Reason, and Reality.* Chicago: University of Chicago Press, 1987.

Brown, William J., and Arvind Singhal. "Ethical Dilemmas of Prosocial Television." *Communication Quarterly* 38 (1990): 268–80.

Bryson, Lyman, ed. *The Communication of Ideas.* New York: Harper, 1948.

Buber, Martin. *I and Thou.* Trans. Walter Kaufmann. New York: Scribner's, 1970.

Buhler, Patricia. "Understanding Cultural Diversity and Its Benefits." *Supervision* 54 (July 1993): 17–19.

Burawoy, Michael. *Manufacturing Consent.* Chicago: University of Chicago Press, 1979.

Burch, Robert W. *A Peircean Reduction Thesis: The Foundations of Topological Logic.* Lubbock: Texas Tech University Press, 1991.

Burke, Edmund. "Speech to the Electors of Bristol, On Thursday, the 3rd of November, 1774." In *The Works of the Right Honourable Edmund Burke.* Vol. 2. London: Oxford University Press, 1906.

Burke, Kenneth. *Counter-Statement.* Rev. ed. Berkeley: University of California Press, 1968.

———. *A Grammar of Motives.* Berkeley: University of California Press, 1969.

———. *Language as Symbolic Action: Essays on Life, Literature, and Method.* Berkeley: University of California Press, 1966.

———. *Permanence and Change: An Anatomy of Purpose.* 3d ed. Berkeley: University of California Press, 1984.

————. *The Philosophy of Literary Form: Studies in Symbolic Action.* 3d ed. Berkeley: University of California Press, 1973.

————. *A Rhetoric of Motives.* Berkeley: University of California Press, 1969.

————. *The Rhetoric of Religion: Studies in Logology.* Berkeley: University of California Press, 1970.

Burks, Don M., ed. *Rhetoric, Philosophy, and Literature: An Exploration.* West Lafayette, Ind.: Purdue University Press, 1978.

Campbell, James. *The Community Reconstructs: The Meaning of Pragmatic Social Thought.* Urbana: University of Illinois Press, 1992.

Campbell, Karlyn Kohrs. "The Ontological Foundations of Rhetorical Theory." *Philosophy and Rhetoric* 3 (1970): 97–108.

————. "The Rhetorical Implications of the Axiology of Jean-Paul Sartre." *Western Speech* 35 (1971): 155–61.

Campbell, Karlyn Kohrs, and Kathleen Hall Jamieson, eds. *Form and Genre: Shaping Rhetorical Action.* Falls Church, Va.: Speech Communication Association, 1976.

Cheney, George. "The Rhetoric of Identification and the Study of Organizational Communication." *Quarterly Journal of Speech* 69 (1983): 143–58.

Chesebro, James W., ed. *Extensions of the Burkeian System.* Tuscaloosa: University of Alabama Press, 1993.

Christians, Clifford G., Kim B. Rotzoll, and Mark Fackler. *Media Ethics: Cases and Moral Reasoning.* 3d ed. New York: Longman, 1991.

Cohen, M. D., J. G. March, and J. P. Olsen. "A Garbage Can Model of Organizational Choice." *Administrative Science Quarterly* 17 (1972): 1–25.

Colapietro, Vincent M. *Peirce's Approach to the Self: A Semiotic Perspective on Human Subjectivity.* Albany: SUNY Press, 1989.

Condit, Celeste Michelle. "Crafting Virtue: The Rhetorical Construction of Public Morality." *Quarterly Journal of Speech* 73 (1987): 79–97.

Cope, E. M. *An Introduction to Aristotle's Rhetoric.* London: Macmillan, 1867.

Dallmayr, Fred R. *Polis and Praxis: Exercises in Contemporary Political Theory.* Cambridge, Mass.: MIT Press, 1984.

Day, Louis A. *Ethics in Media Communications: Cases and Controversies.* Belmont, Calif.: Wadsworth, 1991.

Deely, John. *Basics of Semiotics.* Bloomington: Indiana University Press, 1990.

Deetz, Stanley. "Keeping the Conversation Going: The Principle of Dialectic Ethics." *Communication* 7 (1983): 263–88.

————. "Reclaiming the Subject Matter as a Guide to Mutual Understanding: Effectiveness and Ethics in Interpersonal Interaction." *Communication Quarterly* 38 (1990): 226–43.

Denton, Robert E., ed. *Ethical Dimensions of Political Communication.* New York: Praeger, 1991.

Derrida, Jacques. Afterword. *Limited Inc.* Translated by Samuel Weber. Evanston: Northwestern University Press, 1988.

————. *Of Grammatology.* Translated by Gayatri Chakravorty Spivak. Baltimore: Johns Hopkins University Press, 1976.

————. *Speech and Phenomena and Other Essays on Husserl's Theory of Signs.* Translated by David Allison. Evanston: Northwestern University Press, 1973.

de Saussure, Ferdinand. *Course in General Linguistics.* Edited by Charles Bally, Albert Sechehaye, and Albert Riedlinger. Translated by Wade Baskin. New York: McGraw-Hill, 1966.

Dewey, John. *Experience and Nature.* 2d ed. La Salle, Ill.: Open Court, 1971.

————. *The Public and Its Problems.* Athens, Ohio: Swallow, 1954.

————. *Reconstruction in Philosophy.* Boston: Beacon, 1948.

————. *Theory of Valuation.* Foundations of the Unity of Science 2. Chicago: University of Chicago Press, 1939.

Dewey, John, and James H. Tufts. *Ethics.* Rev. ed. New York: Henry Holt, 1932.

Di Zenzo, Silvano. "A Many-Valued Logic for Approximate Reasoning." *IBM Journal of Research and Development* 32 (1988): 552–65.

Duncan, Hugh Dalziel. *Communication and Social Order.* London: Oxford University Press, 1962.

Ebben, Maureen Majella. "Women on the Net: An Exploratory Study of Gender Dynamics on the Soc.women Computer Network." Paper presented at the annual meeting of the Speech Communication Association, New Orleans, La., November 1994.

Eco, Umberto. *Semiotics and the Philosophy of Language.* Bloomington: Indiana University Press, 1984.

————. *A Theory of Semiotics.* Bloomington: Indiana University Press, 1976.

Ehninger, Douglas, ed. *Contemporary Rhetoric: A Coursebook.* Glenview, Ill.: Scott, Foresman, 1972.

Ellis, John M. *Against Deconstruction.* Princeton: Princeton University Press, 1989.

Fagenson, Ellen A. "Is What's Good for the Goose also Good for the Gander? On Being White and Male in a Diverse Workforce." *Academy of Management Executive* 7 (November 1993): 80–81.

Farrell, Thomas B. *Norms of Rhetorical Culture.* New Haven: Yale University Press, 1993.

Ferré, John P. "Communication Ethics and the Political Realism of Reinhold Niebuhr." *Communication Quarterly* 38 (1990): 218–25.

Ferry, Luc, and Alain Renaut. *French Philosophy of the Sixties: An Essay on Antihumanism.* Translated by Mary Schnackenberg Cattani. Amherst: University of Massachusetts Press, 1990.

Fisher, Walter R. *Human Communication as Narration: Toward a Philosophy of Reason, Value, and Action.* Columbia: University of South Carolina Press, 1987.

Fletcher, Joseph. *Situation Ethics: The New Morality.* Philadelphia: Westminster Press, 1966.

Foss, Sonja K. *Rhetorical Criticism: Exploration and Practice.* Prospect Heights, Ill.: Waveland, 1989.

Foucault, Michel. *The Foucault Reader.* Edited by Paul Rabinow. New York: Pantheon Books, 1984.

———. *The Order of Things: An Archaeology of the Human Sciences (Les mots et les choses.)* New York: Random House, 1970.

———. *Politics, Philosophy, Culture: Interviews and Other Writings, 1977–1984.* Edited by Lawrence D. Kritzman. New York: Routledge, 1988.

———. *The Use of Pleasure.* Vol. 2 of *The History of Sexuality.* Translated by Robert Hurley. New York: Pantheon, 1985.

Freeman, Eugene, ed. *The Relevance of Charles Peirce.* LaSalle, Ill.: Hegeler Institute, 1983.

Gadamer, Hans-Georg. *Truth and Method.* New York: Seabury, 1975.

Galison, Peter. "The Ontology of the Enemy: Norbert Wiener and the Cybernetic Vision." *Critical Inquiry* 21 (1994): 228–66.

Gilligan, Carol, Janie Victoria Ward, and Jill McLean Taylor, with Betty Bardige, eds. *Mapping the Moral Domain: A Contribution of Women's Thinking to Psychological Theory and Education.* Cambridge, Mass.: Harvard University Press, 1988.

Golden, James L., Goodwin F. Berquist, and William E. Coleman, eds. *The Rhetoric of Western Thought.* 3d ed. Dubuque: Kendall/Hunt, 1983.

Goodheart, Eugene. *The Skeptic Disposition in Contemporary Criticism.* Princeton: Princeton University Press, 1984.

Greene, Nathanael, ed. *Fascism: An Anthology.* Arlington Heights, Ill.: AHM Publishing, 1968.

Greenlee, Douglas. *Peirce's Concept of Sign.* The Hague: Mouton, 1973.

Gregg, Richard B. "The Ego-Function of the Rhetoric of Protest." *Philosophy and Rhetoric* 4 (1971): 71–91.

———. *Symbolic Inducement and Knowing: A Study in the Foundations of Rhetoric.* Columbia: University of South Carolina Press, 1984.

Grimaldi, William M. A. *Studies in the Philosophy of Aristotle's Rhetoric. Hermes:* Zeitschrift für klassische Philologie, Einzelschriften, Heft 25. Wiesbaden: Franz Steiner Verlag GMBH, 1972.

Grumley, John E. *History and Totality: Radical Historicism from Hegel to Foucault.* London: Routledge, 1989.

Guthrie, W. K. C. *The Sophists.* Cambridge: Cambridge University Press, 1971.

Habermas, Jürgen. *Justification and Application: Remarks on Discourse Ethics.* Translated by Ciaran P. Cronin. Cambridge, Mass.: MIT Press, 1993.

———. *The Structural Transformation of the Public Sphere: An Inquiry into a Category of Bourgeois Society.* Translated by Thomas Burger and Frederick Lawrence. Cambridge, Mass.: MIT Press, 1989.

Hare, R. M. *The Language of Morals.* 1952. Oxford: Oxford University Press, 1964.

Hart, Roderick P. *Modern Rhetorical Criticism.* Glenview, Ill.: Scott, Foresman, 1990.

———. "An Unquiet Desperation: Rhetorical Aspects of 'Popular' Atheism in the United States." *Quarterly Journal of Speech* 64 (1978): 33–46.

Hart, Roderick P., and Don M. Burks. "Rhetorical Sensitivity and Social Interaction." *Speech Monographs* 39 (1972): 75–91.

Harvey, Irene E. *Derrida and the Economy of "Différance."* Bloomington: Indiana University Press, 1986.

Hauser, Gerard A. "The Example in Aristotle's Rhetoric: Bifurcation or Contradiction?" *Philosophy and Rhetoric* 1 (1968): 78–90.

Heidegger, Martin. *The Basic Problems of Phenomenology.* Rev. ed. Translated by Albert Hofstadter. Bloomington: Indiana University Press, 1982.

———. *Being and Time.* Translated by John Macquarrie and Edward Robinson. New York: Harper and Row, 1962.

Herrick, James A. "Rhetoric, Ethics, and Virtue." *Communication Studies* 43 (1992): 133–49.

Hill, Forbes. "Conventional Wisdom—Traditional Form—The President's Message of November 3, 1969." *Quarterly Journal of Speech* 58 (1972): 373–86.

Hirschman, Albert O. *The Rhetoric of Reaction.* Cambridge, Mass.: Belknap Press of Harvard University Press, 1991.

Horne, Janet. "Rhetoric after Rorty." *Western Journal of Speech Communication* 53 (1989): 247–59.

Hoy, David Couzens, ed. *Foucault: A Critical Reader.* Oxford: Basil Blackwell, 1986.

Hume, David. *An Inquiry Concerning the Principles of Morals.* Indianapolis: Bobbs-Merrill, 1957.

———. *An Inquiry Concerning Human Understanding.* Indianapolis: Bobbs-Merrill, 1955.

Infante, Dominic A. "Aggressiveness." In *Personality and Interpersonal Communication.* Edited by James C. McCroskey and John A. Daly. Beverly Hills: Sage, 1987.

James, William. *The Writings of William James: A Comprehensive Edition.* Ed. John J. McDermott. Chicago: University of Chicago Press, 1977.

Jamieson, Kathleen Hall. *Dirty Politics: Deception, Distraction, and Democracy.* New York: Oxford University Press, 1992.

Jensen, J. Vernon. "Ethical Tension Points in Whistleblowing." *Journal of Business Ethics* 6 (May 1987): 321–28.

Johannesen, Richard L. *Ethics in Human Communication.* 3d ed. Prospect Heights, Ill.: Waveland, 1990.

Johannesen, Richard L., ed. *Ethics and Persuasion: Selected Readings.* New York: Random House, 1967.

Johnstone, Christopher Lyle. "An Aristotelian Trilogy: Ethics, Rhetoric, Politics, and the Search for Moral Truth." *Philosophy and Rhetoric* 13 (1980): 1–24.

Johnstone, Henry W., Jr. "Rationality and Rhetoric in Philosophy." *Quarterly Journal of Speech* 59 (1973): 381–89.

———. "Toward an Ethics of Rhetoric." *Communication* 6 (1981): 305–14.

Kant, Immanuel. *Grounding for the Metaphysics of Morals.* Trans. James W. Ellington. Indianapolis: Hackett, 1981.

———. *The Philosophy of Kant: Immanuel Kant's Moral and Political Writings.* Edited by Carl J. Friedrich. New York: Random House, 1949.

Keller, Paul W. "Interpersonal Dissent and the Ethics of Dialogue." *Communication* 6 (1981): 287–303.

Kerferd, G. B. *The Sophistic Movement*. Cambridge: Cambridge University Press, 1981.

Kierkegaard, Søren [Johannes Climacus]. *Concluding Unscientific Postscript to the Philosophical Fragments*. Trans. David F. Swenson and Walter Lowrie. Princeton: Princeton University Press, 1941.

———. *The Point of View, Etc*. Trans. Walter Lowrie. London: Oxford University Press, 1939.

Kinneavy, James L. *A Theory of Discourse: The Aims of Discourse*. 1971. New York: Norton, 1980.

Kosko, Bart. *Fuzzy Thinking: The New Science of Fuzzy Logic*. New York: Hyperion, 1993.

Kramarae, Cheris. *Women and Men Speaking: Frameworks for Analysis*. Rowley, Mass.: Newbury House, 1981.

Kuhn, Thomas S. *The Structure of Scientific Revolutions*. 2d ed. Chicago: University of Chicago Press, 1970.

Lasswell, Harold. "The Structure and Function of Communication in Society." In *The Communication of Ideas*. Edited by Lyman Bryson. New York: Harper, 1946.

Laszlo, Ervin. *Introduction to Systems Philosophy: Toward a New Paradigm of Contemporary Thought*. New York: Gordon and Breach, 1972.

Lester, Tom. "A Woman's Place." *Management Today* (April 1993): 46–50.

Lundberg, Craig. "Open Letter to Karl Weick." *Journal of Applied Behavioral Science* 18 (1982): 113–17.

Lyne, John R. "Rhetoric and Semiotic in C. S. Peirce." *Quarterly Journal of Speech* 66 (1980): 155–68.

Lyotard, Jean-François. *Libidinal Economy*. Translated by Iain Hamilton Grant. Bloomington: Indiana University Press, 1993.

———. *The Postmodern Condition: A Report on Knowledge*. Translated by Geoff Bennington and Brian Massumi. Minneapolis: University of Minn Press, 1984.

McArthur, Tom, ed. *The Oxford Companion to the English Language*. Oxford: Oxford University Press, 1992.

McCroskey, James C., and John A. Daly, eds. *Personality and Interpersonal Communication*. Newbury Park, Calif.: Sage, 1987.

McGee, Michael Calvin. "Text, Context, and the Fragmentation of Contemporary Culture." *Western Journal of Speech Communication* 54 (1990): 274–89.

McGuire, Michael. "The Structure of Rhetoric." *Philosophy and Rhetoric* 15 (1982): 149–69.

MacIntyre, Alasdair. *After Virtue: A Study in Moral Theory*. 2d ed. Notre Dame, Ind.: University of Notre Dame Press, 1984.

———. *A Short History of Ethics*. New York: Macmillan, 1966.

———. *Whose Justice? Which Rationality?* Notre Dame, Ind.: University of Notre Dame Press, 1988.

McKerrow, Raymie E. "Critical Rhetoric: Theory and Praxis." *Communication Monographs* 56 (1989): 91–111.

———. "The Repressive Voice of Modernity in a Postmodern Rhetoric." Paper presented at the annual meeting of the Southern States Communication Association, Norfolk, Va., April 1994.

McNeil, Daniel, and Paul Freiberger. *Fuzzy Logic.* New York: Touchstone, 1993.

Malcolm X and Alex Haley. *The Autobiography of Malcolm X.* New York: Ballantine, 1973.

Maruyama, Magoroh. "The Second Cybernetics: Deviation-Amplifying Mutual Causal Processes." *American Scientist* 51 (1963): 164–79.

Maurer, Hohn G., ed. *Readings in Organization Theory: Open System Approaches.* New York: Random House, 1971.

Minnick, Wayne C. "A New Look at the Ethics of Persuasion." *Southern Speech Communication Journal* 45 (1980): 352–62.

Mitchell, Gillian. "Women and Lying: A Pragmatic and Semantic Analysis of 'Telling It Slant.' " *Women's Studies International Forum* 7 (1984): 375–83.

Moore, George Edward. *Principia Ethica.* Cambridge: Cambridge University Press, 1903.

Morrison, Grant, Charles Truog, and Mark Farmer. "Deus ex Machina." *Animal Man* 26 (August 1990).

Newfield, Christopher. "What Was Political Correctness? Race, the Right, and Managerial Democracy in the Humanities." *Critical Inquiry* 19 (1993): 308–36.

Nietzsche, Friedrich. *On the Genealogy of Morals and Ecce Homo.* Translated by Walter Kaufmann and R. J. Hollingdale. New York: Random House, 1967.

Nilsen, Thomas R. *Ethics of Speech Communication.* 2d ed. Indianapolis: Bobbs-Merrill, 1974.

Nilsen, Thomas R., ed. *Essays on Rhetorical Criticism.* New York: Random House, 1968.

Norris, Christopher. *The Contest of Faculties: Philosophy and Theory after Deconstruction.* London: Methuen, 1985.

———. *Deconstruction: Theory and Practice.* London: Methuen, 1982.

Ornstein, Robert. *The Evolution of Consciousness.* New York: Prentice Hall, 1991.

Osborn, Michael. "Archetypal Metaphor in Rhetoric: The Light-Dark Family." *Quarterly Journal of Speech* 53 (1967): 115–26.

———. "The Evolution of the Archetypal Sea in Rhetoric and Poetic." *Quarterly Journal of Speech* 63 (1977): 347–63.

Ouchi, William G. *Theory Z: How American Business Can Meet the Japanese Challenge.* New York: Avon Books, 1982.

Pagels, Heinz R. "Uncertainty and Complementarity." In *The World Treasury of Physics, Astronomy, and Mathematics.* Edited by Timothy Ferris. Boston: Little, Brown, 1991.

Parks, Malcolm R. "Interpersonal Communication and the Quest for Personal Competence." In *Handbook of Interpersonal Communication,* 171–201. Edited by Mark L. Knapp and Gerald R. Miller. Beverly Hills: Sage, 1985.

Pefanis, Julian. *Heterology and the Postmodern.* Durham: Duke University Press, 1991.

Peirce, Charles S. Manuscript L75. Edited by Joseph Ransdell. Peirce Tele-community Project, Electronic Peirce Consortium. Available on Internet via Gopher from Georgetown University.

————. *Peirce on Signs.* Edited by James Hoopes. Chapel Hill: University of North Carolina Press, 1991.

————. *Philosophical Writings of Peirce.* Edited by Justus Buchler. New York: Dover, 1955.

————. *Selected Writings (Values in a Universe of Chance).* Edited by Philip P. Wiener. New York: Dover, 1966.

Perelman, Chaim. *The Realm of Rhetoric.* Trans. William Kluback. Notre Dame, Ind.: University of Notre Dame Press, 1982.

————. "Rhetoric and Politics." *Philosophy and Rhetoric* 17 (1984): 129–34.

Pribble, Paula Tompkins. "Making an Ethical Commitment: A Rhetorical Case Study of Organizational Socialization." *Communication Quarterly* 38 (1990): 255–67.

Richmond, Virginia P., and James C. McCroskey. *Organizational Communication for Survival.* Englewood Cliffs, N.J.: Prentice Hall, 1992.

Ricoeur, Paul. "Ethics and Culture: Habermas and Gadamer in Dialogue." *Philosophy Today* 17 (1973): 153–65.

Robbins, Bruce, ed. *The Phantom Public Sphere.* Minneapolis: University of Minnesota Press, 1993.

Roethlisberger, Fritz J., and William J. Dickson. *Management and the Worker.* Cambridge, Mass.: Harvard University Press, 1939.

Rorty, Richard. *Objectivity, Relativism, and Truth.* New York: Cambridge University Press, 1991.

————. *Philosophy and the Mirror of Nature.* Princeton: Princeton University Press, 1979.

Ruben, Brent D., and John Y. Kim, eds. *General Systems Theory and Human Communication.* Rochelle Park, N.J.: Hayden, 1975.

Ruether, Rosemary Radford. *Sexism and God-Talk.* Boston: Beacon Press, 1983.

Rybacki, Karyn, and Donald Rybacki. *Communication Criticism: Approaches and Genres.* Belmont, Calif.: Wadsworth, 1991.

Sallis, John, ed. *Deconstruction and Philosophy: The Texts of Jacques Derrida.* Chicago: University of Chicago Press, 1987.

Sass, Hans-Martin. "Ideational Politics and the Word Tolerance." *Philosophy and Rhetoric* 11 (1978): 98–113.

Schilpp, Paul Arthur, and Maurice Friedman, eds. *The Philosophy of Martin Buber.* The Library of Living Philosophers 12. La Salle, Ill.: Open Court, 1967.

Schrift, Alan D. *Nietzsche and the Question of Interpretation: Between Hermeneutics and Deconstruction.* New York: Routledge, 1990.

Schudson, Michael. *Discovering the News: A Social History of American Newspapers.* New York: Basic Books, 1978.

Scott, Joan Wallach. "The Campaign Against Political Correctness: What's Really at Stake." *Radical History Review* 54 (1992): 59–79.

Silverman, Hugh J., ed. *Derrida and Deconstruction.* New York: Routledge, 1989.

Smith, Craig Allen. *Political Communication*. San Diego: Harcourt Brace Jovanovich, 1990.

Solomon, Robert C. *Morality and the Good Life: An Introduction to Ethics through Classical Sources*. New York: McGraw-Hill, 1984.

Spender, Dale. *Man Made Language*. 2d ed. London: Routledge and Kegan Paul, 1985.

Spitzberg, Brian H., and William R. Cupach. *Interpersonal Communication Competence*. Beverly Hills: Sage, 1984.

Spivak, Gayatri Chakravorty. *In Other Worlds: Essays in Cultural Politics*. New York: Methuen, 1987.

Steffenson, David Conrad. "A Foundational Model for an 'Ecological Social Ethic.' " Ph.D. diss., Union for Experimenting Colleges and Universities, 1984.

Stevenson, Charles L. *Ethics and Language*. New Haven: Yale University Press, 1944.

Taylor, Frederick W. *Principles of Scientific Management*. New York: Harper and Row, 1911.

Thorne, Barrie, Cheris Karamarae, and Nancy Henley, eds. *Language, Gender and Society*. Rowley, Mass.: Newbury House Publishers, 1983.

von Bertalanffy, Ludwig. *General System Theory: Foundations, Development, Applications*. New York: George Braziller, 1968.

———. *A Systems View of Man*. Ed. Paul A. LaViolette. Boulder, Colo.: Westview, 1981.

Wander, Philip. "The Ideological Turn in Modern Criticism." *Central States Speech Journal* 34 (1983): 1–18.

Warnick, Barbara. "The Narrative Paradigm: Another Story." *Quarterly Journal of Speech* 73 (1987): 172–82.

Washell, Richard F. "Towards an Ecology of Communicative Forms." *Philosophy and Rhetoric* 6 (1973): 109–18.

Weaver, Richard. *The Ethics of Rhetoric*. South Bend, Ind.: Regnery/Gateway, 1953.

Weber, Max. *The Theory of Social and Economic Organization*. Translated by A. M. Henderson and Talcott Parsons. Glencoe, Ill.: Free Press, 1947.

Weick, Karl E. "Educational Organizations as Loosely Coupled Systems." *Administrative Science Quarterly* 21 (1976): 1–18.

———. *The Social Psychology of Organizing*. 2d ed. Reading, Mass.: Addison-Wesley, 1979.

White, James Boyd. *When Words Lose Their Meaning: Constitutions and Reconstitutions of Language, Character, and Community*. Chicago: University of Chicago Press, 1984.

Wieman, Henry Nelson, and Otis M. Walter. "Toward an Analysis of Ethics for Rhetoric." *Quarterly Journal of Speech* 43 (1957): 266–70.

Windt, Theodore Otto, Jr. "The Diatribe: Last Resort for Protest." *Quarterly Journal of Speech* 58 (1972): 1–14.

Witt, Charlotte. *Substance and Essence in Aristotle: An Interpretation of Metaphysics VII–IX*. Ithaca: Cornell University Press, 1989.

Wittgenstein, Ludwig. *Tractatus Logico-Philosophicus.* Trans. C. K. Ogden. London: Routledge and Kegan Paul, 1981.

Wood, Ellen Meiksins, and Neal Wood. *Class Ideology and Ancient Political Theory: Socrates, Plato, and Aristotle in Social Context.* Oxford: Basil Blackwell, 1978.

Wood, Julia T. *Gendered Lives: Communication, Gender, and Culture.* Belmont, Calif.: Wadsworth, 1994.

Index

About the Series

STUDIES IN RHETORIC AND COMMUNICATION
General Editors:
E. Culpepper Clark, Raymie E. McKerrow, and David Zarefsky

The University of Alabama Press has established this series to publish major new works in the general area of rhetoric and communication, including books treating the symbolic manifestations of political discourse, argument as social knowledge, the impact of machine technology on patterns of communication behavior, and other topics related to the nature or impact of symbolic communication. We actively solicit studies involving historical, critical, or theoretical analyses of human discourse.

About the Author

James A. Mackin, Jr., is Associate Professor of Communication at Tulane University. He received his bachelor's degree from The University of Oklahoma, Norman, Oklahoma; his master's from Regents University, Virginia Beach, Virginia; and his doctorate from The University of Texas, Austin, Texas.